Mental Health and Wellbeing
in Primary Education

A Practical Guide and Resource

Dr Laura Meek, Joanna Phillips and Dr Sarah Jordan

Mental Health and Wellbeing in Primary Education

© Pavilion Publishing & Media Ltd

Published by:
Pavilion Publishing and Media Ltd
Blue Sky Offices
Cecil Pashley Way
Shoreham by Sea
West Sussex
BN43 5FF
Tel: 01273 434 943
Email: info@pavpub.com

Published 2020

A catalogue record for this book is available from the British Library.

ISBN: 978-1-912755-92-9

Pavilion Publishing and Media is a leading publisher of books, training materials and digital content in mental health, social care and allied fields. Pavilion and its imprints offer must-have knowledge and innovative learning solutions underpinned by sound research and professional values.

Authors: Laura Meek, Joanna Phillips and Sarah Jordan
Production editor: Ruth Chalmers Pavilion Publishing and Media Ltd
Cover design: Phil Morash, Pavilion Publishing and Media Ltd
Page layout and typesetting: Emma Dawe, Pavilion Publishing and Media Ltd
Printing: CPI Anthony Rowe

Contents

About the authors iv

Acknowledgements v

Foreword vii

Introduction 1

Section 1: Putting Mental Health and Wellbeing First in Schools 15

    Chapter 1: Identification, Responses and Intervention 17

    Chapter 2: Ready to Learn 35

    Chapter 3: A Whole-School Approach to Mental Health and Wellbeing 51

Section 2: Wellbeing 71

    Chapter 4: Wellbeing for All 73

    Chapter 5: Building Emotional Intelligence.. 89

    Chapter 6: Managing and Mastering Screens... 109

Section 3: Mental Health Presentations and Conditions 119

    Chapter 7: Anxiety, Panic and OCD.. 121

    Chapter 8: Low Mood... 143

    Chapter 9: Behaviours That Challenge – Anger and Defiance................... 151

    Chapter 10: Attachment Difficulties and Trauma 167

    Chapter 11: Autism Spectrum Condition 183

    Chapter 12: Difficulties with Attention, Hyperactivity,

    Impulsivity and Tics 199

    Chapter 13: Onset of Puberty and Gender Identity.................................... 213

    Chapter 14: Eating Disorders 221

Section 4: Transitions 231

    Chapter 15: Transition into the Early Years Foundation Stage................. 233

    Chapter 16: Daily Transitions... 239

    Chapter 17: Yearly Transitions 249

    Chapter 18: Transition to Secondary School 257

Section 5: Resources and Lesson Plans..269

    Chapter 19: Resources and Lesson Plans... 271

    Further Reading and Guidance 307

    Glossary of Terms 311

    Index 321

About the authors

Dr Laura Meek is a Consultant Child Psychiatrist. She has an interest in supporting teachers and empowering young people to take charge of their mental health. Laura has written articles for the Huffington Post, Juno Magazine and the Metro and is the author of Be Your Own Superhero (Penguin, 2019). She lives in Yorkshire with her husband and two sons.

Joanna Phillips is a primary teacher and aspiring children's author who was previously a doctor in the NHS. She is currently a Learning Mentor and Nurture Teaching Assistant, supporting children with a variety of needs. Joanna writes online about reading, books and mental health and she has an interest in how stories can be used to support children with their emotional wellbeing. She lives in Hertfordshire with her husband and two children.

Dr Sarah Jordan is a mother and highly specialised Clinical Psychologist currently working in Child and Adolescent Mental Health Services. Sarah has worked with children and families for 18 years. She specialises in the assessment, diagnosis and interventions for children on the autism spectrum.

Acknowledgements

We would like to extend our sincerest gratitude to the schools who have welcomed, encouraged and inspired us on the journey of writing this book. Without you, this would not have been possible. For every interview, for every idea shared, for every discussion that challenged us and spurred us forward – thank you so very much. As professionals we all have a vast amount of knowledge to share with each other, yet this type of interdisciplinary learning sadly does not happen often enough. You are all beacons of hope for our children and our school system. We are honoured to have been able to witness the marvellous work you are doing to support the mental health and wellbeing of the children you teach.

Aspire Academies Trust
Vicky Parsey, CEO
Lyndon Evans, Executive Principal

Bedmond Academy, Bedmond, Watford
Miss J Harris, Principal

Bovingdon Primary Academy, Hemel Hempstead
Mrs S Breslin, Principal

Broadfield Academy
Ms Bijal A Shah, Principal
Ellie Nolan, Assistant Principal and Inclusion Lead
Nicki Buchanan, Families and Safeguarding Lead,
John Nanson, Teacher
Pat Stone, Jigsaw Hub Lead
J Bulpit, Higher Level Teaching Assistant and Jigsaw Hub Teacher

The Grove Academy, Watford
Mohamed Mohamed, Principal
Sarah Longden, SENCO
Emer Douglas, Art Therapist and Pastoral and Therapeutic Support

Knutsford Academy, Watford
Eileen Anderson, Principal
Nicola Beaumont, Deputy Principal
Annette McConnon, Inclusion Support Worker

Hammond Academy, Hemel Hempstead
Eileen Anderson, Interim Principal
Deborah Bloomfield, SENDCO

Boxmoor Primary School, Hemel Hempstead
Emma Argiolas, SENCO and Class Teacher
Chantal Breckell, Class Teacher

Chiltern Hills Academy, Chesham
Suzanne Jackson, Director of Learning Support

Newtown School, Chesham
Julia Antrobus, Headteacher
Toni East, Nurture Practitioner
Tony Hooper, Nurture Practitioner

Sauncey Wood Primary School, Harpenden
Steve Lloyd, Headteacher
Jenny Byford, SENCO
Sally Pattrick, SENCO
Mrs Vass, Teaching Assistant
Nicky Allen, Teaching Assistant

St. Richard Reynolds Catholic Primary, Twickenham
Velia Hartland, Inclusion Manager and SENCO
Emma O'Byrne, EYFS Coordinator
Sarah Taylor, Emotional Literacy Support Assistant (ELSA) and Class Teacher

St. Thomas More Catholic Primary School, Berkhamsted
Maddy Loria, SENCO

Westfield Primary School and Nursery, Berkhamsted
Adrian Bethune, Year 4 Teacher

Foreword

It's essential that all children and young people have the opportunities they need to achieve their full potential and grow into happy and healthy adults. Good mental health is a vital part of developing the skills and character they need to do that. Young people face many challenges ranging from stress and anxiety about exams, to complex, serious and debilitating long-term conditions. Everyone who works with children and young people has a vital role to play in identifying any mental health needs they may have early on and helping them get the required support. Early intervention is key to combat this and more needs to be done to help schools and professionals develop knowledge around mental health, identifying issues when they arise and taking action as soon as possible. In 2017, about 1 in 10 children aged 5 to 16 had a diagnosable mental health need. This can have an enormous impact on quality of life, relationships and academic achievement. Sadly, in many cases it is life-limiting.

Promotion of positive mental health and wellbeing for the whole school community (children, staff, governors, parents and carers) is therefore essential. As is the recognition of how important mental health and emotional wellbeing are to our lives, in just the same way as physical health. We must all recognise that children's mental health is a crucial factor in their overall wellbeing and can affect their learning and achievement.

The Department for Education recognises that: 'In order to help their children succeed; schools have a role to play in supporting them to be resilient and mentally healthy' (DfE, 2018, *Mental Health and Behaviour in Schools*).

Schools can be, and I believe should be, a place for children and young people to experience a nurturing and supportive environment that has the potential to develop self-esteem and provide positive experiences for overcoming adversity and building resilience. For some, school will be a place of respite from difficult home lives and offer positive role models and relationships, which are critical in promoting children's wellbeing and can help engender a sense of belonging and community.

Our role in school is to ensure that children are able to identify and manage times of change and stress, and that they are supported to reach their potential or access help when they need it. We also have a role to ensure that children learn what they can do to maintain positive mental health, what affects their mental health, how they can help reduce the stigma surrounding mental health difficulties, and where they can go if they need help and support.

The aim of all adults who work with children should be to help develop the protective factors which build resilience to mental health problems and to be a school where:

- All children are valued.

- Children have a sense of belonging and feel safe.

- Children feel able to talk openly with trusted adults about their problems without feeling any stigma.

- Positive mental health is promoted and valued.

- Bullying is not tolerated.

In addition to promoting children's wellbeing, we recognise the importance of promoting staff mental health and wellbeing. This too remains a high priority for any education setting.

I believe that schools are much more than centres of learning. They can and do provide the most reliable conduit to address the worrying increase in mental health difficulties, and only they can set us back on track. However, for schools to succeed in helping their pupils, our priorities as a nation must be realigned, and the education system must rebalance academic learning and emotional wellbeing. This is what our children and young people want, it is what our teachers and school leaders want and it is what our parents want. More to the point, it is what our children and young people deserve. They deserve an excellent education that prepares them academically and emotionally for the challenges they will face inside the classroom, and for the ever-changing world that they will experience at each transition in both education and the wider world.

There is already exceptional work being done, but these efforts remain isolated and undervalued. It should be the opposite. Such work should be at the crux of our educational system and recognised at the highest level. I believe that each child deserves a dedicated place to learn to care for their own mental health, and it is our duty as a society to provide this. With schools at the helm, we can create a generation of resilient, healthy and confident individuals.

A massive thank you and well done goes to the creators of this book. It is time that we take stock of the current situation and continue to do all we can to ensure that children's mental wellbeing remains high on the agenda for all schools. It has been a pleasure to work alongside the authors and again it reaffirms and reignites in me a passion to help and support each and every child both academically, but even more importantly, emotionally. If this book can reach even half of the schools across the UK, I know that there will be a positive impact on teacher practice, and this will result in an immensely positive impression on our children.

Our children need to feel safe, secure and valued – we must get them to the point that they are 'ready to learn' before we get them to learn. This can be done by ensuring that a child's mental health is in a good place and they are emotionally secure. Again, having an invaluable resource such as this book will equip professionals with the knowledge and understanding they need to ensure this can happen and that children are in the best place they can be emotionally.

Mental Health and Wellbeing in Primary Education: A practical guide and resource is a truly remarkable book and collection of resources for all people involved in the education of children; not just teachers. This book will provide you with the practical support you need to improve the mental health and wellbeing of your pupils, prevent minor problems from escalating into more serious long-term issues and intervene earlier, providing a cultural change for a whole-school approach.

We must continue to do what we can to get this right for the next generation of young people.

Steve Lloyd, Headteacher, Sauncey Wood Primary School

Online resources

The resources and lesson plans in Chapter 19 are also available to download from
www.pavpub.com/mental-health-and-well-being-in-primary-education-resources

Introduction

Setting the scene

Policy is finally attempting to catch up with what education and healthcare professionals working with children and young people have been noting for years: that the incidence and severity of mental health difficulties they see in these groups is rising, and that resources in the community to effectively support and manage these problems are lacking (NHS Survey, 2018).

In our different fields of work, as a teacher, psychiatrist and clinical psychologist, we believe that overall attitudes towards mental health difficulties are shifting and policy is gradually reflecting this, which can only be seen as a positive. Everybody, from the Royals to the latest social media 'influencer', is talking about mental health in a way that could barely have been imagined even a decade or two ago. We now have an annual Mental Health Awareness Week which encourages discussion and openness, alongside many high-profile campaigns such as 'Heads Together' which aim to change the conversation around mental illness.

The term 'parity of esteem' regarding mental and physical health – that the two should be considered and treated as equals – has been used with increasing frequency and remains the ultimate goal. This was reflected in the 'No health without mental health' slogan which was the title of a 2011 government strategy document outlining proposals to improve mental wellbeing across all age groups and sectors of society (DoH, 2011). It aimed to raise the profile of mental health, encouraging greater appreciation of the role of good mental health for our overall wellbeing, where previously physical wellness has been held in higher esteem.

In 2015, NHS England and The Department of Health joined forces to produce *Future in Mind*, a document outlining an ambitious five-year plan for the transformation of children's mental health services (DoH and NHS England, 2015). Key themes included promoting resilience, improving access to services and developing the national workforce. This proposal also included outlines to develop lesson plans on mental health (delivery of which will become statutory for schools by September 2020) and increased support for teaching staff to help them identify problems in students and to offer support. Although this plan is beginning to come to fruition, progress remains patchy and unequal across the UK. Schools are currently free to decide for themselves the amount of mental health support that is provided to pupils, and there is no central database collating information on which mental health difficulties are being addressed within the school environment and how. A recent increase in funding to support the initiatives in schools will hopefully accelerate the progress of improvement.

What do we mean by 'mental health and wellbeing'?

In its simplest form, 'mental health' is the state of wellbeing experienced in the absence of mental illness. But it is more than simply an *absence* of illness. We, as education and healthcare professionals (who are also all parents), believe that having good mental health means having a range of skills and resilience to cope with stress and change, to have self-belief and self-worth and engage in purposeful and meaningful activities. This involves developing the ability to make relationships with others (outside immediate attachment relationships), and to learn from personal experiences and those of others. An individual who has good mental health feels safe, valued and comfortable with their identity. They are likely to feel a sense of purpose and contribution in their life. They are likely to be engaged in a process of learning and growth – both in relation to themselves and to the world around them. Having a positive outlook on life makes it more likely for a person to develop a growth mindset. A growth mindset involves the underlying belief that we have control over our abilities; we can change, learn and improve – as opposed to having a fixed, innate level of ability (Dweck, 2017).

Children who are mentally healthy will be able to:

- form healthy, loving relationships with adults and peers
- be aware of others and their feelings
- enjoy having some time alone
- tackle challenges they may face and learn from them
- engage in learning and play
- develop in all domains including socially, intellectually, emotionally and physically.

The term 'wellbeing' has taken on new significance in recent years. It is defined in various and subtly different ways: 'physical, psychological, or moral welfare' (Oxford English Dictionary) or 'the condition of being contented, healthy or successful' (Collins Online). All definitions point towards it being a desirable state that we are encouraged to strive for. In the media it is currently closely linked to the concept of self-care and the terms are often used interchangeably. For the purposes of this book, we consider *wellbeing* as a precursor to having good mental health and also a state that supports our mental health as it fluctuates in line with life's challenges. There are many activities we can engage in and ways in which we can structure our lives that will support our mental health. There is much that can be done in a school to educate children about wellbeing and the practices they can use to support its development. Some of these practices are the same for everyone – good sleep, adequate nutrition and hydration, regular exercise. But many will be unique to the individual and their interests. We will explore the variety of ways in which schools can foster wellbeing for children and staff in **Chapter 4: Wellbeing for All**.

Are mental health difficulties increasing in children?

To those working with children and young people it certainly feels as if the frequency and severity of mental health difficulties is increasing, but what do the statistics tell us? Major surveys of the mental health of children and young people in England were carried out in 1999 (Meltzer *et al*, 2000) and 2004 (Green *et al*, 2005), but there was then a gap in data until 2017. The latest survey was funded by the Department of Health and Social Care, commissioned by NHS Digital and carried out by multiple agencies, including the Office for National Statistics and Youthinmind. This showed that the incidence of mental health difficulties had indeed increased. In general, the prevalence of mental health difficulties in young people has been underestimated and services underfunded when compared to adults. Currently, mental health services for children and young people get around 6.4% of mental health spending, and just 0.7% of overall NHS spending (Young Minds, 2019). One of the key findings in 2017 was that emotional disorders (one of four broad categories of mental health difficulties) had become more common in 5–15 year old school children, increasing from 3.9% of the population in 2004 to 5.8% in 2017. The research also found that one in eight 5–19 year olds (12.8%) had at least one mental disorder.

The reasons for this increase are the subject of speculation and discussion. There is likely to have been some increase in the reporting of difficulties, with stigma finally reducing and conversations about mental health becoming more commonplace. But it is also important to recognise that our world has changed and the pressures on our children and young people are immense. The Social Metrics Commission report that 14.3 million people are living in poverty[1] in the UK. This includes 8.3 million working-age adults and 4.6 million children. The last three years have

---

1   Poverty refers to when a person's resources are well below their minimum needs, including the need to take part in society (Mental Health Foundation, 2016).

seen a concerning trend in poverty rates evidencing that people in lone parent families, people in families with three or more children and child poverty have all increased (Social Metrics Commission, 2019). Living in poverty increases the risk of mental health difficulties, and can be both a causal factor and a consequence of mental health difficulties within families (Fell & Hewstone, 2015). Young people age 10-15 years with low socioeconomic status have been reported to have a 2.5 fold higher prevalence of anxiety and depressive disorders than their peers from higher socioeconomic groups (Lamstra *et al*, 2008). Additionally, children and young people today face different challenges that we could not have imagined when we were at their stage of life. As professionals, and as parents of young children, we personally know this to be true. Their world is exciting and terrifying in equal measure. All children, no matter their specific needs and family circumstances, are growing up in a world of high academic expectations, digital overload and online trials and tribulations, prominent celebrity culture and fears related to climate change and the political situation across the world – sadly, these are the building blocks of their lives at present. It is no wonder that we are noticing an increase in mental health presentations.

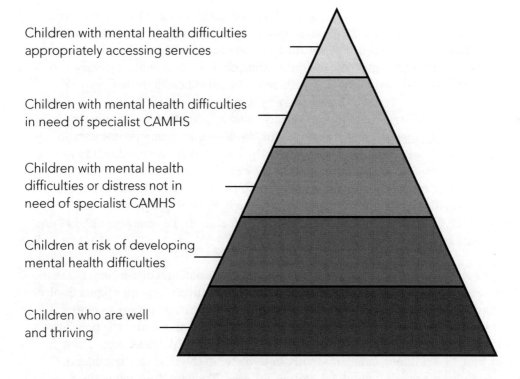

Children with mental health difficulties appropriately accessing services

Children with mental health difficulties in need of specialist CAMHS

Children with mental health difficulties or distress not in need of specialist CAMHS

Children at risk of developing mental health difficulties

Children who are well and thriving

Figure 1: The pyramid of need

Despite this increase, there remains a significant amount of unmet need. The children presenting to mental health services such as Child and Adolescent Mental Health Services (CAMHS) are just a fraction of those who are experiencing difficulties (see Figure 1). In some cases, this is in a child's best interests – there may be a myriad other family, friends and non-healthcare professionals who are better placed to support them. For others, this represents a failing on a higher level, with a lack of adequate government funding and focus on services to help maintain good mental wellbeing. Sadly, this has meant that timely access to appropriate treatment and support for mental health problems has not always been available – this cannot continue. Thankfully, the tide appears to be turning and awareness of these issues is now so great that it is impossible to justify not investing in mental health services for children and young people. Ultimately, mental health is not just an issue for the NHS: it is an issue for the whole of society.

What is the potential impact of mental health difficulties in children?

Although one in eight young people in England have a diagnosable mental health condition, around one in five reported waiting over six months for contact with a mental health specialist (NHS Digital, 2018). With half of all mental illness beginning by the age of fourteen (WHO, 2018), it is imperative that support and services for this age group improve to enable young people to reach their potential.

Untreated, mental health problems in children are associated with poor educational outcomes, family discord and antisocial behaviour, which has considerable impact on both the individual and their family. This in turn places increased demands on wider society and services including schools, social care and youth justice teams. For example, it has been estimated that preventing conduct disorders in those children who are most affected would save around £150,000 per case in lifetime costs. In addition, the promotion of positive mental health in children with moderate mental health difficulties would yield benefits over the lifetime of around £75,000 per case (Friedli & Parsonage, 2007). Despite this, spending on mental health promotion remains low and the role of schools in promoting good mental health has not been fully utilised, despite recommendations (Annual Report of the Chief Medical Officer, 2012).

Both schools and health professionals want children to have sound mental health and the ability to learn and achieve their full potential within the school environment. Maslow (1943) introduced the term 'self-actualisation', which refers to the drive within all of us to strive towards fulfilment of one's talents and potentialities. Before this is possible, many other needs must be met. We know that children need their basic physiological and safety needs met at home and at school before they are able to develop loving connections with others and positive self-esteem. Without adequate sleep and nutrition and a sense of safety and security, no child is able to fully engage all their senses in the learning experience and progress towards their full potential. It is clear that when the natural process of meeting these needs is interrupted, and mental health difficulties arise, the impact on the child's future can be huge.

Mental health and wellbeing in schools

Mental health policy reforms

Following on from 'Future in Mind' (DoH & NHS England, 2015), the 2017 Green Paper 'Transforming Children and Young People's Mental Health Provision' laid out detailed plans to improve the wellbeing of children in the school setting (Department of Health and Social Care & DfE, 2017). This strategy puts the focus on schools and colleges as key players in early intervention with regard to children's mental health, with more collaborative working between health and education. Plans include the need for a trained Designated Senior Lead (DSL) for mental health in every school by 2025; new Mental Health Support Teams, who will work with clusters of schools and be jointly managed by both sectors; and a pledge to reduce waiting times for specialist mental health services. The paper asserts: *'We want to put schools and colleges at the heart of our efforts to intervene early and prevent problems escalating'*. This is promising and long overdue.

Another anticipated change for schools is the new statutory guidance on Health Education, alongside Relationships and Sex Education, which comes into effect from September 2020. However, schools were encouraged to implement this from September 2019. In primary schools, this will include learning regarding:

- mental wellbeing and the importance of this alongside physical health
- that it is common to have mental health problems and that these can be resolved with support
- understanding and discussing emotions
- benefits of physical exercise
- approaches to wellbeing and self-care
- loneliness and bullying
- how to seek support

(Relationships Education, Relationships and Sex Education (RSE) and Health Education, July 2019)

We will explore this guidance in more detail in later chapters.

In June 2019, as part of a commitment to provide better mental health education for many sectors, then-Prime Minister Theresa May pledged particular support for schools in a number of areas (Prime Minister's Office, Press Release, June 2019). This would involve: updated teacher training on mental health; specific support for mental health leads helping children struggling with self-harm and risk of suicide; and support and resources for teachers implementing the new Health Education curriculum guidance. Whether or not all these specific pledges are met over the coming years, the fact that our politicians are moving mental health up the agenda is encouraging.

The Ofsted Education Inspection Framework

The changes to the Ofsted Education Inspection Framework, which came into force in September 2019, also offer some hope for the immediate future (Education Inspection Framework, May 2019). The phrasing of the new judgement focuses (quality of education, behaviour and attitudes, personal development and leadership and management) and the removal of the term 'assessment' suggests that a wider, and more holistic, view of children's education will be taken in forthcoming inspections. Under the personal development judgement, it is encouraging to see mention of learners discovering their individual interests and talents, as well as the requirement for schools to support children to keep 'physically and mentally healthy'. Another positive addition is the requirement that 'leaders engage effectively with learners and others in their community', which encompasses families and external agencies. However, as the Mental Health Foundation has asserted in its comprehensive response to the Framework, there is no explicit expectation that a whole-school approach to mental health and wellbeing be developed (Mental Health Foundation Consultation Response, April 2019). This is something which we regard to be essential. Overall, however, it is to be welcomed that Ofsted has begun to shift its expectations and joined the necessary conversation around children's mental health.

How can schools respond to the policy changes?

The intention to support children with any additional need has been a priority in schools for many years and yet each school can face challenges when implementing the support. With regard to mental health and wellbeing, many schools have been developing new approaches in these areas for some time and many more are currently endeavouring to do the same. However, the external support for this across the country has been patchy.

Decreasing levels of additional adult support in schools can be a barrier to change. There are countless members of teaching staff already making a difference in children's lives every day, and countless schools who wish they could provide more members of staff for all who need them. But recent years of austerity have left their mark on the budgets and staffing levels in our schools. Adults that were once on hand to provide the extra support and interventions are not available in the numbers they once were. The existing systems are stretched thin, and sadly, so are many of the adults that work within them. Another concern is the aforementioned link between poverty and mental health difficulties. It must be acknowledged that there are significant challenges for schools in socioeconomically deprived areas. Each school is different, with a unique demographic and as such, each will teach children with varying levels of need.

Despite these challenges, all of us working in the health and education sectors still want to improve outcomes for the children in our care. We want them to be safe, to be happy, to be able to learn in the present and to grow towards their future potential. The schools we have visited are welcoming the anticipated policy and curriculum changes. They are long overdue. But what do they mean in a practical sense for schools overall and in daily life in the classroom? How can schools develop their role as the starting place for the difficult conversations that are needed, and continue to build effective partnerships with families, as they design individual approaches for children with additional needs?

Undoubtedly, many teachers are exhausted and disillusioned with the state of our education system and the thought of yet more things to do can cause great stress. We believe that the key to navigating this mounting pressure and answering the difficult questions above, is matching up the ethos of wellbeing that many teachers are striving for in their classrooms, with a corresponding ethos of wellbeing for the whole school. Fundamental shifts in school culture, that are supported by all staff, will be the driving force behind sustainable change.

How to use this book

We have written this book for all education professionals working with children in a school environment. We hope that senior leadership teams, special educational needs coordinators (SENCOs), teachers, teaching assistants (TAs) and students will all find it useful in their daily practice and when planning for the expected changes to mental health policy in schools. Because it is also written with students in mind, there may be sections where we have covered foundational aspects of school life that experienced teaching staff already know well. Even so, if you are one of those experienced members of staff, we still hope that in these sections you will find some insight or reflections that inspire you to develop your practice even further. This book may also be read by other professionals, such as psychologists or CAMHS psychiatrists and practitioners. For these individuals, we hope that the details regarding school life will provide you with extra knowledge and understanding to support your work with children, families and teaching staff.

We begin with the big picture discussions regarding mental health and wellbeing. In **Section 1: Putting mental health and wellbeing first in schools**, we consider the importance of the early identification of mental health needs and the support that is offered to schools from external agencies; what being 'ready to learn' looks like for all children; and how a whole-school culture centred on wellbeing can be developed. **Section 2: Wellbeing** addresses how this culture of wellbeing could look in practice; it examines the concept of emotional intelligence and how we can cultivate this for children and staff; and there is an exploration of one of the biggest pressures for all children today: screens and the online world. **Section 3: Mental health presentations and conditions** focuses on the specifics of the key mental health concerns that you may see in a primary school. Each chapter gives detailed information about the presentations and their management in CAMHS, how these may look in school and the strategies that can be used to help children overcome the subsequent barriers to learning. Information regarding the management of each condition in CAMHS is also given. In **Section 4: Transitions**, we explore the importance of significant transitions for all children: as they begin the EYFS, throughout daily life in school, as they move from one year group to another, and as they move from Year 6 to secondary school. Finally, **Section 5: Resources and lesson plans**, provides a variety of resources specifically linked to the text. Many of these are directly photocopiable or can be adapted to suit the needs in your classroom. Section 5 also contains our glossary of terms and suggested further reading.

A few notes on the language we have chosen to use regarding the various adults involved in supporting children with mental health difficulties:

- When we talk about 'senior leadership in schools', this usually encompasses the headteacher or principal, the deputy or assistant headteachers, the SENCO and any other members of staff with the role of Designated Senior Person for Child Protection (DSP) (who may also be members of a pastoral support team).

- When we use the term 'teaching staff', we are referring to all teachers and teaching assistants (TAs).

- When we talk about the 'school community', this refers to children, parents, governors and all members of school staff.

- When we refer to 'external agencies', this encompasses health, mental health, social care and voluntary organisations who may be involved in supporting a child and their family with their mental health and wellbeing.

- When we talk about 'CAMHS', we are generally referring to specialist Child and Adolescent Mental Health Services (CAMHS) at Tier 2 and 3 level rather than all services aimed at supporting children's mental health.

In the midst of busy daily life in school, it is not practical to suggest that this book be read and digested from start to finish in one go. We recommend that you read the first few chapters fully to gain an overview of how a whole-school change in the area of mental health and wellbeing could be achieved. After that, dive in when and where you need support. This may be:

- when you are getting to know your new class at the start of the year

- when a change is noticed in a child

- when you begin to gather information and evidence to pass on

- when you learn that a child has a specific mental health difficulty and/or diagnosis and you are planning how to best help them move forward with their learning

- when you are striving to boost wellbeing for all the children in your school or class

- when you are considering how best to engage with families and provide support when home circumstances are challenging.

Always keep in mind that every child is unique and at a different stage of their learning journey. Therefore, despite everyone's best intentions and hard work, not every strategy and approach will work for every child. This is a hard reality for us all – there is no one 'right answer' to any of the difficult situations we face in our practice each day. We must move forward with open minds, always willing to listen, learn and adapt. We must also never forget that we are not alone and that one adult cannot work in isolation. We must seek support from our colleagues, engage in the right conversations and share our stresses when it all gets too much. As we introduce new strategies and initiatives we must also remember not to change too much at once. Bringing in many new ideas at the same time will prove confusing and overwhelming for children and it will also be hard to identify what has had a positive impact and what hasn't.

Message from the authors

We have written this book in response to the mental health policy changes, but, more importantly, we have written it to reinforce the idea that change is needed and possible. Therefore, our message is ultimately one of hope. Wherever a child is on their journey, this book is here to provide schools with support. We have drawn on our own professional teaching and clinical experiences and we have also gathered wisdom from many other experts and practitioners. We are living these words in our daily lives as professionals and as parents. The strategies in this book all flow from some core principles: creating safety in school, cultivating an ethos centred on wellbeing and providing space for each child to be their own unique and wonderful self. There are many practical strategies that we can implement in our daily interactions and teaching practice that can be transformative for children. We have endeavoured to make our suggestions manageable and realistic. Some are subtle tweaks to language that can make a big difference. Some take practise and a commitment to changing our own attitudes and behaviours. Some are larger scale whole-school changes and require mindful consultation and planning with the whole-school community. We have listened to the voices of many different members of school staff. We have witnessed these approaches in action in the schools we have visited and seen the positive change they can bring about for all children, but especially those with mental health difficulties.

One very important message to convey concerns the continuum of mental health need. Not all children with mental distress will have a diagnosable mental health condition. We must exercise great caution with the labels we give – ideally, schools shouldn't be labelling children at all. To the untrained eye, it is exceptionally hard to differentiate between a typical, expected behaviour in a certain difficult circumstance and that which has crossed over into a mental health difficulty. Again, this is not for schools to decide and we must therefore always be mindful that referring children for specialist assessment is a really significant step and never to be taken lightly.

We must also be cautious when considering what the role of schools and teaching staff is in helping children to manage their distress and ensure they can work within the boundaries of their role and training. Primarily, their role should be to help children feel they are in a safe place to learn and grow. We will later consider the impact of significant attachment difficulties and trauma. It is important to note a need, with this level of psychological disturbance, for a child to be well contained and safe within a therapeutic space, supported by a trained professional (such as a therapist or clinical psychologist). A child should not be exposed to others' unrealistic expectations to explore their trauma within a school setting and a teacher should not be expected to step into the role of a therapist.

Furthermore, we do understand the frustrations of teaching staff who feel that they are expected to solve all of society's problems, in addition to their job of teaching the curriculum. And we acknowledge that we cannot do it all and we do not have all the answers. Change needs to be supported by sensible and realistic messages from government, but also, change must happen in partnership with parents. Both of these required elements present many challenges. But no matter what the perceived and actual barriers are, education and healthcare professionals need to continue to strive to find ways of working in effective partnership with each other. We need to create sustainable shifts in attitude and practice for all children and staff. We need to acknowledge each child's reality and commit to working alongside families and other agencies to discover what will help them. We also need to develop ways of offering protection for the future to children with no apparent mental health difficulties. It is our job to support them to navigate the evolving landscape of childhood and develop the skills and resilience to walk out the other side into adolescence and adulthood, equipped with skills for the rest of their lives. This is all a huge undertaking and responsibility, but we believe that this cannot be seen as 'someone else's job'. Looking after our children's mental health is everyone's job.

We would very much like to continue the conversation we have begun here. Let us know what is working for you, what you adapt and what new ideas you develop. Our philosophy is one of sharing good practice and encouraging each other – we talk and the children benefit.

Find us at:

Dr Laura Meek @mentalhealthforschools and @mindfuldoctoring on Instagram, @drlaurameek on Twitter.

Dr Sarah Jordan @drsarahclinicalpsych on Instagram and Dr Sarah Jordan on Facebook.

Joanna Phillips @fromthepageswegrow on Facebook and Instagram and @fromthepageswe1 on Twitter.

References

Children's Society (2008) *The Good Childhood Inquiry: Health research evidence*. London: Children's Society.

Department for Education (2019) *Relationships Education, Relationships and Sex Education (RSE) and Health Education. London: DfE.*

Department of Health (2011) *No Health without Mental Health: A cross-government mental health outcomes strategy for people of all ages*. London: D.H.

Department of Health and Department for Education (2017) *Transforming Children and Young People's Mental Health Provision: A green paper. London: DoH / DfE.*

Department of Health and NHS England (2015) *Future in Mind: Promoting, protecting and improving our children and young people's mental health and wellbeing. London: DoH / NHS England.*

Dube S, Felitti V, Dong M, Giles, W *et al* (2003) The impact of adverse childhood experiences on health problems: Evidence from four birth cohorts dating back to 1900. *Preventative Medicine* **37** (3) 268–277.

Dweck C (2017) *Mindset - Changing the Way you Think to Fulfill your Potential*. London: Robinson, Constable & Robinson Ltd.

Fell B & Hewstone M (2015) *Psychological Perspectives on Poverty*. Available from: http://www.jrf.org.uk/report/psychological-perspectives-poverty.

Friedli L & Parsonage M (2007) *Mental Health Promotion: Building an economic case*. Belfast: Northern Ireland Association for Mental Health.

Ginsburg G, Becker-Haimes E, Keeton C *et al* (2018) Results from the Children/Adolescent Anxiety Multimodal Extended Long-Term Study (CAMELS): primary anxiety outcomes. *Journal of the American Academy of Child and Adolescent Psychiatry* **57** (7) 471–480.

Green H, Maginnity A, Meltzer H et al (2005) *Mental Health of Children and Young People in Great Britain*. London: TSO.

Healthwatch (2017) *Children and young people with autism: Findings from the Healthwatch network* (online). Available from www.healthwatch.co.uk/sites/healthwatch.co.uk/files/children_and_young_people_with_autism_-_findings_from_the_healthwatch_network_0.pdf

Lemstra M, Neudorf C, D'Arcy C, Kunst A, Warren L & Bennett N (2008) A systematic review of depressed mood and anxiety by socioeconomic status in adolescents aged 10–15 years. *Canadian Journal of Public Health* **99** (2) 125–129.

Long R, Bellis A & Steele S (2018) *Mental Health and Wellbeing in Schools – Debate Pack*. Available from researchbriefings.files.parliament.uk › CDP-2018-0265 › CDP-2018-0265

Maslow AH (1943) A theory of human motivation. *Psychological Review* **50** (4) 370–396.

Meltzer H, Gatward R, Goodman R *et al* (2000) *The Mental Health of Children and Adolescents in Great Britain*. London: TSO.

Mental Health Foundation (2016). *Poverty and Mental Health: A review to inform the Joseph Rowntree Foundations' anti-poverty strategy*. Available from: https://www.mentalhealth.org.uk/sites/default/files/Poverty%20and%20Mental%20Health.pdf

Mental Health Foundation Consultation Response (2019) Ofsted: Education Inspection Framework 2019 – inspecting the substance of education.

Murphy M & Fonarg P (2012) Mental Health Problems in Children and Young People in Annual Report of the Chief Medical Officer. *Our Children Deserve Better: Prevention pays*. London: Department of Health.

National Institute for Health and Care Excellence (2011) *CG128: Autism spectrum disorder in under 19s: recognition, referral and diagnosis*. London: NIHCE.

National Institute for Health and Care Excellence (2013) *CG170: Autism spectrum disorder in under 19s: support and management*. London: NIHCE.

Mental Health Foundation Consultation Response (2019) *Ofsted: Education Inspection Framework 2019 – inspecting the substance of education*. London: MHF.

Murphy M & Fonarg P (2012) *Mental Health Problems in Children and Young People in Annual Report of the Chief Medical Officer. Our Children Deserve Better: Prevention pays*. London: DoH.

NHS Digital (2018) *Mental Health of Children and Young People in England, 2017 [PAS] – NHS Digital*. [online] Available from https://digital.nhs.uk/data-and-information/publications/statistical/mental-health-of-children-and-young-people-in-england/2017/2017

Ofsted (2019): The Education Inspection Framework. Reference no: 190015. Available from https://assets.publishing.service.gov.uk/government/uploads/system/uploads/attachment_data/file/801429/Education_inspection_framework.pdf

Prime Minister's Office (2019) 10 Downing Street and The Rt Hon Theresa May MP. *Press Release: PM launches new mission to put prevention at the top of the mental health agenda* (online). Available from www.gov.uk/government/news/pm-launches-new-mission-to-put-prevention-at-the-top-of-the-mental-health-agenda

Social Metrics Commission (2019) *Measuring Poverty 2019*. A report of the Social Metrics Commission. Available from www.socialmetricscommission.org.uk

World Health Organisation (2018). *Child and Adolescent Mental Health*. Available from www.who.int/mental_health/maternal-child/child_adolescent/en/ Geneva: WHO.

YoungMinds (2019). *Children's Mental Health Funding Not Going Where It Should Be – YoungMinds* [online]. Available from https://youngminds.org.uk/about-us/media-centre/press-releases/children-s-mental-health-funding-not-going-where-it-should-be London: Young Minds.

Section 1: Putting Mental Health and Wellbeing First in Schools

Chapter 1: Identification, Responses and Intervention

The importance of early intervention

Mental health problems in children occur at a time of rapid development in several important domains – physical, social, emotional and cognitive. Without early detection and intervention, mental illness can potentially alter the trajectory of a child's life in all of these domains and have lasting effects into adulthood. Childhood mental illness is linked to higher rates of relationship difficulties, to educational outcomes and to employment prospects (Goodman *et al*, 2011).

Identification of children with mental health needs

Noticing

All school staff have an essential role to play in noticing and tuning in to what is going on for children regarding their mental health and emotional wellbeing. Throughout our daily interactions with children, teaching staff notice, and are likely to be the first to observe, subtle and significant changes. They may notice emotional states, behaviours and levels of engagement with peers and with learning. They may notice changes, patterns and triggers on an individual level – perhaps a child has begun to show frustration or anger in situations where they previously had coped well, or perhaps a child is becoming anxious at the same time every day. Changes can also be detected on a bigger scale, when multiple children are struggling with particular situations – perhaps there is a concern that a group of children are not engaging with their learning as a result of low self-esteem, or perhaps several children are struggling with their evolving friendship groups in the playground. When time is taken for mindful observation of the interactions and events in the classroom, it is easier to notice changes as soon as they arise.

We know that there is a vast spectrum of potential events that may affect a child. Adverse childhood experiences (ACEs) such as abuse, neglect, exposure to domestic violence or parental separation are known to be highly likely to have an impact on mental health (Felitti *et al*, 1998). The higher the number of adverse experiences, the worse the later physical and psychological outcomes for children and young people are (Hughes *et al*, 2017). More common experiences such as moving house, the death of a pet, family illness or difficulties with a sibling can also contribute to, possibly more transient, reduced levels of mental wellbeing. The extent to which the smaller scale events will impact on a child will vary greatly, dependent on their individual circumstances and existing level of resilience and how the events are managed by the adults around them. Having awareness of children's lived experiences and fostering a good relationship with the child puts teaching staff in a good position to spot patterns and recurring triggers.

Recording and reporting

It is hard to keep track of the vast number of observations made in a school day. In addition to using the formal reporting systems discussed below, teaching staff should try to develop an ongoing system of recording small daily observations that works for them – in a notebook, on a spreadsheet or in an individual learning folder for each child. This method needs to be as easy and accessible as possible so that insights are not forgotten. These daily observations will then support the process of formally reporting concerns.

Once a change in a child's emotional or behavioural presentation is noted, make it a priority to share as soon as possible. There are several potential courses of immediate action, dependent on the extent of the change and the circumstances of the child. There may be an urgent situation that needs to be immediately reported and help sought; for instance, a previously well child who begins to show signs of self-harm in the classroom. There may be a small-scale change, such as gradual withdrawal from peer interactions, but in the context of a known parental separation. In this case, sensitive discussion with the parents and timely involvement of the SENCO is warranted. Remember that other staff members may hold information you are not aware of and your observation may be a key piece of the overall picture that they are building about this child's circumstances. Equally, a small-scale change may arise for a child with no past history of mental health difficulties. In this case, conversations with the parents and monitoring the situation within class would be appropriate.

No matter what the specific situation, early involvement of, and effective communication with, parents and colleagues is essential. A school can support this process by creating a culture of trust and openness, where all members of the community believe that they will be listened to and their concerns taken seriously. It is also important that everyone knows that they can raise a concern about a child's mental health – staff, parents and the children themselves. Everyone needs to understand their responsibilities and know their first point of contact when reporting a concern. Designated Safeguarding Persons for Child Protection will be familiar with the thresholds for child protection reporting and the referral pathways, as set out by their local safeguarding partners (these being the local authority, Clinical Commissioning Group and the chief officer of police (HM Government, 2018)). The bi-annual Designated Safeguarding Lead training, in line with *Keeping Children Safe in Education* (DfE, 2019), should equip them to feel confident about how all types of abuse (physical, emotional, neglect and sexual) present in children and young people.

All staff in school are legally required to complete statutory and mandatory training in safeguarding, but the systems used by each school for recording and monitoring may differ. Some schools use paper-based systems, whereas others have moved to electronic monitoring. The various child protection and safeguarding software options offer a comprehensive way to log concerns, monitor patterns and communicate with colleagues. All staff members can have access to record child protection concerns, but they also allow information about Special Educational Needs and Disability (SEND), behaviour and pastoral matters to be noted, classified and tracked over time. Crucially, senior members of staff with a high level of access are able to view all entries related to an individual child and see the overall chronology and pattern of events. This is extremely helpful when building a complete picture of the factors that are affecting a child and the impact of these factors on the child's learning and wellbeing. These systems offer huge value to staff in terms of the ease of timely recording and communication with colleagues, which in turn contributes to improved safeguarding. Schools must pay an annual fee for use of such a system, which is generally dependent on the size of the school and may be a limiting factor for its use in some areas. Details of some of the available options can be found in *Chapter 19: Resources and lesson plans* on p271. Whichever system of recording a school uses, all staff must ensure they follow the chosen procedures for reporting, monitoring concerns and taking appropriate actions.

Methods for identifying mental health needs

Schools are likely to use a combination of formal and informal methods of identification of mental health needs. In 2017, the Department for Education published the findings of their Survey of Mental Health Provision of Schools and Colleges (Marshall *et al*, 2017). Of the 2780 institutions that completed the survey, it was found that although almost all (93%) systematically tried to identify children with particular needs, only 24% conducted targeted mental health screening and only 15% conducted screening for all. There are benefits to be found in both formal and informal methods of identification, but we would encourage all schools to consider using a formal method that allows the tracking of concerns over time, and allows effective repeat screening at intervals or after targeted interventions.

Formal methods of identification

The Boxall Profile is an online tool for the assessment of children's emotional, behavioural and social development and levels of need (The Nurture Group Network Ltd., 2018). It was first introduced in the 1960s and it is now the most commonly used formal method for measuring mental health and wellbeing in children (Marshall *et al*, 2017). Adults in school who know a child best, complete two checklists: the first, measuring how factors relating to the child's cognitive, emotional and social development are affecting their learning; and the second, measuring behaviours that challenge and how these are impacting on their social and academic functioning. The outcomes of the assessment provide insight into a child's individual needs and they prompt consideration of the potential reasons behind behaviours. This information can then be used to plan appropriate support and interventions for the child. The Boxall Profile is especially useful for the early identification of needs and can be used as a screening tool for all children, not just those about whom concerns have been raised. Schools are able to utilise a variety of subscription options of the Boxall Profile in order to meet their specific requirements.

The Strengths and Difficulties Questionnaire (SDQ) is a brief behavioural screening questionnaire for use with children aged 3–16 years (Goodman, 1997). Along with the Boxall Profile, it is one of the most commonly used tools in school to identify children with emotional difficulties (Marshall *et al*, 2017). There are various versions which can be completed by children (aged eleven or above), parents or teaching staff. It is quick and easy to complete, and includes 25 items covering five areas: emotional problems, conduct problems, hyperactivity/inattention, peer relationships and prosocial behaviours. In a similar way to the Boxall Profile, the outcomes of the SDQ can give an overall picture of a child's social and emotional presentation.

Local education authorities and other external agencies , such as Thrive® (see **Further Reading and Guidance**), also provide various assessment tools to assist schools in the formal identification of social, emotional and mental health needs.

Informal methods of identification

There are also a number of more informal ways in which schools can identify children who are struggling with, or at risk of, mental health difficulties. There is great benefit to simply being present where the children and their families are and taking time to connect and notice. This may look like the headteacher or other member of senior leadership being out in the playground or on the gate in the morning to welcome the children and their families into school each day. Or it may look like a teacher remaining at the classroom door for a time and chatting informally with parents at the end of the day. These are daunting tasks at times, when teachers' days are already very full. But so much important background information about what is going on in children's lives can be picked up on by simply being there, saying hello and listening when someone wants to talk. Additionally, the connections that are made in these times are invaluable in terms of building overall partnership with parents. These methods are more likely to work effectively if they are consistent across the school and happening as often as possible.

Having an open-door culture in classrooms is beneficial to children and staff. If members of senior leadership are welcome to pop in and out, without any pressure or particular expectations, they are able to check in with children and monitor how they are doing. This doesn't need to be a source of anxiety for teachers, as long as the messages about the purpose of the visit are properly communicated. This can be part of an overall culture of trust and openness between staff across the school. As previously mentioned, it is important that teaching staff feel able to raise concerns in a relaxed manner and know they will be received without judgement. All members of staff need to be appropriately sharing information that will help form that complete picture of need for a particular child.

End of year handover procedures also offer another valuable opportunity to raise concerns about a child and ask for input from colleagues. The class handover meeting and pupil progress meetings (PPMs) or equivalent will be discussed further in *Chapter 17: Yearly Transitions*.

Developing systems by which children can self-refer concerns about their own mental health is also important. It is necessary not only to help them to understand what good mental health looks like and help them tune in to their emotional state, but also to support them in alerting adults when they feel something is wrong or they are struggling. We will explore some of these in more detail in *Chapter 5*.

The graduated approach to intervention

The graduated approach of Assess Plan Do Review (APDR), as described in the Special educational needs and disability (SEND) code of practice (SEND Code of Practice, 2015), can provide a template for the initial response to mental health concerns. This approach will hopefully have already begun in the classroom, as described above, with teaching staff noticing, talking, providing initial support and monitoring the impact of this support. It is important to share this stage of the process with the SENCO before they begin their own observations. Note that there will always be a period of observation before any child is added to the SEND register. The SENCO may then carry out further assessment, as described above, continue more detailed conversations with the parents; and consider the impact of other factors. They can then plan, in partnership with the child, parents and teaching staff, the appropriate support to put into place. After an agreed period of time, during which strategies and interventions are actioned, all parties should then be involved in the review process.

Seeking external assessment and support

If it is decided that there has been little or no improvement in the child's presentation, the SENCO will then make a judgement about how to proceed. Again in partnership with parents, a decision will be made as to whether it is appropriate to continue to use a graduated approach to manage the concern within school, or whether it is necessary to seek external expertise. This may take the form of seeking advice and support from other agencies; or it may take the form of an application for further assessment. There are various routes that may be taken:

- Education, Health and Care (EHC) needs assessment: When a child continues to make less progress than expected or there is no improvement in a concern, despite support being put into place in school, an EHC can be requested (SEND Code of Practice, 2015). Assuming that the local authority agrees that an EHC is necessary, they will follow a person-centred approach to assessment and subsequent planning, considering the views of all parties. If it is deemed that the child needs more support than can be provided through standard school SEND support, then an Education, Health and Care Plan (EHCP) will be drawn up to provide detailed guidance on how to meet their needs. The SEND Code of Practice lays out very specific timescales that local authorities must follow at all stages of this process.

- Early Help Assessment (EHA): The recent publication *Working Together to Safeguard Children* (HM Government, 2018) stipulates that an EHA could be led by a teacher, a school nurse or a SENCO within schools. This is designed to identify what help a child and their family needs in order to prevent a situation escalating to a level where a statutory assessment under the Children Act 1989 would be necessary. These replace the Common Assessment Framework (CAF), but similarly involve identifying additional needs and offering support to families.

- Direct referral to specialist mental health services, if the concerns are primarily around a child's mental health (see further details later in this chapter).

If external expertise is sought, there will be a period where the school needs to continue its graduated approach while they await the response or further assessment. These routes are not mutually exclusive – some children may have an EHCP and/or an EHA and also be open to CAMHS, or any combination of these three, depending on their needs.

It is helpful to clarify here which areas of need fall under the umbrella of SEND. Children with SEND are those defined as having a learning difficulty or a disability which calls for special educational provision to be made. The broad areas of need defined within the SEND Code of Practice (communication and language; cognition and learning; social, emotional and mental health; sensory and/or physical needs) bring mental health presentations under the umbrella of SEND (SEND Code of Practice, 2015). A child has a learning difficulty or disability if he or she has a significantly greater difficulty in learning than the majority of others of the same age, or has a disability which prevents or hinders him or her from making use of facilities of a kind generally provided for others of the same age in mainstream schools (Section 20, Children and Families Act, 2014). This book is not intended to inform teaching staff about different learning difficulties, such as dyslexia, dyspraxia or sensory processing impairments, nor physical health conditions. However, it is worth noting that all of the above will be covered under the SEND definition if a child requires special educational provision.

Diagnosis vs formulation

Psychiatry has traditionally emphasised the importance of diagnostic categories, with the implication that these offer a reliable guide for treatment options and predictions of outcomes. Diagnosis is primarily a system of classification within a biomedical model to understand a child's difficulties. In contrast, formulation is primarily a process of understanding using a psychosocial model to hypothesise reasons for a child's presentation and factors that maintain these difficulties.

Formulation is a key competence in UK training curriculums for both psychologists and psychiatrists, but the two professions often differ in their approach. Psychological formulation refers to an understanding of a child's current presentation and should draw equally from two different sources of evidence: the family's information regarding their life, experiences, relationships and circumstances and the mental health practitioner's knowledge, derived from theory, research and clinical experience. In this way, it is a tool that relates theory to practice (Butler, 1998) and should always be co-constructed and collaborative. Psychiatric formulation will include biological, social and psychological factors which may predispose, trigger or prolong the experience of a particular diagnosable mental illness, as well as factors which may be protective (Royal College of Psychiatrists, 2013).

The diagnostic model (and also some psychotherapeutic models) has been criticised for its tendency to individualise difficulties and therefore locate the problem within the child (and their biomedical differences), rather than finding the problem to be a product of wider familial, environmental or societal factors that have contributed to a child's emotional, social and cognitive presentation.

Much has been written about the importance of the formulation approach within mental health services. Furthermore, there is significant value in communication and involvement of teachers within the formulation process regarding school-age children. As previously noted, teachers, who see a child daily, can provide mental health clinicians with key information that can inform the process of formulation. A best practice formulation highlights a child's strengths and skills – areas which teachers already focus on. Teachers are also well placed to challenge unfounded 'myths' or beliefs about a child; for example, where a child is able to demonstrate a skill or strength within the school environment but not at home. While a teacher is not responsible for co-constructing a psychological formulation, multi-agency communication regarding a specific child's presentation can support a school to manage difficulties and risk. Formulations can increase the team around a child's understanding, empathy and reflectiveness, raise staff morale and convey messages to staff about hope for positive change (Division of Clinical Psychology, 2011).

Despite widespread use of formulations, services tend to use diagnostic classifications in order to structure service pathways. Parents continue to seek out diagnoses in a predominantly medicalised culture and diagnoses such as autism spectrum condition (ASC) and attention deficit hyperactivity disorder (ADHD) continue to be instrumental in accessing support and services. In the UK, the International Statistical Classification of Diseases and Related Mental Health Problems, 10th edition (ICD-10) and the Diagnostic and Statistical Manual of Mental Health Disorders, 5th edition (DSM V) continue to be widely used, and these diagnostic manuals (despite significant criticism) continue to be revised and updated. The ICD-11 was published in 2018 and is due to come into clinical use in 2022. In this book, we have classified areas of need using some diagnostic labels so that we can support teachers' understanding regarding presentations that might be given a diagnosis. However, all the chapters in *Section 3* can be accessed on a symptom level as well. So, for example, if you are supporting a child with significant attention difficulties, the chapter regarding ADHD may be helpful to you, even if that child does not meet all the criteria for a clinical diagnosis.

A diagnosis can be viewed in several different lights. In some circumstances, a diagnosis can provide relief and understanding for parents and teachers who have been trying to support a child with complex needs. It can be the route to accessing the external services that are needed, such as access to specialist advisory teams or to specific types of therapy. It can channel a school's attention in the right direction and they can begin to implement helpful strategies. However, any diagnostic label that a child may be given should not be used to narrow expectations of them – we need to use our understanding of conditions to help children learn and thrive in a way that is appropriate for them as an individual. We should also use this understanding to support children to find ways to promote their cognitive, social and emotional development using different ideas and strategies. It is important to not always associate a particular condition with a specific child with this diagnosis. No two children with the same condition will present in the same way. Rather than approaches being one-size-fits-all, individualised strategies and techniques to promote learning and development are most likely to be effective. Overall, it must be remembered that the child and their needs remain the same, regardless of the diagnostic label that may or may not be given.

Overview of current mental health care for children

In the Introduction, we began to consider the vital role that schools can play in supporting a child with mental health difficulties. Of course, a school cannot and should not work in isolation. A network of professionals working in the child's best interests is essential. This may include staff from social care, physical health and mental health services.

Currently in the UK, there are a number of agencies who support children with their mental health, with CAMHS often taking a lead role. Exact referral pathways differ across the country, but often families will seek support and advice from their child's school or from their general practitioner (GP), who can then refer on to other agencies, including CAMHS. Most CAMHS services accept referrals from GPs and other healthcare professionals, as well as from education and social care professionals. Some services also accept self-referrals direct from families, so it is helpful to check local procedures online.

Historically, mental health services for children in the UK have been based around a 'tier system', with different levels of support and types of intervention being offered by each tier. More recently, there has been a push to move away from the tier-based model to a more holistic framework, which is needs-led and person-centred, rather than being dependent on a particular service. This approach is outlined in the THRIVE model below.

The tier system of mental health support

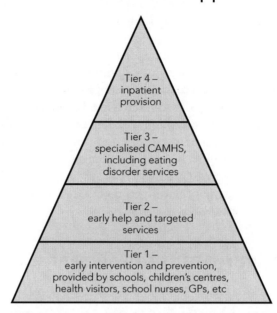

Figure 2: The tier system of mental health support (Integrated Care Pathways for Mental Health, Division of Clinical Psychology for Mental Health, 2011)

Tier 1: These are the services aimed at early intervention and prevention, and are provided by staff that are working in universal services (available to all) and not specifically mental health-trained. This includes health visitors, school nurses, teachers and GPs. They can help to support general mental wellbeing, identify early problems and refer to more specialist services.

Tier 2: These services are more targeted and aimed at providing early help for mental health and wellbeing difficulties. They may be delivered in a range of settings, such as schools and GP surgeries. Tier 2 level interventions may be offered by CAMHS primary mental health workers in some parts of the UK (sometimes called 'CAMHS practitioners'), but educational psychologists, school counsellors and voluntary organisations such as MIND also offer this level of intervention.

Tier 3: This tier is composed of specialist CAMHS, including eating disorder services, specific diagnostic teams (e.g. for ADHD or ASC) and early intervention for psychosis services. Support may include individual, family or group-based therapies such as cognitive behavioural therapy (CBT) and medication. Children requiring medication for their mental health will usually be open to a Tier 3 service, as those under 18 require specialist monitoring.

Tier 3.5: This is a term sometimes used to describe intensive community support aimed at preventing an in-patient admission, including assertive outreach, home-based treatment and crisis team support.

Tier 4: Tier 4 involves inpatient or day unit treatment. This may include children's units (under 13 years), adolescent units (13–18 years), psychiatric intensive care units (providing a higher level of security and containment of risk), or other specialist units, including CAMHS learning disability or eating disorder units. These services are commissioned by NHS England, whereas lower tiers are funded by Clinical Commissioning Group and local authority budgets.

The THRIVE model

The tier system has been criticised by some who argue that it strengthens divisions between services (Wolpert *et al*, 2014). The THRIVE model is now part of the NHS Long Term Plan (NHS, 2019). It moves away from the tier system towards a more needs-led approach, meaning that the mental health needs are agreed collaboratively between all involved, and not based purely on severity, diagnosis or health care pathways (Anna Freud Centre, 2019). The THRIVE model provides a set of principles to guide communities to use their resources most efficiently in the support of the mental health of children, young people and families.

Figure 3: The THRIVE model of mental health support (Anna Freud Centre)

The THRIVE model places children and young people into one of five needs-based groupings:

- Getting advice
- Getting help
- Getting risk support
- Getting more help
- Thriving

Thrive is gradually being implemented across the UK and commissioners are being supported in how best to adapt services and resources to be more in line with this approach (National i-Thrive Programme). On a practical level for children and families, this should mean faster access to the most appropriate sources of support for their mental health needs.

Child and Adolescent Mental Health Services and other agencies

Child and Adolescent Mental Health Services (CAMHS) is usually the term used when referring to tier 2 or 3 NHS services, but may also be used as a broad term for all services that work with children and young people who are having difficulties with their emotional or behavioural wellbeing. Professionals working within an NHS CAMHS team may include psychiatrists (medical doctors specialising in the diagnosis and treatment of mental illness), clinical psychologists (psychologists specifically trained in the assessment and treatment of mental, emotional and behavioural disorders), mental health nurses and other professionals, including occupational therapists and social workers. Increasingly, CAMHS teams employ 'CAMHS practitioners', who may be from a diverse range of professional backgrounds, but all of whom will be involved in assessing and treating children with mental health problems.

Many CAMHS services now use a pathway approach to the assessment and triage of children and young people. Following referral, further information is usually sought direct from the family or referrer and a decision made as to whether or not CAMHS is the most appropriate place for the referral. Once accepted, there is usually an initial assessment appointment during which a formulation of the child and family's difficulties is produced collaboratively. Following this appointment, if accepted into the service, a child will usually be allocated to a particular pathway, such as 'emotional difficulties' or 'ADHD'. In some cases, such as possible ADHD or

ASC, further specialised assessment will be required within that pathway. Others, for example a child experiencing low mood and anxiety, may be allocated or placed on the waiting list for a particular evidence-based intervention such as group or individual CBT, or family therapy. It is usual for psychological therapy to be offered before medication is considered (if appropriate), as evidence suggests that talking therapies should be the first line of treatment offered for many mild to moderate mental health difficulties – this part of of the National Institute for Clinical Excellence (NICE) 'stepped care' approach recommended for most mental health problems (NICE guidance, 2011).

Alongside direct work with children and families, CAMHS staff will also work with the wider network around a child. This includes liaison with schools and attendance at meetings where possible, working with social care and family support teams (particularly where there are safeguarding concerns), and working with other specialist teams, such as youth justice or forensic services.

Other agencies and support

School-based support

Current provision for supporting young people with their mental health within schools varies immensely across the UK. In addition to pastoral support, some schools can also access additional school-based wellbeing support, which may be jointly funded by health, social care and education. Typically, a wellbeing worker would cover a cluster of schools and work with staff and young people around emerging and developing mental health needs. They seek to support those with difficulties that may not be at the threshold for treatment within CAMHS, but are above the remit of school pastoral care. In other areas, this service may be offered by third party organisations.

Paediatrics

Paediatricians may be involved in both detecting and managing different aspects of a child's emotional and mental health. In some areas, paediatrics will be the leading agency (as opposed to CAMHS) in the assessment and diagnosis of some neurodevelopmental conditions such as ASC and ADHD, depending on how services are commissioned. Paediatricians can assess a child's overall development and they may refer onto other professionals, such as occupational therapists and speech and language therapists. They may be jointly involved with CAMHS in managing the physical aspects of eating disorders, such as anorexia nervosa, with some young people requiring admission to a paediatric ward. In the case of overdoses and self-harm, young people who present to A&E will often be admitted to a paediatric ward.

Social care and local authority services

Local authority services may be involved in supporting the whole family unit. This may encompass giving parenting advice and practical support, which can have a preventative function regarding mental health difficulties. This could happen at an early stage through prevention services and family support workers, or through children's social care if there are specific identified needs or safeguarding concerns. As looked after children (LAC) are known to have higher rates of mental health difficulties, there is a need for social workers to work together with mental health staff in supporting these children. Some areas have specialist LAC CAMHS teams, which usually include staff from both CAMHS and social care in recognition of the high needs of this particular group.

Third sector

There are many organisations offering free and accessible support to children and families across the UK outside of NHS services. This includes organisations such as MIND, the mental health charity which offers counselling, advice and mentoring; and online platforms, such as Kooth. These are increasingly being promoted by the NHS as alternative routes to accessing help in a bid to reduce pressure on an overstretched system. Further details of these organisations are given in ***Further Reading and Guidance***.

Therapeutic interventions

If a school is keen to access specific therapeutic support for a child, for example art, play or music therapy, parental consent would always need to be gained first. Some schools have in-house therapists and others have regular weekly timetable slots for visiting therapists. Therapies tend to be time-limited, usually 6–12 sessions. However, this could be extended at the discretion of the therapist if they feel longer is needed. Sometimes it can take a long time for a therapist to gain a child's trust. There is a need to be flexible and let things evolve at the child's pace. Once the course of therapy has finished, assuming parents are consenting, the therapist may be able to offer further sessions if or when necessary.

All models of therapy will have certain explicit boundaries. Some might even have written contracts. For example, during a play therapy session, various play resources are provided and the child knows they are allowed complete control over what they select. The only rules are: they may not hurt themselves or the therapist, and they may not break anything on purpose. It is very important that they are allowed to make a mess.

If the therapist works permanently in a school setting, they are likely to become one of the child's trusted adults, whom they can speak to at any time about their worries.

The therapist may be able to step in to support a child they work with at times of high emotional need; not just in their regular sessions. This is obviously an advantage to having an in-house therapist and will not be possible in all schools.

Crucially, therapy should always respect the boundaries of confidentiality in order to promote the psychological safety of the child within the therapeutic space. The principle of confidentiality is based on mutual respect, trust and honesty but it is not an absolute. Confidentiality can be breached with specific permission granted by the child and should always be breached in order to safeguard a child. Information regarding risks to the self and others should always be communicated. It is also important to note that a child may ask the therapist to speak to their parents on their behalf, perhaps because they predict that their parents may not react emotionally towards the therapist in the same way that they might towards the child. Additionally, if the therapist feels that it would be useful to share some information with the child's teaching staff, they should seek permission from the child first, explaining why they think this would be helpful.

Working within the system

No single teacher, CAMHS practitioner, therapist or social worker can have a complete picture regarding a child's needs, family and circumstances without all the adults around the child communicating and sharing information. If children and families are to receive the right help at the right time, everyone who comes into contact with the child has a role to play in identifying concerns and taking proactive, prompt action.

Legislation, such as the Children Act 2004, as amended by the Children and Social Work Act 2017, and most recently *Working Together to Safeguard Children* (HM Government, 2018) strengthens the need for key agencies to communicate, share information and work effectively together, in order to both safeguard and protect the welfare of children. Partnership between schools and other agencies is essential in order to:

- protect children from maltreatment
- prevent impairment of children's health and development
- ensure that children grow up in circumstances consistent with the provision of safe and effective care
- take action to enable all children to have the best outcomes.

(Children and Social Work Act, 2017)

However, there is no getting away from the fact that communication between different systems and cultures (for example, between schools and CAMHS) is often difficult due to both teaching staff and health professionals having significant workloads and time pressures. Some areas have set up regular consultation slots between such services or have regular communication based on the individual relationships within local areas which have developed over time. Frequently, communication is on a case-by-case basis, which means that there is great disparity regarding how much the 'team around the child' communicates for different children. This often reflects level of concern, clinical presentation or the extent of risk of harm to the child or other people. As we all know, high workloads are not a sufficient reason to explain a lack of information sharing in relation to protecting the welfare of children. Unfortunately, serious case reviews repeatedly highlight missed opportunities to share information in a timely manner, and to record and understand the significance of pieces of information.

General data protection regulation

It is also worth highlighting that new data protection legislation (the Data Protection Act 2018 and the General Data Protection Regulation, or GDPR) should not be a barrier to sharing information regarding a child in order to safeguard and promote the welfare of children. Even very personal and sensitive information can be shared if this is felt it will contribute to safeguarding a child. Although it is good practice to do this with the consent of parents, this is not necessary if there are concerns that gathering this consent from parents would be detrimental to the child's welfare.

Accessing support

It is important to be aware of local sources of help and support and how to access them. Arrangements will vary across the country, with many CAMHS teams now operating a 'Single Point of Access' number which can be used for both referrals and advice. Some areas may have specific advice lines for other professionals. Waiting times for face-to-face assessments and interventions can be long, but you may also be signposted to other helpful resources or agencies. Take the time to become familiar with your local practices and procedures. Schools must also be familiar with the local services that support families via an Early Help Assessment. The directory can usually be found on the local authority's website. Taking the time to network with colleagues in other agencies, such as those listed above, and build strong relationships is very important. Setting up regular local network meetings can be really beneficial for the process of reviewing vulnerable children and families.

Summary

- Early identification of emotional and mental health needs in children is essential if we are to reduce their future impact.

- Taking time to mindfully observe children is key – notice the changes and develop an effective system for remembering your observations.

- Following the graduated approach of Assess, Plan, Do, Review gives a sound foundation to responding to mental health difficulties in the classroom.

- Ensure that school procedures and policies for recording and reporting concerns are followed in a timely manner.

- Although some children will have specific diagnoses, every child is unique. The strategies in this book can be used regardless of diagnosis.

- Various agencies can support a child and their family with their mental health, ranging from universal, available-to-all services to more specialised, targeted services such as CAMHS.

- CAMHS is usually the term used when referring to tier 2 or 3 NHS services.

- The Thrive model is moving mental health support towards a more needs-led, collaborative approach.

- It is vital for the support system around a child to work together and find a way to communicate concerns to ensure information is shared effectively.

- Processes for accessing advice and support will vary. It is important to be familiar with local practices and procedures.

References

American Psychiatric Association (2013) *Diagnostic and statistical manual of mental disorders* (5th Ed). Washington DC: APA.

Anna Freud Centre (2019) *THRIVE Framework for System Change*. Available from: www.annafreud.org/media/9254/thrive-framework-for-system-change-2019.pdf

Butler G (1998) Clinical formulation. In: AS Bellack & M Hersen (Eds) *Comprehensive Clinical Psychology*. Oxford: Pergamon.

Children's Society (2008) *The Good Childhood Inquiry: Health research evidence*. London: Children's Society.

Department for Education (2019) *Keeping Children Safe in Education: Statutory guidance for schools and colleges*. Available from: https://assets.publishing.service.gov.uk/government/uploads/system/uploads/attachment_data/file/835733/Keeping_children_safe_in_education_2019.pdf

Division of Clinical Psychology (2011) *Good Practice Guidelines on the Use of Psychological Formulation*. Leicester: British Psychological Society.

Felitti M, Anda R, Nordenberg M *et al* (1998) Relationship of childhood abuse and household dysfunction to many of the leading causes of death in adults: The Adverse Childhood Experiences (ACE) Study. *American Journal of Preventative Medicine* **14** (4) 245-258.

Goodman A, Joyce R & Smith JP (2011) The long shadow cast by childhood physical and mental health problems on adult life. *Proceedings of the National Academy of Sciences of the United States of America* **108** (15) 6032–6037.

Goodman R (1997) The Strengths and Difficulties Questionnaire: A research note. *Journal of Child Psychology and Psychiatry*, **38**, 581–586.

HM Government. Children and Social Work Act (2017). Available at: http://www.legislation.gov.uk/ukpga/2017/16/contents/enacted.

HM Government (2018) *Working Together: Transitional guidance - Statutory guidance for Local Safeguarding Children Boards, local authorities, safeguarding partners, child death review partners, and the Child Safeguarding Practice Review Panel*. Available from: https://assets.publishing.service.gov.uk/government/uploads/system/uploads/attachment_data/file/722306/Working_Together-transitional_guidance.pdf.

HM Government (2018a) *Working Together to Safeguard Children: A guide to inter-agency working to safeguard and promote the welfare of children*. Available from https://assets.publishing.service.gov.uk/government/uploads/system/uploads/attachment_data/file/779401/Working_Together_to_Safeguard-Children.pdf.

Hughes K, Bellis M, Hardcastle K *et al* (2017) The effect of multiple adverse childhood experiences on health: A systematic review and meta-analysis. *The Lancet: Public Health* **2** (8) 356–366.

Marshall L, Wishart R, Dunatchik A & Smith N (2017) *Supporting Mental Health in Schools and Colleges*. Quantitative Survey. Nat Cen Social Research. Department for Education. Available from: https://assets.publishing.service.gov.uk/government/uploads/system/uploads/attachment_data/file/634728/Supporting_Mental-health_Case_study_report.pdf

National i-Thrive Programme, UK. Available from http://implementingthrive.org/about-us/i-thrive-implementing-thrive/

NHS Long Term Plan (2019). Available from https://www.longtermplan.nhs.uk/wp-content/uploads/2019/08/nhs-long-term-plan-version-1.2.pdf

NICE guidance (2011) *Common Mental Health Problems: Identification and pathways to care. Clinical guideline* [CG123]. Available at: https://www.nice.org.uk/guidance/cg123.

Royal College of Psychiatrists Core Curriculum (2013) *Formulation*. Available from www.rcpsych.ac.uk/docs/default-source/training/curricula-and-guidance/curricula-core-psychiatry-curriculum-april-2018.pdf?sfvrsn=881b63ca_2

SEN Code of Practice 0–25 years Statutory Guidance (2015). Available from www.gov.uk/government/publications/send-code-of-practice-0-to-25

The Nurture Group Network Ltd (2018) *The Boxall Profile*. Available from https://www.nurtureuk.org/introducing-nurture/boxall-profile

Wolpert M, Harris R, Jones M et al (2014) THRIVE: The AFC–Tavistock model for CAMHS [online]. Available from www.annafreud.org/media/2552/thrive-booklet_march-15.pdf

World Health Organisation. *ICD-10*. Available from www.who.int/classifications/icd/icdonlineversions/en/

World Health Organisation. *ICD-11*. Available from www.who.int/classifications/icd/en/

Chapter 2: Ready to Learn

As we begin to consider how our daily practices can support all children to overcome barriers in their learning and boost their wellbeing, including those with mental health difficulties, it is helpful to pause and consider what an individual child needs to become 'ready to learn'.

Imagine a class in front of you as the day begins, each child displaying signs that they are fully engaged and ready to learn. This is the ideal – the holy grail of teaching. And it doesn't exist. Every child brings their unique tendencies, strengths and needs into the classroom with them each morning. Every morning is different from the last. The class as a whole is ever evolving and bubbling along. Each unique child bounces off the other, in positive and less positive ways: unpredictable, challenging and hopefully inspiring to those who teach them. But how do we consider them all and guide them to a place where they are able to engage fully with the activities of the day?

The idea of a child being 'ready to learn' can be explored through several different lenses – many factors can be considered when personalising learning opportunities. This chapter looks at the 'big picture' concepts – the prerequisites that research shows are non-negotiable for learning and the mindsets and motivations that we need to foster in children. The chapter will explore how to view the uniqueness of each child in a positive way and consider how to help them bring their strengths to the process of learning. It looks at how creating a nurturing environment, focused on the connection between staff and children, can move children closer to the point of readiness. Finally, it considers how we can best engage parents to support children in their learning.

What does a child need before they can learn?

The Introduction briefly explored Maslow's Hierarchy of Needs (Maslow, 1943) with regard to the impact that mental health difficulties can have on a child's ability to meet their self-fulfilment needs. We know that schools must provide for a child's basic physical and psychological safety needs before expecting learning to take place. Promoting safety in the classroom encompasses communicating clear expectations of the rules and boundaries of the space. Routines and rituals built into children's daily experiences help make the world more predictable, and therefore safe. How to create this nurturing classroom ethos of safety will be explored later in this chapter and in **Chapter 4: Wellbeing for All**. We must provide for children's psychological needs; that is, fostering secure attachment with adults and peers and helping them to develop a sense of belonging in school. These ideas will be explored again in **Chapter 4**. Children also need to experience accomplishment and recognition in order to develop healthy self-esteem. This is explored further in **Chapter 5: Building Emotional Intelligence**. In order to progress towards self-actualisation, children need rich opportunities to learn, create and develop. This needs to occur in a supportive environment, where they are allowed to make mistakes and encouraged to recover from these setbacks. Ways to do this are outlined below.

It is important to highlight that although high levels of stress are detrimental to the learning process, learning should not be so passive that the appropriate connections in the brain are not made. Learning something new causes the brain to build connections between brain cells (neurons). Neuroplasticity refers to the brain's ability to change and make new connections throughout life. Children's brains are especially plastic. Active learning, that engages multiple senses, is what all teachers are striving for. An optimum level of autonomic arousal (or stress) enables you to learn better. However, a brain that is flooded with stress neurochemicals, such as cortisol, will struggle to take on new information.

Learning mindsets and motivation

Helping all children develop effective mindsets and motivations for learning is essential, but it will be especially beneficial for those who are facing barriers in their learning due to mental health difficulties.

Self-efficacy

Bandura introduced the concept of self-efficacy, which refers to an individual's belief in their capacity to execute behaviours necessary to produce specific performance attainments (Bandura, 1997). Self-efficacy makes a difference to how an individual feels, thinks and acts. It is not an all-or-nothing state and will fluctuate and develop over time. Fostering self-efficacy in children is likely to be beneficial, as individuals with high self-efficacy are more likely to view difficult tasks as challenges to be mastered (and less likely to utilise avoidance). They are more likely, compared to those with low efficacy, to develop a deeper interest and stronger sense of commitment to the activities they participate in. Crucially, they recover from setbacks and disappointments quicker too. Bandura discussed four main conditions necessary to foster self-efficacy:

- Mastery experiences: Having the experience of success supports developing self-efficacy. This highlights the need for appropriate scaffolding so students have sufficient levels of support to experience a positive sense of achievement.

- Social modelling: We are more likely to believe we can achieve and perform well if we observe others (especially those we perceive as similar to ourselves) successfully completing tasks.

- Social persuasion: Verbal encouragement or persuading others that they do have the skills and capabilities necessary to complete a task can be effective.

- Psychological responses: How we perceive and interpret our emotional state (e.g. our moods, feelings, stress levels and physical cues) can also impact on our beliefs about our capabilities.

Growth mindset

Carol Dweck has described how a fixed mindset, or personal belief system, in which one believes they only possess a certain amount of a particular quality leads to an individual having an all-consuming need to prove themselves (Dweck, 2017). She explains the doubt that can exist in every situation they encounter:

Will I succeed or fail? Will I look smart or dumb? Will I be accepted or rejected? Will I feel like a winner or a loser? (Dweck, 2017)

All teachers will have seen how these questions can play out in the classroom in the form of obvious worries and a reluctance to try, or perhaps masked with anger and challenging behaviours. Dweck also highlights that when an individual is focused on questions such as these, they are unable to focus on the actual task and enjoyment of learning. With a mindset of growth, however, your innate intelligence, talents and temperament are simply the foundations from which you can grow – through effort, experience and drawing on the support of others.

Many schools have begun teaching the concept of growth mindset to children and we would encourage every teacher to seize opportunities to discuss it with their classes. When faced with a difficult situation, we can help children to think through the possible responses and guide them towards positive solutions, rather than admitting defeat or reacting negatively. Children also need to know that they are allowed to make mistakes, whether these be in their learning or in their behaviour. We need to support them through the process of recovering from these mistakes and restoring what needs to be restored (this is explored further in *Chapter 3: A Whole-School Approach*). 'Seeds of Hope', a lesson plan relating to these ideas, can be found in *Chapter 19: Resources and Lesson Plans* in Section 5.

Motivation

The Theory of Motivation suggests that there are two types of motivation – intrinsic, in which an individual is motivated to behave in a certain way as a result of their values, interests or morality; and extrinsic, in which motivation instead comes from external factors, such as the expectations of others or the promise of rewards (Ryan & Deci, 1985). The Self-Determination Theory develops this model further, differentiating between autonomous motivation, which includes intrinsic motivators and extrinsic motivators which align with an individual's values; controlled motivation, whereby an individual strives for rewards or where there is fear of punishment; and introjected regulation, in which individuals may endeavour to avoid shame or seek approval (Deci & Ryan, 2008).

How does this theory translate to the classroom? In the vast range of behaviours and attitudes to learning that occur in the classroom each day, we see all these types of motivation in action – but to really understand which motivator causes a child to act in a certain way, we need to take time to get to know them well. A child may consistently follow the rules and always give full effort to learning activities – but is this because they love learning; because they have a strong sense of right and wrong; because they are desperate to move up a reward chart; or because they are seeking the approval of adults? A child may consistently break the rules, show challenging behaviours and refuse to engage with their learning – but is this because they see no value in learning; because there is no reward system that inspires them; or because they are struggling with more complex needs that must be addressed before learning is possible?

'Does it matter?', some may argue. How can we possibly understand every motivator for all the children in our classes? This is a valid point – of course, we cannot know it all and motivators will evolve with time. But there is value in understanding this theory and using it to consider what may be going on when a child is struggling with their motivation for learning. By gradually exploring the ideas around motivation with our classes, we can support them to engage further with learning and challenge unhelpful beliefs about punishment, rewards and approval. Ideally, it is healthy for children to work towards developing intrinsic and autonomous motivation – in this way they will have a drive to continue lifelong learning and act in a way which aligns with their core values and morals. However, often our systems for rewards and punishments in schools can undermine this. Traditional reward charts and behaviour systems encourage children to act in a certain way in order to gain a reward. They may work in the moment, but there is evidence to suggest their long-term effect on motivation may be limited (Fabes *et al*, 1989). At times, especially with very specific and restrictive charts on which children can be moved up and down a scale, they may actually harm self-esteem and motivation.

A child who never gets to experience success or have their efforts acknowledged is unlikely to develop a growth mindset and feel a drive to push themselves further in their learning. They will not believe that it is possible for them. We believe that all learning is an individual journey and no child's journey needs to be publicly compared to that of another child. However, having said that, it is important to note that children with ASC may have an increased need for tangible reinforcers as they are more likely to have reduced motivation to please others. This is related to delays in the development of their theory of mind – the ability to understand that others' thoughts, feelings and experiences are (or may be) different from our own.

Overall it is helpful to move towards a culture of acknowledgement of effort and progress rather than simply rewarding for success. Having positive recognition is often what children are looking for anyway – this doesn't always need to be connected to a reward or prize. Praise can be particularly important for children with behavioural problems or neurodevelopmental problems, such as ADHD, whose undesired behaviour may often become the focus, and they can easily develop a negative view of themselves. If they overcome these difficulties to show effort, the recognition of this can be beneficial for their self-esteem and self-image. Another caveat however: some children, for instance those with Oppositional Defiant Disorder (ODD) or attachment difficulties, can find it difficult to receive praise. It may cause suspicion, anger or rejection of the praise, or the individual giving the praise. Caution and sensitivity must be shown in these circumstances. It may be that the child will only be able to accept the recognition some time after the event or perhaps by 'overhearing' an indirect acknowledgement from one adult to another. If the child struggles especially with direct verbal praise, this could be avoided and they could be given the choice to display a piece of work on a recognition board.

The above ideas can be linked to a whole-school system for positivity, which we will explore further in *Chapter 3: A Whole-School Approach to Mental Health and Wellbeing*. The 'Thinking about…' box in Chapter 3 explores how to give praise and recognition in ways that can increase intrinsic motivation and support learning and prosocial behaviours, without comparison or shaming of others.

Reframing the unique child

Knowing the child in front of you

When teachers meet their classes, full of different characters and individual needs, everything and everyone seems important and worthy of their attention. It can be overwhelming and difficult to know where to begin. We advocate beginning with the unique child and reframing their individuality. Discovering their needs is essential, of course, but so is discovering their strengths. We need to move away from an attitude of 'they always' or 'they never' and putting them in a box that limits and disempowers. Instead, we need to shift to an attitude of acceptance of who they are – valuing and nurturing their interests and strengths, acknowledging their dislikes and struggles and being prepared to enter into their learning journey with them as an individual. Teaching staff can reframe the child, and can also reframe the challenge – it is an opportunity and a privilege to help children achieve their potential and discover who they truly are.

We must also remember that different members of teaching staff can have different perspectives on the same child. Colleagues may not always agree on what is going on for a child or what they need. As humans, we are all vulnerable to unconsciously basing our decisions and opinions on common stereotypes e.g. gender and socio-economic variables. We also bring our own experiences and bias into each situation, without intention. We can navigate this by really seeing the child we have in front of us and with honest and open communication. It is not easy – it takes practice and needs a supportive whole-school culture, where discussion is valued.

In Chapter 1 we discussed that it can be a real challenge to keep track of all insights gathered as teachers get to know a class. Trying to hold it all in our heads may work for some, but inevitably, some gems of information will get forgotten. Keeping a record of ongoing notes is not only useful from the point of view of safeguarding and recording concerns, but can also be used as a tool to boost connection with a class or individual child. Teaching staff can remember something significant they have said or an achievement from outside school. They can ask the class or child about their interests or get them to teach a new skill they have learnt. They can show them that they matter. It is also important to remember those children who may not respond in the expected way to what most perceive as exciting events in the school year. Dress down days, productions and visits may be a source of worry to some – we will explore these further in *Chapter 4: Wellbeing for All*. In *Chapter 17: Yearly Transitions*, we explore considerations related to school and family holidays in more detail.

Of course, it must also be acknowledged that it is not possible to personalise absolutely everything. There are times in the school day when a child will need to take part in activities that are not best suited to their personality, preferred learning styles or interests. This is unavoidable at times and also necessary. As well as providing for their individual preferences, it is the responsibility of teaching staff to show children that they are part of a wider community – a community in which there are lots of individuals working and learning together, all with different needs and wishes.

Personality or temperament?

Personality is a socio-cultural concept. Developmental psychologists generally interpret individual differences in children as an expression of temperament rather than personality (Rothbart *et al*, 2000). Traits develop and change throughout our lifespan. There are five broad dimensions commonly used to describe the human personality, according to the Big 5 Personality Theory (Digman, 1990). These are:

- Openness to experience
- Conscientiousness
- Extroversion
- Agreeableness
- Neuroticism

Personality develops throughout childhood – it is not fixed. For this reason, it is actually more helpful to think in terms of a child's temperament, rather than personality. This allows us to move away from restricting labels, as described above. Rather than dictating that a child is 'very shy', we can reframe this as 'tends towards introversion'. A 'very shy' child can become limited by the inadvertent messages we give – 'Oh, he's so shy! He won't want to do this. I'll give this part in the play to someone more confident.' If we understand that the child has a tendency towards introversion, we see their 'shyness' in less fixed terms. We can offer them chances to step outside of their comfort zone, while acknowledging their preferences and skills. We can express a learning opportunity in a positive way and emphasise their talents: 'How would you like to take some funny lines in the play? I think you'd deliver them really well as you have such a good sense of humour.'

At the very least, tuning into a child's temperament can help teaching staff understand why certain learning situations work well for the child and others don't. For a child with a temperament tending towards introversion, the prospect of working in a group situation or taking part in a class assembly may cause worry, but they may feel unable to express this to an adult. Conversely, for a child with a temperament that tends towards extroversion, the prospect of working on tasks quietly and independently may frustrate them. By beginning relaxed conversations about personality and temperament in the classroom, teaching staff can raise children's awareness of traits they may have and give them insight into why they may feel the way they do in certain situations. Opportunities can then be provided to help children discover information about themselves and this can be used in partnership with them to personalise their learning.

Learning styles or learning preferences?

We are all familiar with the idea of 'learning styles' and it is likely that all teaching staff have given at least some thought to the preferred learning styles of those they teach. The VARK learning style model encourages us to think about which stimuli or activity help children (and adults) learn most effectively: visual, auditory, reading and writing or kinaesthetic (Fleming & Mills, 1992). However, a review of the research into the benefits of teaching according to learning styles has found little evidence that it improves learning outcomes (Pashler *et al*, 2008).

Whatever the debate concludes, teaching staff instinctively know that it is sensible to provide a range of different learning activities across each day and week. We would also argue that practical (or kinaesthetic) learning is beneficial for all, especially for children with additional needs who may find it hard to concentrate on auditory or written information. As we have described above, it is more important to tune in to the individual interests and strengths of a child and follow these in order to allow them to better access learning. Children will of course have notable preferences for learning activities, however, and it is helpful to work with them to discover what these are. See **Chapter 19: Resources and Lesson Plans** for 'How I like to learn', a photocopiable frame to support this process.

Interests and strengths

We have acknowledged that it is vital to get to know children and to understand their unique interests and innate strengths. Following the spark of a child's curiosity is likely to engage them and motivate them in their learning. Providing opportunities for them to demonstrate and develop existing talents allows them the chance to experience learning within their comfort zone and experience mastery (Valentine, *et al* 2004). Additionally, getting to know a child's likes and dislikes is a great opportunity to boost connection. It is also important to discover what a child believes are the areas they need to practise and improve, and especially which of these they are currently keen to work on. See **Chapter 19** for 'This is me' and 'All about school', photocopiable frames to help children share important information about their interests, strengths and areas of need.

Significant dates and events

Having a knowledge of significant dates in a child's life is very important. Not only does it allow positive connection – relating to birthdays, for instance; it also allows adults to prepare for and anticipate difficult anniversaries. These might include bereavements (of family members, friends or pets) or parental separations. These events may trigger emotional or behavioural changes for the child. Perhaps adults at home are thinking or talking about them, or the child associates the event with a particular time of year or something in their environment. Being aware that dates are approaching allows teaching staff to prepare and be sensitive to the child's needs at this time.

Connection and nurture

We have mentioned above about the importance of getting to know children well – but why is this connection so important in schools? There is much literature concerning the science of connection within the parent–child relationship and how this leads to secure attachments. But how can this be applied to our connections with the children we teach? In her book *Why Love Matters*, psychotherapist Sue Gerhardt describes how the interactions between a parent and child in the early years of life literally wire the child's brain and can support or undermine their future emotional wellbeing (Gerhardt, 2004). There is a wealth of helpful information in this book, but here we will consider two elements of these interactions that we can take into our practice. First is the power of positive looks. She highlights research that suggests that positive looks are vitally important to growing a socially and emotionally intelligent brain (Schore, 1994). Smiles from parent to child trigger hormonal changes which help neurons to grow. The old teaching adage 'don't smile until Christmas' suggests we should withhold warmth from children in order to assert authority and show a class you mean business – hopefully most teachers would find this laughable today, but this research reminds us that our smile, our sense of humour and our ability to create a connection with children holds power. Children need this connection in order to feel safe and in order to learn. Second, Gerhardt discusses the importance of adults being well attuned to children and giving quality verbal feedback to support their emotional development. In practice, this involves taking time for the acknowledgement of emotions and giving the child the appropriate words to express them. For some children this experience in a school environment may not be replicated at home, which elevates its importance. We will explore how we can do this in school in ***Chapter 5: Building Emotional Intelligence***.

Secure relationships and connection between individuals fosters cooperation (Markham, 2015). Clinical psychologist Dr Laura Markham explains that when children have strong connections with adults, they actually *want* to cooperate with them. Strengthening connections can ultimately decrease defiance and challenging behaviours. There are so many ways to build connections and community in schools – on an individual level, with a class or with the whole-school community. In subsequent chapters, we will dive into these in detail. Supporting some children, for example those with attachment difficulties, to make these connections and trust others may take considerably more time, skill and patience.

Connection is one of the many things we can achieve through using nurturing practices in school. Nurtureuk describe nurture as highlighting:

'... the importance of social environments – who you're with, and not who you're born to – and its significant influence on social and emotional skills, wellbeing and behaviour.'

The nurture movement began in the late 1960s, through the pioneering work of educational psychologist Marjorie Boxall and headteacher Sylvia Lucas, who were working to support children from difficult socioeconomic backgrounds in London (nurtureuk.com). The six core principles of nurture are:

- Children's learning is understood developmentally
- The classroom offers a safe base
- The importance of nurture for the development of wellbeing
- Language is a vital means of communication
- All behaviour is communication
- The importance of transition in children's lives

(Lucas *et al*, 2006)

Schools are well placed to provide targeted opportunities to children who may, for whatever reason, have missed out on early attachment, emotional and social experiences at home. By thoughtfully and carefully addressing these needs as a priority, we can enable children to thrive in school and later in life. It is important to note that we can all be practitioners of nurture and we can all prioritise connection in our interactions with children. In the schools we have visited, we have seen that is possible to embed such provision and care into all classroom and school practices. Achieving this is no easy task and time must be taken to ensure that all staff are on board with the principles of such an approach, such as those outlined below. Appropriate training for all and consistency from adults are key. Sometimes the parents that we encounter may benefit from a nurturing approach as well.

These principles give schools a strong foundation to work from when considering how to support children with their emotional and social needs. Schools that wish to take further steps in this area can undertake various training programmes, for example through the National Nurturing Schools Programme and the Thrive® Approach. Details can be found in ***Further Reading and Guidance***.

Parental engagement and support

Parents play a pivotal role in helping their children become ready to learn. We cannot control what happens when a child heads home at the end of the day, but we can put systems and strategies in place that will help parents to help their children. Working in partnership with parents and families is something we all strive for. Great benefits are reaped when all adults are working in a supportive team around a child. But achieving this takes work on both sides. When we are supporting children with mental health needs, it is especially vital that we keep working to build strong relationships with parents – and to support and encourage their relationships with other professionals, too. Let's consider some of the factors we need to think about when engaging with parents.

On the part of the parent, a number of conscious and unconscious barriers may exist to full engagement with their child's learning. These include:

- time
- their spoken language
- understanding and acceptance of additional needs
- interest and motivation
- willingness to accept and follow advice
- their own personal history of school and contact with professionals.

We need to view these without judgement, be sensitive to the implications and offer or direct them to appropriate support where we can. If a parent had a negative experience of school, this may colour their judgements and reactions without them even realising. Consider the occasional response of 'What has he/she done now?' when a teacher asks to see a parent at the end of the day, when in actual fact that teacher wanted to tell them something positive. By making a point of sharing specific praise more frequently, we can gradually demonstrate that a child is having positive experiences at school that outweigh the negatives. The 'Thinking about...' box on parental engagement below considers various different ways of doing this.

On the part of teaching staff, barriers to full engagement with parents may also exist. These include:

- time
- confidence
- knowledge and training
- approachability.

Simply being approachable at the classroom door and ready to chat goes such a long way. It builds the foundations of strong connections that will be beneficial for all children, whether they have additional needs or not. However, having the time to talk at length with parents (which is often what is needed) is immensely difficult at the beginning and end of the school day. Schools can support teaching staff by having a system in school to allow for necessary meetings, providing training on specific areas and having clear policies on systems for communicating with parents.

When it is difficult to engage and communicate with parents, step back and take time to consider what is happening. Think about:

- What may be going on for them at that time – in their present life or in their memories of past experiences. As we have said, consider if their own experience of school may now be impacting on their child. To help in this situation, always make any advice about the child, rather than the parent. They need to feel supported, not reprimanded.

- Taking opportunities to address any misconceptions as soon as possible. Teaching staff should be open and honest about mistakes or things that have been forgotten, and be quick to apologise when necessary. We all value this when things go awry. Avoid grudges forming on either side. A child should never be made to feel stuck in the middle between a school and their parents. We all need to be on the same side.

Thinking about ... parental engagement

Think creatively about strategies for engaging parents with their child's learning and with the whole-school community. Some ideas to consider:

- **Classroom**
  - Make time for the little and the big conversations on the door and in the playground.
  - Make it a habit to pass on specific praise and new progress at the end of the day, especially for those with mental health needs and challenging behaviours.

- Be consistent with communication and homework. Putting notes in the window or in the reading diary takes moments, but it really matters. Stick to a chosen homework routine and ensure it gets marked each week.

- Use the windows – display a weekly timetable, a star learner board and other systems to recognise effort, and a PSHE target of the week e.g. *We are learning to offer help to our classmates*. Make it easy for parents to know what is going on in the classroom.

- Invite parents to help in the classroom as often as possible, with reading, theme days and visits. Make them feel welcome and valued. Send thank you emails or cards after specific events.

- If difficult messages need to be conveyed about a child's day, or overall issues that have arisen in class, pass these on as soon as possible, be it in person, by phone or by email (for whole class concerns, for example, if a difficult conversation about a particular subject has arisen in PSHE).

Assemblies and productions

- Invite parents to special assemblies (class assemblies, celebration assemblies, music or singing performance assemblies and significant events such as Remembrance Day). Ask children to make and write the invitations themselves. Post them if there is enough time.

- Make a fuss of parents when they arrive for assemblies and productions. Have children welcoming them in and handing out programmes. Provide drinks and biscuits. Provide an area with toys and books for younger siblings at the back of the hall. Make it easy and enjoyable for the whole family to be there.

Meetings

- Meet the Teacher – these meetings are standard practice early in each academic year. Have an open forum for questions at the end. If possible, repeat daytime meetings in the evening to allow working parents to attend. Ensure that all information given is available to parents unable to attend. Make it easy for parents with younger children to attend these meetings by offering a creche.

- Parent–teacher consultation – at the initial meeting in the Autumn term try not to launch in with all the things you need to convey. Ask the parent for their views on how things are going first (and ask the child too if they are present). Try asking: 'What three important things would you like me to know about your child?' Use the opportunity to get to know the child's interests and strengths.

- Individual meetings – having an agreed system or venue for meetings with parents is helpful: perhaps a comfortable and cosy space that is not in the classroom. It is important to be able to talk in a private, neutral and relaxed environment, where the child and siblings can play freely if necessary.

→

■ **Whole-school**

- ■ Promote parent volunteering wherever possible and have a system for extending thanks on a regular basis.

- ■ If possible, have a member of the senior leadership on the gate or in the playground every morning (see further discussion of this in Chapter 1).

- ■ Have a variety of systems for sending positive messages home to parents, over and above the usual 'star of the week'. School postcards can be posted home with specific praise from class teachers or other members of staff. This is especially powerful for children who may find verbal feedback difficult, or for those parents who you often need to speak to about difficult issues at the end of the day.

- ■ Have an ongoing system for asking for positive feedback from parents. Regular formal surveys are helpful but an informal public system in the entrance hall is morale boosting for all. Parents could share things that are going well for their child on a white board or on 'sticky notes'. Also, if more appropriate, encourage parents to email positive comments to the office that can be passed directly to the class teacher.

- ■ Run regular parent workshops – these could be related to learning or pastoral issues. Many external providers will run workshops on online safety and other similar subjects, but there is great value in the headteacher or other member of the school community leading these. This helps to build trust and relationships within the school community. Additionally, parents who find it more difficult to accept direct advice may find this format of information sharing easier. Learning workshops could also involve children from Upper KS2 – a great opportunity for developing their leadership skills.

- ■ Whole-school events, such as open evenings and fairs, are a wonderful opportunity to meet with parents in a relaxed setting. All staff can use these times to connect with children and parents.

Some of the strategies in the 'Thinking about…' box may feel like they will take a lot of time and energy, when you are already stretched for both. We can't always remember to do everything, but even if things do just happen occasionally and even if they are small scale, they still matter to parents and children and they are remembered. It's the small things that are the foundations of strong relationships.

Summary

■ Consider the child in front of you: What do they need to be ready to learn? Remember this will be different from the child sitting next to them.

- Gently challenge fixed learning mindsets whenever you can.

- Consider how to develop each child's intrinsic motivation to learn.

- Use the small moments of your day to build connection – with children and parents.

- Think about how you can develop nurturing practices that support a child's ongoing emotional and social development – begin with making your classroom a safe space to be.

- Think creatively about the best ways to engage parents.

References

Bandura, A (1997) *Self-efficacy. The Exercise of Control*. New York: W.H. Freeman and Company.

Deci EL & Ryan RM (2008) Self-Determination Theory: A macrotheory of human motivation, development, and health. *Canadian Psychology / Psychologie Canadienne* **49** 182–185. doi:10.1037/a0012801

Digman JM (1990) Personality structure: Emergence of the five-factor model. *Annual Review of Psychology* **41** 417–440.

Dweck C (2017) *Mindset - Changing the Way you Think to Fulfill your Potential*. London: Robinson, Constable & Robinson Ltd.

Fabes RA, Fulse J, Eisenberg N *et al* (1989) Effects of rewards on children's prosocial motivation: A socialization study. *Developmental Psychology* **25** 509–515.

Fleming ND & Mills C (1992) Not another inventory, rather a catalyst for reflection. *To Improve the Academy* **11** 137–155. Available from https://digitalcommons.unl.edu/cgi/viewcontent.cgi?article=1245&context=podimproveacad

Gerhardt S (2014) *Why Love Matters: How Affection Shapes a Baby's Brain*. Abingdon: Routledge. pp. 41-43 and 50-52.

Lucas S, Insley K & Buckland G (2006) *Nurture Group Principles and Curriculum Guidelines Helping Children to Achieve*. The Nurture Group Network.

Markham L (2012) *Peaceful Parent, Happy Kids*. New York: Perigee Book. pp. 40 and 61-63.

Maslow AH (1943) A theory of human motivation. *Psychological Review* **50** (4) 370–396.

Nurtureuk.org (2019) *nurtureuk | An inclusive education for all*. [online] Available from www.nurtureuk.org

Pashler H, McDaniel M, Rohrer D *et al* (2008) Learning styles: Concepts and evidence. *Psychological Science in the Public Interest* **9** (3) 105–119. Available from https://pdfs.semanticscholar.org/6275/2ca4c446ca7328f8c284f5385f1af1c4212e.pdf

Rothbart MK, Ahadi SA & Evans DE (2000) Temperament and personality. Origins and outcomes. *Journal of Personality and Social Psychology* **78** (1) 122–135.

Ryan RM & Deci EL (1985) *Intrinsic Motivation and Self-Determination in Human Behavior*. New York: Plenum Press.

Schore A (1994) *Affect Regulation and the Origin of the Self*. Hillsdale: Lawrence Erlbaum Associates.

Valentine J, DuBois D & Cooper H (2004) The relation between self-beliefs and academic achievement: A meta-analytic review. *Educational Psychologist* **39** (2) 111–133.

Chapter 3: A Whole-School Approach to Mental Health and Wellbeing

Shaping whole-school culture

A culture of supporting and prioritising children's mental health and wellbeing must be embedded throughout an entire school. It must now become the expectation and the norm, and therefore be reflected throughout policies, daily practice and interactions. A teacher attempting to create a new culture in their classroom cannot work in isolation and as with any initiative in school, the chances of success are increased if a whole-school approach is taken (Bennett, 2017). An important consideration here is the integration of whole-school values, which is considered in detail in the 'Thinking about…' box below. It is also helpful to assume the collective benefit of many of the strategies and approaches suggested in this and the following chapters. Where a strategy is put in place to support the needs of a child with a mental health condition, the rest of the class may benefit too. For example, reducing environmental sensory stimulation for a child with a diagnosis of ASC will mean that all children experience a calmer and less cluttered classroom, which in turn will also support their learning. Keeping this in mind supports staff in understanding the significance of particular strategies, some of which may seem time consuming or difficult to implement.

This chapter begins by exploring how the language choices and communication styles we make as adults impact on children. It then looks in detail at how a school can create a behaviour policy that encompasses its core values, with a focus on restorative practice rather than discipline. How to plan for all needs is then explored, which involves supporting and upskilling TAs and designing effective interventions for those with additional needs. This chapter also considers how to approach assessment for children with mental health difficulties. Finally, it explores how to bring all this together with the new changes in policy, to create an ethos centred on wellbeing. For all the areas discussed in this chapter, we advocate consistency. Consistency and predictability contribute to a sense of safety for children. Uncertainty about how an adult will respond to a behaviour or an emotion will lead to additional stress for a child.

❓ Thinking about ... school values

Whole-school values can encapsulate the ethos of a school and provide a means to communicate this to all members of the school community. To be successful and to really make a difference to the children, these need to be fully integrated and embedded into daily practice and throughout all policies and procedures. Consider the following:

■ Whatever values a school chooses, they need to be more than just a slogan for the website. This needs to be the beating heart of the school and every member of the school community should understand what they mean.

■ Some suggestions to consider:

   ■ Respect, happiness, safety, partnership, generosity, kindness, perseverance, honesty, reflection, curiosity, cooperation, community ... the list could go on.

   ■ The values could be linked to an overall theme: perhaps focused on confidence and building resilience; perhaps focused on knowing oneself and striving to reach one's potential; perhaps focused on fostering a love of learning that will stay with a child for life.

■ We suggest a maximum of five core values so that they can be easily recalled by children. Linking them to child-friendly characters can support understanding and integration into daily school life.

■ The values can then feed into many areas of school life:

   ■ Policies

   ■ Assemblies

   ■ Systems for praise and recognition

   ■ Linking to conversations about learning and behaviour

   ■ Displays in classrooms and around school

   ■ Daily reflections

   ■ Linking to current events in our country and world

   ■ Values awards for children who have demonstrated a value well

There are many values worth choosing and many creative ways to explore them in school. Each school will know what is right for them, depending on their exact circumstances.

Communication and language

Teaching staff are constantly moderating their communication styles and language as they teach. The idea that careful thought is needed in this regard is nothing new. But there is definitely a more recent shift in the understanding of the kind of language that is most beneficial to children – in home and school environments. The words used and the manner in which they are delivered have a lasting impact on children. Language choice should build children up, rather than undermine them; it should communicate belief and hope, rather than shame.

We fully support 'no shouting' policies, which many schools are already adopting. While we recognise that teachers and parents are all human, shouting demonstrates an element of dysregulation on the adult's part. Children learn through social modelling. If teachers are able to effectively model how to manage negative emotions – that is, how to recognise and name them – they can then demonstrate to children how to modify their thoughts and behaviours, in order to gradually change a negative emotional state into a positive one. We must always remain conscious of the need to regulate our own emotions, in order to be able to support children to regulate theirs. We will explore this further in ***Chapter 5: Building Emotional Intelligence***.

Teaching staff also need to move away from using negative labels for children and their behaviours, such as 'naughty' or 'bad'. If a negative or distress behaviour is 'branded' in a certain way and attributed to a child's personality, a child (who's sense of self is still developing) will begin to believe that they are actually like that. This language becomes a self-fulfilling prophecy.

So overall, what kinds of language choices should teaching staff be striving to avoid?

- Shaming or humiliating language
- Threats
- Commands and demands
- Negative labels (as described above)

The 'Thinking about...' box below considers how we can make language choices that show we value children and also engages their cooperation. These are important for all children, but they are especially vital for a child with mental health difficulties.

🤔 Thinking about … communication and language choices

Positive communication and language choices to consider:

- **Non-judgemental listening:** Be a good listener – Teachers with multiple demands on their time will understandably have challenges when it comes to giving children time and 'patient hearing' to their stories. But all children need attention and non-judgemental, patient hearing is most likely to make them feel confident and secure in your company.

- **Reframe disappointments:** Consider how disappointment in a child's achievement or behaviour is expressed in your classroom. Any language that could inadvertently send the message that a child is inherently not good enough or that compares them with others should be avoided. Reframe disappointments by turning them into an opportunity for growth and helping a child to identify their unique strengths. Mistakes are learning opportunities and can be celebrated as such; the 'marvellous mistakes' that children demonstrate can enable others to learn from them and enrich class discussion.

- **Engage cooperation:** In their book *How to Talk So Kids Will Listen and Listen So Kids Will Talk*, Adele Faber and Elaine Mazlish describe various ways in which parents can engage their children's cooperation without resorting to the negative language choices listed above (Faber & Mazlish, 2013). Two of these ways that are particularly applicable to everyday classroom practice and can be used in a huge variety of situations are:

  - *Describe the problem* – Rather than saying 'Clear up this mess!' try 'Your table is not tidy yet'.

  - *Give information* – Rather than saying 'If you draw on the table one more time, you are going to lose your breaktime!' try 'Tables are not for drawing on. Paper is for drawing on. Would you like some paper?'

- **Open and relaxed body language:** As far as possible, stay on the child's level and make eye contact (if appropriate for the child). Avoid towering over a child, especially when giving difficult messages. Keep an open posture and think about your proximity to the child – stay at a safe distance when a child is very dysregulated, but it may be appropriate to move closer as they calm down. Not only does using open and relaxed body language help children, but it also helps adults to regulate their own emotional state.

- The PACE approach to communication, designed by Dr Daniel Hughes for use in dyadic developmental psychotherapy (DDP network), focuses on the whole child. It supports them to feel safe with adults and establish an attitude of reflection and growth in relation to their emotions and behaviours. It also enables adults to identify the child's strengths that lie underneath challenging behaviours. Despite the approach being developed primarily for children with attachment difficulties, it is a helpful framework to use when thinking about our interactions with all children. PACE stands for:

  - Playfulness – Interact with lightness and fun in your voice, tone and actions. This can help to diffuse difficult situations, help children to practise processing positive feelings (which for some can be as difficult as negative feelings) and creates connection.

  - Acceptance – Increase a child's sense of safety by offering full acceptance of them and their emotions. This doesn't mean all behaviours are accepted, but limits can be placed on behaviours while still accepting the feelings behind them.

  - Curiosity – Be curious about what feelings and motivations lie beneath a behaviour. Using phrases such as 'I wonder what…' or 'what do you think…' rather than demanding to know why a child did something brings a lightness and attitude of non-judgement to this process.

  - Empathy – Allow a child to feel your compassion for them. Demonstrate that you hear their feelings and you will be with them as they move through the distress.

For consistency in communication to be achieved across the school, the messages need to come from senior leadership. One teacher may be able to change the culture of language used in their classroom, but this needs to be embedded in the practice of all staff for it to have a true positive effect on the children.

Creating a behaviour policy that works for all

As we move away from the concept of 'the difficult child' to the ideas that all behaviour is a form of communication and all children are accepted, we need to ensure that school policies, especially the behaviour policy, reflect this. Many schools are achieving this using a therapeutic approach, centred on reflection, restoration and reconciliation. A behaviour policy also needs to be implemented using a graduated approach for those with SEND and mental health difficulties. When teaching staff examine the reasons behind a behaviour – the message that the child is trying to communicate – they will be better able to choose personalised strategies and interventions to support them to engage in prosocial behaviours.

It is important that the behaviour policy is underpinned by the whole-school ethos and core values, and as a new policy is being developed, staff, children and parents need to be involved as much as possible. Teaching staff need to be consulted and appropriate training and discussion opportunities provided regarding new concepts and ideas. The process of ensuring that all adults follow a therapeutic approach and avoid reactive strategies is not always easy, and it will take time. For the children, if they are able to give their views, and also give the policy a positive and child-friendly name, they will have more ownership over it and hopefully engage with it further.

Prosocial behaviours and recognition

A cornerstone of a behaviour policy that works for all is a framework of desired attitudes and behaviours and a system for recognising these, and therefore fostering positivity. As well as supporting children who are struggling with difficult behaviours, we need to encourage them to behave in a more positive manner and acknowledge those children who are always doing the right thing. As discussed in Chapter 2, traditionally, this acknowledgement has been achieved by using reward systems that are potentially shaming and humiliating for those not always doing the right thing. It is crucial that rewards are not in any way a form of bribery, and overall we should be aiming for rewards to take a higher priority than consequences.

Prosocial behaviours are those which benefit the individual and everyone around them. They help children to foster positive relationships with others, view mistakes as opportunities for growth and consider the impact of their actions on those around them. They include appropriate tone of voice, body language and positive language choices (even when communicating needs or frustrations). We have explored many of these above. By actively teaching and praising prosocial behaviours, we can help children make connections between what is happening now and the subsequent impact on others. We can also demonstrate that they are a valued and important part of something bigger than themselves – the class, the school community and the wider world.

The 'Thinking about...' box below considers how to give praise and recognition in ways that can support learning, prosocial behaviours and intrinsic motivation, without comparison or shaming of others.

❓ Thinking about ... how to give praise and recognition

How can we recognise effort with learning and prosocial behaviours and increase a child's intrinsic motivation? Some ideas to consider:

- Give daily personalised acknowledgement and praise of effort and prosocial behaviours in the classroom and around the school.

- Make praise specific. Avoid using the phrases 'good boy' or 'good girl'. 'Good job' is an alternative, but only if we expand this to fit the situation, for example 'Good job with your handwriting!'.

- Take this a step further by praising the process rather than the outcome. 'You worked hard to keep those letters on the line' or 'You have really taken time to picture this story setting in detail'.

- Praise the values shown by children. These may be traits you see them developing and want to encourage, or perhaps they link in with the core values of the school, for example, kindness, resilience or empathy.

- Relate praise to specific learning behaviours, for example, listening well, choosing resources that work for them, striving to edit or improve their work.

- House points can be awarded for specific behaviours or achievements that are significant for the child. Once awarded, they should not be taken away. Celebrate house point totals in assemblies – not for the sake of competition, but as a motivator for individual children that helps them to see their contribution to their house.

- Give healthy class rewards at the end of the day or week for whole-class effort in relation to specific behaviours or learning e.g. extra time outside or time for a favourite game, song or story. Try to avoid using food as a reward.

- Provide opportunities to work with younger children or take on extra roles and responsibilities.

- Ensure regular celebration and recognition of achievements and behaviour in assemblies.

- Offer special head teacher or governor awards for significant achievements or demonstrating school values.

- Provide opportunities for informal celebrations with the head teacher or other member of senior leadership. This is especially important for those children who may often see these adults for negative reasons.

- Share praise and recognition with parents (see **Chapter 2** for more details).

For those children who struggle with direct praise, explore indirect methods, such as sharing acknowledgement with other teaching staff so the child can 'overhear', sending a postcard home, offering the child a chance to show their work to a trusted adult or display their work on a recognition board in the classroom (see **Chapter 2** for further discussion).

Managing difficult behaviours

So how can teaching staff create consistency in their responses to difficult behaviours? A behaviour document with levelled behaviours linked to educational consequences and protective consequences can be used consistently by all adults. We recommend using the term 'consequence' rather than 'sanction', which suggests punishment. The term consequence should help children make the connection between their actions and the subsequent outcomes. A ladder of proportionate responses is another approach to managing difficult behaviours. This might include:

1. Using positive language, redirect the child towards an alternative activity.

2. Give limited choices that are acceptable to you. This could include self-direction to a different workspace or a calm area.

3. Give adult direction to an alternative workspace.

4. Provide a debrief opportunity for the class following challenging situations.

5. Use educational and protective consequences.

6. Follow with opportunities for reflection, restoration and reconciliation.

Further details are given in the 'Thinking about...' creating a behaviour policy that works for all' box overleaf.

We would argue that there is no one perfect system, and the above examples are not mutually exclusive. Each school must determine what is right for them. The number of children and the level of additional need will probably determine how structured a system needs to be. What is important, however, is that the consequences given follow naturally on from the original behaviour. Through a process of joint reflection, the child needs to be supported to see the outcome of their actions. This may include the effect on the environment or on the other children or adults involved, and, crucially, the effect on their own learning. Remember that this process needs to be graduated appropriately for those with SEND or mental health difficulties that prevent them from fully engaging or understanding it.

With regard to low-level silly or 'attention-seeking' behaviours, a collective effort must be made by all staff to help children learn more appropriate ways of getting the attention they need. Remember that for some children with mental health difficulties, such as ADHD and Tourette's, some 'silly behaviour', such as making noises, is best understood as impulsive behaviour, not always within their conscious control. Again, a graduated approach is essential.

In terms of managing more difficult and challenging behaviours, it is essential to have an agreed and consistent response that is put into place by all adults. Teaching staff need to be empowered to handle these behaviours appropriately and the child needs to feel the safety that comes from every adult responding in the same way. There are many excellent local policies and guidance available to support schools with this.

Some key considerations are:

- When a child is dysregulated, angry and aggressive, their stress response is activated – they are unable to listen to and process lots of language. Keep words to a minimum and ensure the ones you do use deescalate the situation rather than provoke it further. Use nurturing practices to support agreed ways of speaking to children at these times.

- If a child is throwing objects or displaying dangerous behaviour, one or two adults need to remain with the child and a third should evacuate the other children from the space rather than remove the child. If this is not possible, and the child needs to be removed for their safety or the safety of others, two adults (ideally) should follow agreed procedures regarding physical contact and handling, for example steering and guiding with open hands.

- Allow destructive behaviour to happen. This can be controversial – no one likes to see a room destroyed or displays pulled down. It is distressing for all involved and takes a lot of time to put right again. However, teaching staff should never attempt to physically force a child to stop this behaviour or put themselves in danger by trying to intervene and prevent damage to classrooms. The child needs a calm adult nearby who is supporting them to express their emotions as safely as possible and who will help them to begin to calm by using techniques to de-escalate the situation. Once a child has re-regulated, the adult can take them through steps 5 and 6 in the ladder suggested previously.

- When you see a situation developing or you are aware of a trigger arising for a particular child, try to provide a nurturing intervention as soon as possible before it escalates. Offer the child a break, time in a calm area or a chance to chat. Consider your positioning in the class at these times – ensure you always have a good view of what is happening and don't actively block exits from the classroom. Feeling trapped will not help a dysregulated child to calm down.

- In the heat of a difficult moment, it is hard to remember what to say. Scripts can help to stop you inadvertently saying the wrong thing. They can communicate the clear messages of 'I see you. I am here. I want to help', without using lots of language that may be overwhelming for the child. Scripts can be written on the back of ID badges and around school so they are always accessible.

We discuss a detailed approach for the de-escalation of incidents in ***Chapter 9: Behaviours That Challenge***. In ***Chapter 8: Low Mood***, we will also discuss how to create safe spaces in classrooms and around the school that children can use before they reach the levels of dysregulation described above.

In line with the approach of most schools now, we advocate striving to avoid exclusions whenever possible. Schools need to follow their own local guidance, but an exclusion should be seen as a last resort, when all preventative strategies have been exhausted. A fixed-term external exclusion is likely to damage any progress made in school regarding emotional wellbeing and behaviour (Brookes *et al*, 2007). One option can be a move towards internal exclusions that take place in the company of staff. A child can be given time in a calm and comfortable space to reflect on what has happened. Crucially, the exclusion is an opportunity for supported, focused reflection and not a punishment in the traditional sense of the word. The hope is that the child moves forward from this time with an understanding of what has happened and the impact it has had on themselves and others. They should also be able to express steps to deal with a similar situation differently next time.

❓ Thinking about ... creating a behaviour policy that works for all

Some elements to consider:

- Begin with your overall school ethos and values – integrate these throughout the policy.
- What rights does the child have in school – to feel safe, to learn, to be respected and to feel included?
- Link the behaviour policy to systems for positivity, acknowledgement and recognition. Lay out clear, high expectations for prosocial and learning behaviours.
- Provide a Home–School Agreement for all parties to sign each year. This lays out responsibilities and expectations for the school, teaching staff, children and parents. It can be referred to during the process of reflection and restoration, described below.
- Focus on educational and protective consequences rather than sanctions:
  - Educational consequences demonstrate the connection between a child's action and the outcome. They need to be logical, meaningful and appropriate for the individual and the incident e.g. tidying up the results of destructive behaviour within a specific environment with the support of an adult. They could also include: meetings with the child and parents, opportunities to model prosocial behaviours to younger peers and storytelling or role play to help the child understand triggers for and the impact of their behaviour.

→

- Protective consequences look forward to providing future protection for the child or others in the event that difficult behaviours continue. They should be viewed as measures to keep everyone safe, rather than as a punishment. Possible options include: the planned use of calm areas, increasing staff ratios, limiting access to outdoor space, supervising children as they move around the school or on the playground, sending learning activities home for completion if they haven't been finished or providing a differentiated teaching space.
- Follow with opportunities for:
  - Reflection – Provide supported opportunities for a child to process and understand their behaviour. Guide them towards making better choices and use prosocial behaviours in the future. This may involve reflection sheets in class, visiting a Reflection Bench or having a specific break or lunchtime reflection. This process should always be supported by an adult.
  - Restoration and reconciliation – Restoration and reconciliation occur when educational consequences are put into place (see below). Provide supported opportunities for a child to restore what has been physically disturbed or damaged; and also to restore relationships when these have been harmed by words and actions. Apologies are not easy and we don't recommend that these be forced. If they are to be given, they need to have true intention behind them. Explaining this to a child and modelling it in our own responses is important. A child needs to receive and feel forgiveness themselves before they can understand what it means to someone. Perhaps another gesture or offering to make amends with another child may be appropriate – a picture or letter may be easier than a verbal apology.
- Recognise and acknowledge that the aforementioned approaches take time, resources and energy. These are not necessarily strategies that can be carried out by a class teacher at lunchtime while they prepare to teach their afternoon lessons. If appropriate and possible, assign these responsibilities to staff who have the flexibility in their day to spend the extra time needed, be these TAs, learning or behaviour mentors or members of a pastoral team.
- Include zero tolerance on bullying with a focus on identifying the root cause, providing support for both parties and opportunities for reconciliation.
- Agree the format of de-escalation scripts and make these available for all.
- Provide measures to keep all children and staff safe: radios for staff to call for assistance, evacuation procedures and consideration of protective consequences when necessary.

→

■ Using the graduated approach, identify when situations are not improving and further intervention is necessary e.g. seeking external support or assessment, personalised timetables, behaviour plans or risk assessments. Use agreed strategies for monitoring anxiety and other emotions and understanding how feelings are affecting behaviours.

■ Agree follow up and debriefing procedures concerning: the class or individual children that may have witnessed an incident, a child who has been hurt and parents of all parties. Have consistent systems so that staff know what their responsibilities are with regard to contacting parents. Agree a level at which follow-up will be dealt with by senior leadership.

Overall, try to:

■ **Avoid:** controlling language and approaches, punishment, removing all enjoyable experiences, shaming and humiliating, exclusion.

■ **Promote:** safe relationships, comfort and forgiveness, role-modelling by staff and children, choice, consistency, positive language choices and redirection, prosocial behaviours, positive reinforcement and recognition, reflection, restoration and reconciliation.

This overview gives an insight into some of the principles of a therapeutic approach, but it is not intended to be a comprehensive guide. That is beyond the scope of this book. We strongly advise that schools seek appropriate external training to ensure that all staff fully understand the nature of any new approach to behaviour and can implement it effectively. It is essential that schools take time to consider the causes and functions of a behaviour and invest energy in the process of reflection. The principles of a therapeutic approach need to be implemented correctly, consistently and with confidence, in order to facilitate sustainable change for the children (see *Chapter 9* for a further discussion of functional analysis with regard to behaviours that challenge). As mentioned previously, there are many excellent local policies and training programmes available.

With special thanks to Sauncey Wood Primary School, Harpenden and Westfield Primary School, Berkhamsted for allowing us to draw upon their inspirational behaviour policies.

Planning school-based support for children with mental health difficulties

Where to begin?

Planning and providing for the needs of all children is a daunting task. Here, we will consider how schools can best use the resources they have available to provide support for children with mental health difficulties. **Chapter 1** looked at how to identify children who need additional support using the graduated approach of APDR. Once this cycle has begun, whether or not a child is waiting for an assessment or external support, schools need to ensure that the structure of their learning time is working for them. Some children may be able to remain in the classroom for the whole day, but with extra adult or resource-based support to help them access the learning and address specific problems relating to their mental health condition. Some children may benefit from time out of class for specific interventions relating to the curriculum or their emotional wellbeing, or both. Some children will need more personalised timetables to allow for sessions with external agencies or an in-school pastoral support team. Personalised timetables may also be needed when a child is not able to cope with the whole day in school and needs to reduce their hours for an agreed period of time.

Teaching staff, the SENCO, the child and their parents will ideally work together to arrive at a plan that works for all. There is so much information to consider at this stage and it is helpful to all to have this plan drawn up in child-friendly format. See **Chapter 19: Resources and Lesson Plans** for 'Learning Steps', a sample template for a personalised learning proforma to help children and adults track the different elements of a child's learning journey and provision. Personalised planning like this ensures that schools are providing what each individual child needs and not expecting them to always fit in with the 'normal' rhythm of the school day. The aim should be to eventually help the child reach a position where they can integrate with more whole-class activities and learning, but only when they are ready to do so. Remember that the behaviours or concerns that have led to this point were there for a reason and if children are rushed out of more targeted provision too quickly, progress may be undone. A further consideration that cannot be avoided is assessment. The 'Thinking about...' box below considers the elements that can be adjusted for children with mental health difficulties.

Thinking about … making summative assessment work for all

No matter what our views on them, formal summative assessments are still a reality for most children at primary school. We must support them to access these at their own level and pace, and make it as fun as possible.

■ Build engagement with the testing process. Try fun tests on their interests or general knowledge to build their resilience to the concept of assessment.

■ Prepare children for the practicalities of formal assessments – timescales, noise levels, restrictions on movement and respecting that other children want to keep their answers private.

■ Make arrangements for reasonable adjustments:

   ■ Allow rest or movement breaks for children who need them e.g. those with ADHD. Observe how they settle back to work afterwards.

   ■ Does the child need a scribe? A reader? Extra time to allow for slower processing?

   ■ If anxiety is present, consider if the child needs to complete the assessment in a separate room, especially if their distress will affect other children. Allow the child to practise in the chosen room, ideally with the adult that will be supporting them on the day. Work with them and their parents to discover what decreases their anxiety – perhaps talking through the test, practising past papers, feeling comfortable with the chosen environment, completing questions in small blocks, movement breaks or sensory breaks?

Teaching assistants

TAs and other support staff are absolutely vital to the success of any agreed provision. Sadly, budgets have decreased and there are currently fewer TAs in most schools, but more children needing support. TAs' skills and time must be used wisely and their support targeted where the need is greatest. Of course, this can be controversial at times, when some classes are left without TA support and others seem to have extra adults in and out all day long.

Historically, 1:1 TAs supported the same child all the time. This certainly has its benefits – the adult knows the child very well and the child feels safe and secure. But some schools are moving to a more flexible system whereby several 1:1 TAs move between key children needing support. This prevents children developing overly strong attachments to a particular adult, and in some circumstances it allows each adult a break from the constant and demanding nature of supporting children with challenging behaviour. It also means that several adults know how to support a particular child, which gives flexibility in case of staff absence. TAs can work to upskill each other.

It is really important for TAs to feel supported with planning and for time to be provided for this, if at all possible. Regular meetings between TAs and class teachers are ideal, if not essential – though in reality, snatches of conversation in the corridor may be all that is happening, especially if a TA's hours start and finish within the normal school day. Having a dedicated slot once a week to plan and discuss problems and progress is so beneficial for teaching staff and children. Timetabling this during an assembly may be a good starting point if nothing else is possible. A great strategy to facilitate understanding and communication between teachers and TAs is for them to swap roles on a regular basis. This allows them to see situations from the other's point of view and also allows the teacher focused time with individual children with additional needs.

It is important to note that there are certain situations that all adults in school should have the skills and knowledge to manage. There is of course a need for confidentiality in many situations – some information will be shared only on a need-to-know basis. But TAs and support staff should never be put in a position where they have insufficient knowledge of a child's circumstances, yet are expected to manage challenging behaviours or high levels of distress. There is always a danger (though obviously not through any intention on the part of the adult) that the wrong thing may be said and a negative reaction triggered. Through effective communication about key children, this can be avoided.

Interventions

Once it has been identified that a child with mental health difficulties would benefit from a school-based intervention, several options may be considered. If a child is struggling to access learning in class due to challenging behaviours, a group curriculum-based intervention may be appropriate. Some schools run learning 'Hubs', in which a group of children receive a personalised maths and literacy curriculum. Others take children out of class for shorter periods of time for focused work on curriculum targets. Both of these can take the pressure of teachers during the core learning time of the day. They can focus on the rest of the class for an extended, predictable and consistent period of time. If a child has more significant emotional and wellbeing needs, then a focused 1:1 or group intervention can be offered. This is explored further in *Chapter 5: Building Emotional Intelligence*. However, it is important to recognise that support can still be provided for social, emotional and mental health difficulties within a curriculum-focused session and a nurturing ethos can be embedded throughout. The communication strategies given earlier in the chapter will support this.

The 'Thinking about…' box on curriculum interventions below outlines some important considerations when setting these up for children with mental health difficulties.

 Thinking about … curriculum interventions for children with mental health difficulties

Some factors for SENCOs, teachers and TAs to consider when setting up curriculum interventions for children with mental health difficulties:

■ Set clear expectations for planning and documentation – will this be the responsibility of the teacher or the TA? Develop systems of ongoing communication that work for all – the teacher needs to know what is being taught and how the child is coping in the group; and the TA needs to know if an impact is being seen in class and if learning is being transferred.

■ Seek the views of children and parents at the start and end of the programme to assess their understanding of why the intervention is taking place and their thoughts on progress. Organise regular reviews or check-ins with parents. Keep them updated about the impact of interventions and ask if they are noticing any change at home.

■ Provide opportunities for children to raise and address particular worries about learning. They may feel more comfortable sharing things they are struggling with in a small group situation.

■ Reframe the intervention, perhaps as a 'Power Learning' group, in which they will develop learning powers that they can take back and use in class, and share with their peers.

■ Be clear about routines and expectations around transitions. Will the children be collected from class or are they allowed to meet at the room?

■ Learning activities should be kept short, focused and practical. For the child to benefit and really want to be there, learning needs to be engaging and stimulate curiosity. Enquiry-based learning objectives can work well, through which children can work on individual targets.

■ Use sessions to pre-teach important topic-related vocabulary and concepts that will allow children to access learning in class later.

■ Really take note of progress, however small – celebrate and share this in the group and with their class teacher.

- When children are finding it hard to engage, or refusing to engage with the learning, be flexible, don't make a fuss and avoid confrontation. Ultimately, you want the child to want to be in the room. Be patient and keep trying to gently bring them back to the group.
- Allow diversions at times. Chatter and curiosity boosts connection. Children need the opportunity to share things that are important to them and know that this is interesting to others.

Bringing it all together

When a commitment is made to build a new school ethos centred on wellbeing, changes need to be introduced gradually. Every school will begin in a different place, and the journey is not a race. New approaches and initiatives need time to become embedded. There is a huge amount of helpful information out there and many resources to try. It is easy to end up introducing too many new ideas at once and overwhelming both adults and children. Let the wider school community know that everyone is on this journey together, and that the feedback of all is welcomed. This feedback will support the process of reviewing changes and recognising where a positive impact has been made – both at school and in children's homes. Building a staff team that trusts each other, shares good practice and collaborates for the benefit of the children is vital. We will explore how to look after the wellbeing of staff in *Chapter 4*. Cultivating an overall staff attitude of proactivity rather than reactivity, is key. Expect the unexpected and strive to be unshockable. Above all, respond to all children with calm and kindness, no matter what the situation, and endeavour to create a ripple effect throughout the community. The 'Thinking about…' box on building an ethos centred on wellbeing on p68 provides guidance for whole-school change that can be adapted according to the needs of your school.

Planning for policy changes

All schools need to appoint their new Designated Senior Lead (DSL) for Mental Health by 2025. The person best placed to take on this role will vary from school to school, depending on their size and level of need, and we have seen many different models in the schools we have visited. It could be taken on by the headteacher, the SENCO, the pastoral lead, the nurture lead, the PSHE subject leader, or a teacher with a special interest in wellbeing and mental health. Having two leads, one a member of senior leadership and one a member of support staff, also works well. It has been highlighted that in order for the DSL to fulfil their role, there needs to be 'buy in' from colleagues at all levels – supporting pupils with their mental health cannot purely be the job of the DSL (National Children's Bureau, 2018). It will be for each school to consider how the role of the DSL will fit with existing support structures, including pastoral care, learning mentors, in-house therapists and DSPs for Child Protection. The Department for Education has promised the provision of specific training for the DSL role which should help provide some clarity around this. Schools will also need to consider the training needs of the rest of the staff. Mental health first aid courses are widely available and, again, there will be other local options or various national schemes to buy into. It is likely that with the renewed government focus on mental health, training options will be set to increase. Training for all staff should be revisited annually if possible and new staff members will need full induction into the school ethos and agreed approaches. Mental health and wellbeing can also be prioritised on the INSET and staff meeting programmes to continue the overall upskilling of all adults in school. Schools can also choose to work towards several local and national awards related to mental health and wellbeing. Details of these and various training schemes are given in ***Further Reading and Guidance*** at the end of the book.

All the considerations in this chapter will support schools to fulfil the requirements of the new Ofsted Education Inspection Framework.

❓ Thinking about ... building a whole-school ethos of wellbeing

These ideas will guide schools when they are beginning to think about developing an ethos centred on wellbeing or when considering how to develop mental health and wellbeing provision further:

- Talk to all staff. How do they currently feel about their own wellbeing? How do they feel about the children's wellbeing? What would they like to change? Get staff on board before beginning lots of changes. They need to understand why this is important.

- Talk to all children. Begin to develop shared language of wellbeing that works for the school. What is going well in our school? What would you like to see change? What new things could we try? Do you know where to go or who to speak to when you have a problem?

- Begin with the basics – create safety for all. Identify times and places when children and staff do not feel safe. Address these as a priority.

- Appoint a DSL for Mental Health and ensure they receive the appropriate training for your local area. What will their responsibilities be? Where is the overlap with other roles? What strategies will they use for implementing change? What will be the priorities and what challenges do you expect to encounter?

- Appoint a governor for mental health and wellbeing.
- Consider the training needs of all staff and governors.
- Develop policies to align with the school's core values:
  - Behaviour
  - Mental health (or emotional health) and wellbeing
  - SEND or inclusion
  - PSHE
  - Online safety
- Ensure that policies are understood by all. Encourage a culture where staff and parents feel able to ask questions without receiving judgement.
- Develop procedures for identifying mental health needs and agree a framework for involving parents and seeking external support.
- Choose an existing framework, or develop your own framework, to support the development of emotional intelligence.
- Explore how mental health provision and nurturing practices can be embedded throughout the curriculum.
- Consider how to bring wellbeing practices into daily life in school (see **Chapter 4**).
- Plan regular reviews of the new ethos. Include staff, child and parent surveys.
- Plan to revisit staff training annually and develop systems for training new staff.

With special thanks to Westfield Primary School, Berkhamsted for sharing their journey of developing their whole-school ethos centred on wellbeing.

Summary

- Using a values-based, whole-school approach will support the prioritisation of mental health and wellbeing for all.

- The language we choose to use and our manner of communication matters greatly. By using the PACE model, in addition to other strategies, all our interactions with children can be enhanced and supported.

- Behaviour policies should give high importance to the recognition of positive and prosocial behaviours. When developing an approach to managing difficult behaviours, consider the need for reflection, restoration and reconciliation. These will be supported by implementing educational and protective consequences.

- When planning for the needs of all children, especially those with mental health difficulties, consider the role personalised learning proformas, TAs and curriculum based-interventions can play.

- Cultivate an overall staff attitude of proactivity rather than reactivity.

- Consider the training needs of all staff as you develop an ethos centred on wellbeing.

- Develop the role of the DSL for Mental Health to suit the needs of your school.

References

Bennett T (2017) *Independent Review of Behaviour in Schools: Creating a culture: How leaders can optimise behaviour.* London: Department for Education. Available from https://assets.publishing.service. gov.uk/government/uploads/system/uploads/attachment_data/file/602487/Tom_Bennett_Independent_ Review_of_Behaviour_in_Schools.pdf

Brookes M, Goodall E & Heady L (2007) *Misspent Youth: The Costs of Truancy and Exclusion – a guide for donors and funders.* London: New Philanthropy Capital.

DDP network (2020) *What Is Meant by Pace?* Available from https://ddpnetwork.org/about-ddp/meant-pace/

Faber A & Mazlish E (2013; 30th anniversary edition) *How to Talk So Kids Will Listen and Listen So Kids Will Talk.* London: Piccadilly Press. pp. 56-61.

National Children's Bureau (2018) *Transforming Mental Health Provision for Children and Young People: Summary findings of consultation events with children's sector practitioners and parents.* London: Department for Education.

Section 2: Wellbeing

Chapter 4: Wellbeing for All

When thinking about how to cultivate wellbeing for all, the focus needs to be not only on those children who have mental health difficulties, but also on every other individual within the school community. For a school to establish an ethos centred on wellbeing, practices need to be integrated into daily life for all. The ethos will not be effective if wellbeing is thought of as an 'extra' or an 'add-on'. In 2014, a Public Health England report reviewed evidence regarding the link between health and wellbeing and educational outcomes (Public Health England, 2014). The report acknowledges the difficulties in drawing firm conclusions in an area where there are so many complex relationships between different factors, but it does suggest that children with better health and wellbeing are likely to achieve better academically and have more effective social and emotional competencies, and specifically, that there is a positive association between physical activity and academic attainment. That is not to suggest that increasing levels of attainment should be the primary goal, but clearly this is a very positive link that all schools would wish to encourage.

In 2009, the most recent TellUs survey of school children in England, *TellUs 4*, gathered data from more than 250,000 children in 3699 schools. Compared to TellUs 3, conducted the previous year, there had been a clear decline in emotional health and wellbeing, largely due to a fall in the number of children who felt they could talk to an adult other than their parent if they were worried about something. There had also been a slight drop in the measure for participation in positive activities (DCSF, 2010).

The wellbeing of individual children can also change over time. For example, a Children's Society survey (Rees *et al*, 2009) noted decreases in many aspects of subjective wellbeing as children became older, with happiness with school and family shown to decline, while happiness with friends tended to remain more constant.

In the introduction we defined wellbeing as a desirable state of contentment and a precursor to, and support for, our mental health. There are many helpful frameworks suggested for the cultivation of wellbeing, and for overall happiness – details of some of these are given in ***Further Reading and Guidance***.
For our purposes, this chapter explores whole-school strategies for supporting wellbeing, in relation to the following areas:

- physical health and activity
- curating the various learning environments around school
- relationships and community

We will also specifically address how to look after the wellbeing of staff – an area that was previously neglected, but thankfully is rising up the agenda in most schools. We believe that all the suggestions given are beneficial for both children and adults. ***Chapter 19: Resources and Lesson Plans*** also provides 'My Wellbeing Wings', a photocopiable frame to help children consider and track the things that help boost their wellbeing and the things that drain it.

Physical health and activity

Healthy eating

A child who is well fed and well hydrated will function better both mentally and physically. A key finding of the government pilot of free school meals in 2010 was that children who had a healthy lunchtime meal had more energy, were more alert and were more likely to concentrate in class (DfE, 2011). Not only can a poor diet impact mood and concentration, it has also been linked to wider behavioural issues, including aggression (Bellisle, 2004). Providing access to drinking water for adequate hydration can reduce the consumption of sugary alternatives and may also improve cognitive functioning (Edmonds & Jeffe, 2009).

From 2015, school food and 'an ethos of exercise and healthy eating' became part of the Ofsted Common Inspection Framework, highlighting the important role that it plays in a child's development (Ofsted, 2015). A healthy food culture in schools can help make lunchtimes a more pleasurable experience. The dining hall can be a place to model good manners, for conversations to take place and for a sense of community to develop. For some children this may be the only setting in which they sit at a table to eat and play a part in decisions around what they are eating. Staff can also help by role modelling healthy food choices, possibly via a rota system so that staff are always seated with pupils. Other skills, such as sharing and turn taking, can be developed during meal and snack times. A whole-school ethos around caring for ourselves and others, including looking after our bodies, can be promoted at these times.

It is important that children feel comfortable in the school dining hall environment. This may may be achieved in part by using welcoming wall displays and pictures which the children are involved in choosing or creating. It is important that children have adequate time to eat their meals, as for some the anxiety of feeling rushed can impact on their ability to eat. The noise levels in the dining room can also make it difficult for some children to relax while they eat. Ear defenders could be worn or an alternative space can be offered to these children, again with an adult sitting with them to eat their lunch. If the weather allows, children could eat outside in a designated picnic area.

Sleep

We are all aware of the vital importance of getting enough sleep. The quantity of sleep a child needs varies with age. The National Sleep Foundation suggests that the average 6–13 year old should get between 9–11 hours of sleep per night, which then drops to 8–10 hours during the teenage years (Hirshkowitz *et al*, 2015). Teaching staff should know what is normal for the children in their class in terms of levels of alertness. Look out for the obvious signs that children are particularly tired: excessive yawning, low concentration or heads slumped down onto desks. Sleepy children are often quiet and fly under the radar. Try to identify patterns and speak to the child and parents at the earliest opportunity – a child who is always too tired to learn needs timely support.

Screen use in the evening can be a contributing factor to excessive tiredness. If a child indicates that they are losing sleep due to screen use at bedtime, teaching staff should not delay in contacting the parent. We all worry about having these conversations, but it may turn out that the parent would actually like to receive some advice on how to change things. For example, the simple suggestion of allowing a child to wind down with an audiobook in bed, rather than a screen, may be well received. Signposting parents to appropriate options and resources can be beneficial.

Some children with neurodevelopmental differences, such as ADHD or ASC, appear particularly prone to sleep problems – one study found that around 80% of parents of children with pervasive developmental disorders reported sleep issues (Couturier *et al*, 2005). This can include difficulties falling asleep and/or staying asleep, early morning waking and excessive daytime sleepiness. Some of these children may be prescribed medication to help improve their body's sleep cycle, usually melatonin. This is a synthetic version of the body's own natural sleep hormone that is sometimes used outside of its approved usage licence in children. However, despite the underlying difficulties, these children will benefit from the same sleep hygiene advice and implementation as all children, including a good routine and screen-free time before bed. For more information about managing screen use, see ***Chapter 6***.

Physical education

We know that being physically active helps to promote physical and emotional health and wellbeing (British Heart Foundation, 2013). A review of empirical studies concluded that acute physical exercise enhances executive functioning in preadolescents and adolescents (Verburgh *et al*, 2014). Research has also shown that as little as five minutes of regular physical activity can result in benefits, including improved concentration and attention, alongside the positive effects of sport on confidence and self-esteem (Sullivan *et al*, 2017).

The aims of the National Curriculum for Physical Education (PE) state that as well as developing competence and engaging in competitive activities, children need to be active for sustained periods and be encouraged to lead healthy and active lives (DfE, 2013). There is no statutory requirement for the number of hours of PE which children must take part in each week, but most schools provide at least two hours (Ofsted, 2013). It is argued that it should be made a core rather than a foundation subject to ensure that the time allocated is protected, which would in turn lead to PE going further to improve the physical, mental and personal wellbeing of children (Harris, 2018).

Daily movement

Over and above the expectations for formal PE lessons, children need to move. Building regular movement breaks into the school day is beneficial for all children. Providing an aptly timed five minutes for movement in the classroom, or outside if possible, will allow a much needed break from cognitive tasks and children will return with renewed capacity to concentrate. These breaks can be scheduled or spontaneous, responding to the needs of the class. For those with mental health difficulties, particularly those with ADHD, they are essential. Time for movement can be an effective strategy for interrupting a difficult behaviour cycle that might be escalating, e.g. anger, peer difficulties or anxiety. The caveat here is of course that we want to avoid too many transitions, which are unsettling for many children with mental health difficulties. Establishing routines and boundaries around the transitions is key so that children can return to their learning with renewed focus. (See *Chapter 16: Daily Transitions* for further discussion regarding daily transitions in school).

There are many excellent options to choose from when it comes to designing your movement breaks. There are established initiatives to engage with, such as The Daily Mile and Skip2bFit (see *Further Reading and Guidance* for details); or teaching staff can simply put on a class playlist and dance on the carpet for ten minutes. It is also possible to build in more physical activity on a weekly basis with theme days, such as 'Dance Monday' or 'Yoga Friday', in which the whole school can take part in learning a particular move or pose. Whatever is chosen, it is important to keep the activities social and relaxed. Adults can use the opportunity of a class run to chat with children. This conscious breaking down of barriers supports a truly inclusive community and fosters connection with children who may be struggling.

Specific physical activities that provide a high level of sensory feedback can also be very beneficial for some children with mental health or sensory difficulties, especially when they are dysregulated. This could include using:

- exercise balls to roll, bounce on or squash into safely
- small 'stress' balls or toys to squeeze during learning
- fiddle toys
- stretchy bands
- hammering pegs into holes or pins into cork boards
- eating crunchy foods e.g. carrots, breadsticks or toast.

Curating the learning environment

The structure and nature of the different spaces within a school can have a huge impact on children and adults. Many of us know that feeling of overwhelm and confusion when faced with a desk covered in piles of paper, books and resources. Teaching staff may also notice children struggling when they are expected to concentrate in an untidy classroom. Environmental clutter can affect us deeply, though we may not realise it. Here, we will consider how we can create calm, uncluttered and nurturing spaces around school, which will support rather than undermine other efforts to foster wellbeing for all.

The classroom

A classroom designed with wellbeing in mind takes into account the needs of all children, and adults too. Often, the size of the space or the elements of the room that cannot be changed (for example, door positioning, windows or cloakroom design) may feel restricting and they may limit how the room can be used. But one space can be more than one thing – a book corner can be a purposeful hub for reading and exploring books, but also a relaxing space for a child in need of a break from learning or a cosy and welcoming space for a small group discussion. Sometimes, areas of a classroom can feel awkward, redundant or disconnected, but with careful consideration it is possible to find a useful purpose for a dark corner or cupboard and create a natural flow around the room. As the school year progresses, children can begin to take ownership of the space too and their ideas can shine through. Involving them as much as possible with the daily running of the classroom, for example by scheduling regular tidy-up times during the day and by appointing weekly classroom monitors, supports this ownership and encourages them to take care of what they create.

When setting up a classroom, it is sensible to assume that children with various SEND and mental health difficulties will need to be provided for, and it therefore needs to be an inclusive space for all. Following the handover from the previous class teacher, it will be possible to think ahead in detail about making the space work for particular children. Important considerations will include furniture choices and layout, resource placement and access to adults and quiet spaces. It is really valuable to involve the individual child in this process. This is discussed further in ***Chapter 17: Yearly Transitions***.

The 'Thinking about...' box below outlines a range of elements to consider when designing and reviewing a classroom space. Once the children have settled into a space, a culture should be built in which they feel able to share what is and isn't working for them. Do they all feel comfortable in the space? Would someone rather be positioned near a window or are they less distracted if they face into the room? Perhaps a working wall is now so full with ideas and resources that the children are overwhelmed by it and begin to ignore it. How can you reduce the visual stimulation and make it useful again? Perhaps the book corner has been neglected and children cannot find what they are looking for. Encourage children to play an active role in this process of reviewing the space.

> ### ❓ Thinking about ... designing a classroom that supports wellbeing
>
> In order to create a space that supports wellbeing for all (including adults!), consider the elements below:
>
> - Classroom layout:
>   - Consider the flow of movement in the space and ensure no one is trapped in a corner. Adults also need to be able to get to all children quickly if something is happening. Identify the 'bottlenecks' – where will children bump into each other or push past one another? Rearrange furniture accordingly.
>   - Make your table layout and seating arrangements work for your class. Ask children to consider who they learn best with, but rotate seating plans often. Curved tables that allow an adult to sit supporting many children at once are useful – in this way children have their own space and are not bumping arms with others. As children approach secondary transition, consider moving tables into curved rows facing the front, which more closely resembles the structure of a secondary classroom.
>
> →

- Resources:
  - Give everything a home and label with words and pictures so all can access resources easily. Develop systems for the movement of books and resources around the room. Build in regular tidy-up times during the day when all are responsible for returning things to their homes. Leaving this until the end of the day can create stress for all.
  - Organise resources centrally in one area of the classroom and encourage children to collect what they might need before a lesson begins. Let children know they can use whatever they feel will support them with their learning.
  - Keeping sensory and calming resources in a known location (in classrooms and corridors) is also helpful so children can choose what they need without adult support.
  - Resources need to be kept well organised and be accessible to all.
- Display a visual timetable in a prominent location. See **Chapter 16: Daily Transitions** for more details.
- Additional spaces:
  - Create a calm space in each classroom and in several areas around the school. See **Chapter 8: Low Mood** for a discussion of what this may look like.
  - Create a space for children to work standing up, ensuring that the surface is at a comfortable height. For some children, having the freedom to move while they think and write can aid their concentration. If a child feels restless, they could choose to work there for a period of time.
- Sensory input – Always consider the sensory input that children are receiving in a space and how this can be adjusted to support their wellbeing. What may cause discomfort or distress? What sensory stimuli may be soothing?
  - Auditory – Children with ASC can be acutely sensitive to auditory stimuli. Think about noise levels from electronic equipment, other children, alarms and even music (what you perceive to be calming might not be for every child). Ear defenders can be a great support to children in the various noisy environments around school.
  - Visual – Though well intentioned, highly decorated classrooms can be overwhelming for many children, especially those with mental health difficulties. Be mindful of this potential learning-related clutter. Working walls and beautiful displays are important, but they must add value. Consider how you can use a non-clashing, soft colour palate and plain fabrics to bring calm to the classroom space.
  - Temperature – At certain times of the year it can feel impossible to get the temperature of the classroom just right. If it is too hot, children may struggle to concentrate and regulate their behaviour. If it is too cold, it can be hard to relax and focus. Work to achieve the best balance you can, ideally with cool air flow from outside. On a really hot day, consider if you are able to work outside with your class in a shady area.

Other indoor environments

It is also important to consider how the other indoor areas around school can be designed to support wellbeing. Having open access to several quiet, calming and restorative spaces can support all children, but especially those with mental health difficulties. A corridor that is well ordered and tidy, with the appropriate furniture or resources, can provide an interesting base for learning, a refuge for a child in distress or simply a calm passage for transitions. Walls can hold murals and interactive displays that support learning and encourage engagement with school values. Valuing and showcasing the creativity and ideas of all members of the school community is essential. The library should be a welcoming, comfortable and safe space – for reading and for relaxing. A sensory room and music area can provide a support for children in need of a break from learning or the classroom space and those who are dysregulated. Allowing children to name the various spaces around school can boost their engagement with them and encourage respect and a sense of ownership.

Outdoor environments

The playground

The playground can be a place of fun and friendship for many, but for some children playtimes are a significant source of stress. This may be due to many reasons: perhaps they are feeling lonely and finding it hard to connect and play with other children; perhaps they are seeking to control what happens in the play of others; or perhaps their play can escalate into aggressive behaviours. There is a need for flexible provision at these times. For some children, having the support of an adult in the playground for a time may be enough. Others may need a different space altogether. Having a staffed classroom or nurturing space open for children to have a quieter lunchtime can work wonders to prevent difficult situations occurring. It can also provide companionship and conversation for those who are feeling lonely. This alternative provision needs to be calming and children need to be aware that noisy or boisterous play is not appropriate. A variety of activities could be offered: craft, Lego, colouring and games. Ideally, two adults should be on duty, especially if there are high numbers of children present. Children could also spend time in the library or at lunchtime clubs or be given a helpful job to do, such as watering the school garden.

Regular communication with lunchtime staff can go a long way to support children who are struggling on the playground. The 'I need you to know' card provided in **Chapter 19** can be used to help children convey their needs. Work with children, parents and staff to develop playground strategies for individual children. If possible, make regular observations of these children from afar. This is helpful for monitoring concerns but also to provide evidence of positive playtimes. Give a simple positive gesture to a child that doesn't interrupt their play but shows them that you have noticed things are going well. Keeping the feedback low-key like this reduces any embarrassment that might be felt when an adult is checking in or resistance from children who find verbal praise difficult to receive and/or process.

Outdoor learning

The far-reaching benefits of spending time outdoors, and more specifically in nature, are now increasingly well documented. A review of the health benefits of spending time outdoors found that a wide range of positive physical health outcomes result from exposure to greenspace (Twohig-Bennet & Jones, 2018). Although more research in this area is needed, studies suggest that spending time in nature also has a positive effect on mental health outcomes, including in the areas of self-esteem, stress, resilience and depression (Tillmann *et al*, 2018). A recent report on Forest Schools and outdoor learning recommended that government consider the societal and financial benefits that result from integrating outdoor learning into the curriculum (Sylva Foundation, 2019). It also suggested that new funding avenues be explored in order to overcome barriers to using the outdoor environment.

It is therefore important to find ways to use the other outdoor areas in school for learning and for fostering overall wellbeing. Options could include:

- an outdoor classroom or creative writing area
- a forest school
- a flower or vegetable garden
- a sensory area
- a music area
- a large wooden reading chair or throne.

Although not possible for all schools due to space and budget restrictions, a small outdoor area (covered if possible) is a good extension to the classroom learning environment. It can simply be a bench or small table and chairs, with some quiet activities set up each morning. Of course, this provision is standard practice in the EYFS, but all children will benefit from the opportunity to learn outdoors more often. A class can be given ownership of an area of a garden or vegetable patch. This space can be used as an ongoing opportunity for cross-curricular learning, in which children can plant, build, care for wildlife and explore the natural world.

When working outside, there should always be consideration of those children who may find open space a challenge or those who may not stay in a designated area. All gates should be locked and play equipment out of sight. As always, reasonable adjustments should be made for these children and it should be ensured that there are enough adults to keep everyone safe.

Relationships and community

Secure, supportive and sociable relationships between peers and adults and a strong sense of community are vital to an overall ethos of wellbeing. The 'Thinking about…' box below discusses the wide range of opportunities to build these bonds and foster a feeling of belonging for children and adults. See **Chapter 19** for 'My school village', a lesson plan and photocopiable frame to help children start thinking about their key relationships in school.

 Thinking about … opportunities to build relationships and community

Consider the following areas as you look for opportunities to build relationships and a sense of community for children and adults:

■ Peer and adult relationships

   ■ Encourage conversation among staff, among peers and between them both. Allow time for relaxed but meaningful chatter. Children should know that they can speak to an adult when they need to (having a few identified adults for particular children can be helpful). Giving this time a specific name, such as 'Chatter Time', enhances its meaning and encourages children to make use of the opportunity.

   ■ Provide a range of clubs for children to attend, both after school and during lunchtimes. Ideally, have some that are run by school staff as well as external providers. They provide a great chance for connection and play and allow children to explore new and existing interests. If there are particular needs which could be supported in the setting of a club, attendance could be by invitation only and children could rotate each half-term. Older children could also be invited to attend to help them develop leadership skills (see below). Potential options could include quiet lunch club, curiosity, Lego, choir, beat boxing, craft, games and puzzles, books and stories.

   ■ Enabling adults and children to eat together at lunchtime has wide-ranging benefits (see above discussion about healthy eating).

   ■ Host Awareness Weeks or Days to highlight particular needs within the school community, for example on ASC. Following consultation with parents and children to ensure all are comfortable with the arrangements, provide input and activities that give positive framing for mental health conditions. Enable all children to see the strengths of a condition and celebrate the differences between children. This can facilitate bonding across year groups and between peers who may be struggling to understand behaviours and mannerisms of other children. It may be helpful for the siblings, who will feel less alone once others have a better understanding of a condition. →

- Pupil leadership
  - Finding opportunities to develop leadership skills is beneficial for all. Older children are given a sense of responsibility and ownership within the community and younger children are able to learn from the positive role modelling and have something to aspire to for when they reach Year 5 and 6. Examples include buddy systems, play leaders, prefects, head boy and girl, sports leaders, support for lunchtime clubs, supporting reading or leading assemblies. The 'Thinking about…' box in *Chapter 9: Behaviours That Challenge* discusses how children with mental health difficulties that affect their behaviour may benefit from engaging in leadership activities.
- Residential trips
  - Residential trips are invaluable opportunities for teaching staff to build relationships with children, and for children to connect with each other. Spending time with our classes in a different context allows us to get to know each unique child better.
  - When planning trips, consider what reasonable adjustments children with mental health difficulties may need in order to attend. All adults involved need to feel comfortable with ratios and there need to be agreed plans in place for any potential problems.
- Assemblies and productions
  - Occasions where large sections of the school community join together to learn, reflect and celebrate are vital in giving children a shared sense of identity and belonging.
  - Assemblies can be linked with school values or wellbeing focusses. It can also be helpful to use them to respond to current issues arising with classes or the wider community.
  - Inviting parents to assemblies as often as possible builds relationships and allows shared celebration.
  - Participation in assemblies by children encourages them to develop speaking and listening skills, creativity, confidence and respect for others.
- Pupil voice
  - We need to give children the chance to share their voice and have a positive impact on their community. This can be achieved through the school council, a school parliament, suggestion boxes or pupil voice surveys. Feeling invested in relevant decisions can support those children who find it hard to engage or show respect for others and the environment.
- School pets
  - The presence of animals in school is more often than not a joy for children and adults alike. Class pets could include rabbits, fish, hamsters or ➜

> guinea pigs. Increasingly, schools are welcoming therapy dogs, which either come in with a member of staff each day or attend with a visiting therapist. Children can benefit from stroking and cuddling animals, reading to them, chatting to them or simply being in their safe and predictable presence.
>
> ■ There is some research to suggest that many children with ASC benefit from spending time with animals. Social behaviours increase in children with ASC in the presence of animals, when compared with toys (O'Haire et al, 2013). Pets provide the opportunity to learn responsibility and companionship and many children with ASC demonstrate a bond with animals. They can interact with them in play and/or sharing personal space (Carlisle, 2014). In fact, research indicates that children with ASC who have had a family pet from a young age tended to have greater social skills (Grandgeorge et al, 2012).
>
> ■ Community engagement
>
> ■ Building links and relationships with individuals and groups in the local area creates a sense of belonging to the wider community and broadens children's world view. This could involve visiting care homes or sheltered accommodation to sing or play instruments, attending services at local churches, inviting church leaders or local experts to speak in assemblies or baking or making gifts to share with local residents.

Staff wellbeing

Staff wellbeing is appropriately rising up the agenda in every school. Teaching can be joyful and fulfilling, but at times it can drain individuals of inspiration, energy and resilience. Consideration must be given to how practices and procedures can support, rather than undermine, wellbeing and an individual's capacity to carry out their job properly. Reasonable expectations need to be given around planning, marking, assessment and checking emails – and understanding offered when deadlines cannot be met. It is important that any wellbeing strategies are considered not just for teaching staff, but also for the whole staff team.

A teacher or TA's ability to teach and provide for the children in their schools is wholly dependent on their own mental health and wellbeing. Meeting their own needs must be a priority if each individual is to sustain their engagement and enthusiasm for life in school. See *Chapter 5* for a discussion of adult emotional regulation and how this us helps us to support children.

❓ Thinking about ... staff wellbeing

Consider some of these ways in which schools can boost wellbeing for staff:

- Designing the staff room to be a comfortable space for rest and spending time with colleagues.

- Having a designated, quiet work space for PPA[2] time (ideally not the staff room).

- Having realistic and reasonable expectations around planning and marking.

- Encourage staff to find ways of working that are suited to them and their circumstances. Could there be an option to undertake PPA time at home each week or even a few times a term? Distractions during PPA time can have a huge impact on workloads.

- Have reasonable expectations about time of arrival at school and a set time that teaching staff must leave by at the end of the day.

- Paid leave for a 'wellbeing day'.

- Using an INSET day for report writing.

- Keep staff meetings and briefings to a minimum and consider the timing carefully so teaching staff have adequate time to set up or pack away from the day.

- Provide on-site activities after school, such as yoga, mindfulness and meditation.

- Conduct regular wellbeing surveys and act on the findings.

- Ensure there are good opportunities for supervision and feedback with senior leadership. A member of senior leadership having an open-door policy one afternoon a week for staff to bring concerns is a good informal way of doing this, without putting too much pressure on anyone's time.

- With a largely female workforce, schools need to consider the impact of the menopause on wellbeing. Staff need to feel able to raise concerns without fear of judgement and with the confidence that adjustments to working arrangements might be possible.

- Sending inspirational quotes and 'Dear Team' emails at various points during the week is a simple way to boost morale and belonging.

- Schools can access a range of external support to help with their wellbeing practices. This could include training, surveys of wellbeing and counselling. Details are given in **Further Reading and Guidance**.

---

2   PPA refers to the work of planning, preparation and assessment undertaken by teachers and TAs.

Summary

■ The wellbeing of all members of the school community needs to be prioritised, regardless of whether or not they have existing mental health difficulties.

■ Physical wellbeing can be supported by encouraging healthy eating habits, good sleep routines and high levels of physical activity, both through PE and with more informal movement during the school day.

■ The learning environment needs to be designed and managed to support wellbeing. Key areas to consider are the classroom, other indoor spaces, the playground and other outdoor learning areas.

■ Building relationships and a sense of belonging and community for children and adults is vital to an overall ethos of wellbeing.

■ Ensuring high levels of wellbeing for all staff will boost wellbeing and learning for children. Our own needs must be met so that we can subsequently meet the needs of children.

References

Bellisle F (2004) Effects of diet on behaviour and cognition in children. *British Journal of Nutrition* **92** (2) S227–232.

British Heart Foundation (BHF) National Centre for Physical Activity and Health (2013) *Making the Case for Physical Activity*. Loughborough: Loughborough University.

Carlisle GK (2014) Pet dog ownership for parents of children with autism spectrum disorder. *Journal of Pediatric Nursing* **29** (2) 114–123.

Couturier J, Speechley K, Steele M *et al* (2005) Parental perception of sleep problems in children of normal intelligence with pervasive developmental disorders: Prevalence, severity, and pattern. *Journal of the American Academy of Child & Adolescent Psychiatry* **44** (8) 815–822.

Department for Children, Schools and Families (2010) *Local Authority Measures for National Indicators Supported by the TellUs4 Survey*. Statistical Release OSR 04/2010 London: DfCSF.

Department for Education (2011) *Implementing the free school meals pilot*. National Centre for Social Research. Available from https://assets.publishing.service.gov.uk/government/uploads/system/uploads/attachment_data/file/184037/DFE-RR228.pdf

Department for Education (2013) *Physical education programmes of study: Key stages 1 and 2*. National curriculum in England. London: DfE.

Edmonds C & Jeffes B (2009) Does having a drink help you think? 6–7 year-old children show improvements in cognitive performance from baseline to test after having a drink of water. *Appetite* **53** 469–472.

Grandgeorge M, Tordjman S, Lazartigues A *et al* (2012) Does pet arrival trigger prosocial behaviours in individuals with autism? *Public Library of Science ONE* **7** (8).

Harris J (2018) *The Case for Physical Education Becoming a Core Subject in the National Curriculum*. Loughborough University on behalf of the Physical Education Expert Group. Available from www.afpe.org.uk/physical-education/wp-content/uploads/PE-Core-Subject-Paper-20-3-18.pdf

Hirshkowitz M, Whiton K, Albert S *et al* (2015) National Sleep Foundation's sleep time duration recommendations: Methodology and results summary. *Sleep Health* **1** (1) 40–43.

Ofsted (2013) *Beyond 2012: Outstanding physical education for all. Physical education in schools 2008–12*. Reference no: 120367 [online]. Available from https://assets.publishing.service.gov.uk/government/uploads/system/uploads/attachment_data/file/413187/Beyond_2012_-_outstanding_physical_education_for_all.pdf

O'Haire ME, McKenzie SJ, Beck AM & Slaughter V (2013) Social behaviours increase in children with autism in the presence of animals compared to toys. *Public Library of Science ONE* **8** (2).

Public Health England (2014) *The Link between Pupil Health and Wellbeing and Attainment:* https://assets.publishing.service.gov.uk/government/uploads/system/uploads/attachment_data/file/370686/HT_briefing_layoutvFINALvii.pdf

Rees G, Bradshaw J, Goswami H & Keung A (2009) *Understanding Children's Well-Being: A national survey of young people's well-being.* London: The Children's Society.

Sullivan R, Kuzel AH & Vaandering M (2017) The association of physical activity and academic behaviour: A systematic review. *Journal of School Health* **87** (5):388–398

Sylva Foundation (2019) *Bringing Children Closer to Nature. Report of a survey on Forest School and outdoor learning in England* [online]. Available from https://sylva.org.uk/forestschools/report#

Tillmann S, Tobin D, Avison W *et al* (2018) Mental health benefits of interactions with nature in children and teenagers: A systematic review. *Journal of Epidemiology and Community Health* **72** 958–966.

Twohig-Bennett C & Jones A (2018) The health benefits of the great outdoors: A systematic review and meta-analysis of greenspace exposure and health outcomes. *Environmental Research* **166** 628–637.

Verburgh L, Königs M, Scherder EJA *et al* (2014) Physical exercise and executive functions in preadolescent children, adolescents and young adults: A meta-analysis. *British Journal of Sports Medicine* **48** 973–979.

Chapter 5: Building Emotional Intelligence

What is emotional intelligence and why does it matter?

Emotional intelligence matters because it is closely associated with mental wellbeing. Although there are several models of emotional intelligence, here we use the term to refer to a person's developing ability to:

- recognise their own emotions, which involves tuning into their own physical information and having an awareness of what that means

- use an internal language to label emotions; this specific element of emotional intelligence refers to emotional literacy

- be able to differentiate between different feelings

- recognise the emotions of others, which involves being able to effectively read a range of verbal and non-verbal cues

- use all this emotional information to consciously guide their own thinking and behaviour (Goleman, 1996; Rafaila, 2015; Salovey *et al*, 2002).

By highlighting the multicomponent nature of emotional intelligence, we want to demonstrate how challenging it can be for children to develop the ability to regulate their emotions – that is, to change their emotional state from one to another (for example, calming down). Very young children are not able to calm down independently and rely on their attachment figures to regulate them. Teaching staff, especially in the EYFS, can be particularly instrumental within a child's attachment hierarchy, therefore influencing their developing limbic system. The limbic system refers to several structures within the brain that work together to regulate motivation, emotion, learning and memory. A child's ability to regulate their emotions is related to the security of their attachment relationships, their experiences (particularly those categorised as ACEs), brain development and the interaction between these factors.

Emotional intelligence moderates the relationship between stress and mental health. It is positively associated with the skill of identifying emotional expressions in others, the amount and quality of social support a person has and the use of mood management behaviours (Ciarrochi *et al*, 2001). Research indicates that people who can more easily recognise and manage the emotions of others tend to adapt better to high stress (Ciarrochi *et al*, 2002). It is thought that the specific skills that relate to emotional intelligence can be identified and taught, and in theory, such skills should go some way to protect children from the emotional difficulties that contribute to mental health problems.

Emotions and mental health

According to Erikson's famous Theory of Psychosocial Development, it is in the early school years (6–10 years of age) that children are really developing their own identity, individuality and independence skills. A child's energy during this developmental phase is generally directed towards creativity and productivity. They are striving to accomplish competence with various activities and skills to attain social recognition among peers and adults around them (Erikson, 1963). Of course, all of this striving, with its associated successes and failures, can be an emotional process. During the course of a school day, children can experience a huge range of emotions – there are highs and lows, and everything in between. Children may also be carrying a significant emotional load from home – whether positive or negative, it all impacts on their ability to engage with their learning. Helping children to recognise and name the emotions they experience is a vital first step in building emotional intelligence, and hence guiding them towards the best possible starting point for their learning. In order to do this, we must first understand the full range of human emotions.

Most of the psychologists specialising in the study of emotions and emotional intelligence (e.g. Ekman, 2004; Cosnier, 2007) believe that the basic emotions are happiness, sadness, fear, anger and surprise; to these are added shame, guilt, disgust, despair and curiosity. By the age of four or five, neurotypical children are starting to identify and differentiate between the emotions of others based on verbal and non-verbal behaviours. Vocabulary regarding emotions and feelings tends to increase and diversify with age. However, children with neurodevelopmental differences may (but do not always) have delays in emotional literacy development. These include children with learning disabilities and/or ASC, those with ADHD and those with neurodevelopmental differences as a result of significant neglect, abuse or maltreatment.

Good mental health requires both the ability to manage distress and also to feel positive emotions. Our biological systems process negative and positive emotions using different brain circuitry and hormonal systems. Research shows that those who are more emotionally resilient have a more hopeful outlook and are able to give more meaning to their emotions (Wolff, 1995). Reactions to negative emotions or stressors such as curiosity, perseverance, seeking comfort from another person or in fact protesting, can be positive coping responses and outward signs of emotional resilience (Mandleco & Peery, 2000).

It is vital that children understand that all emotions are acceptable and welcomed. Teaching staff can normalise emotions and help children to be accepting of them when they arise. However, they must also support them to know when it is not acceptable to act on an emotion in a certain way. For example, 'I understand you are angry because … and that is ok. But it is not ok to hit/kick.' We must also support children to regulate their emotional state and move from one state to another e.g. from anger to calm, and give them explicit feedback and praise for managing to do this. Ways to achieve these important aims are discussed further below.

Adult emotional regulation

We have acknowledged the emotional rollercoaster that the average school day can be. This is, of course, not just the case for the children. All school staff are emotionally affected by the events that take place within school. We care about the children and it is only natural that we will at times become emotionally invested in situations. Additionally, like the children, we often bring our own emotional load into school, despite our good intentions to not let our personal lives affect our professional lives. This is to be expected, and it is normal. However, when adults are able to understand, manage and cope with their own emotional responses, they are better able to support the children in their care. They are more likely to be able to build relationships with the children they teach, based on trust, empathy and respect.

Dr Laura Markham, a clinical psychologist who supports parents to connect with their children, describes the essential responsibility of a parent to be mindful of their own inner state (Markham, 2012). Although her work is based on the relationships within the family unit, the principles can be usefully applied within a school setting. She explains:

'If … we can stay mindful – meaning we notice our emotions and let them pass without acting on them – we model emotional regulation, and our children learn from watching us.' (Markham, 2012)

Crucially, this doesn't mean that we won't or shouldn't feel intense emotions while teaching. When a difficult situation in school triggers us, we may indeed feel fear, anger or sadness. But we need to develop our ability to recognise and hold that emotion lightly, eventually allowing it to pass rather than to influence our behaviour in a way that negatively impacts on the children and their learning.

Let's explore the example of a child displaying intense anger in the classroom. Something has triggered them and they are shouting, swearing, perhaps kicking furniture or pulling down displays. They are disturbing the learning of the rest of the class and breaking many school rules. It is only natural to feel anger and outrage. But if the adults present can acknowledge and hold that anger, and instead meet the child's anger with their own calm, they not only model healthy emotional regulation, but they also offer the child a way out of their storm. And perhaps most importantly, the child is given the message that is ok to feel what they are feeling.

A deeper understanding of what is happening in these times of dysregulation can help adults to remain calm. What is often perceived as children having 'meltdowns', or in more derogatory terms referred to as 'kicking off' or 'trashing the place', is more accurately reframed in most instances as distress behaviour and/or children behaving in line with their 'fight or flight' response. When people are triggered into a state of fight or flight their sympathetic nervous system is preparing their bodies for action. In the face of threat (both real and perceived), our blood pressure and heart rate increases, adrenaline is pumped round our systems and stress hormones (such as cortisol) are released. In this state of arousal, a child's brain cannot take on new information – they will often struggle to listen and process. Additionally, being in a state of distress will mean they find it hard to cope with any negative consequences being placed upon them. Generally, it can take up to 90 minutes for adrenaline to completely leave our bodies, suggesting that some time may need to pass after an incident before the child should be expected to reflect on it and manage the consequence that is put in place.

However challenging a situation or however upset or angry a child is, if adults can acknowledge their emotions and model appropriate regulation to the children in their care, they will in turn help the children to build their own emotional intelligence. This approach will be much more effective in promoting emotional intelligence compared to managing a situation by shouting or threatening to give or giving negative consequences at a time of high stress. Note that some children who have experienced maltreatment, witnessed domestic violence or developed insecure attachment styles may be triggered into fight or flight responses as a direct result of hearing adults shouting (see also discussion about language and communication choices in *Chapter 1*). It is recognised that many teachers frequently and consciously make great efforts to regulate their internal and expressive components of emotions appropriately, according to the boundaries of the school environment. This intense effort or 'emotional labour' (Grandey, 2003) requires robust processes to be in place to ensure individuals are able to access sufficient and effective emotional support. There is an extensive body of research on teacher 'burnout' and the related feelings of emotional exhaustion (Ghanizadeh & Jahedizadeh, 2015). (See also the discussion on staff wellbeing in ***Chapter 4: Wellbeing for All***.)

It is also known that a teacher's emotions influence the cognitions, motivations and behaviours of both the teacher and the child (Sutton & Wheatley, 2003) and that, generally speaking, positive emotions provoke positive effects and negative emotions provoke negative effects (Rodrigo-Ruiz, 2016). However, in an effort to teach, model and build emotional resilience (discussed in more detail later), perhaps the most appropriate strategy is not to mask or hide negative emotions, but rather to present them openly in a manner that is sufficient, adequate and consistent to the situation (Kimura, 2010). The teacher's ability to transparently and consciously control their emotions demonstrates emotional intelligence to those that witness it. High levels of emotional intelligence have positive repercussions in different areas of a teacher's life and their educational work (Palomera *et al*, 2008) and, as such, should be prioritised within teacher training and within whole-school support processes.

Helping children to know themselves

Self-awareness

Self-awareness encompasses the knowledge we have about our own fundamental nature and also the knowledge we have about ourselves in the moment – our current state of being. Psychologist Daniel Goleman explains that one of the components of self-awareness is 'recognising a feeling as it happens' (Goleman, 1996). He also describes that it involves recognition of our strengths and weaknesses and viewing oneself in a positive, yet realistic light. Having this understanding of where we may be on our journey of learning is a challenge for most adults, let alone children. Ways to support children with this are explored further below in the discussion regarding self-esteem and self-efficacy.

So how can we help children to tune into their emotions in the moment? We know that children who are surrounded by adults who label their own emotions tend to develop more emotion words within their own vocabulary. Children can struggle to have the language to identify their emotions if they have not been exposed to these words. The first step in increasing self-awareness of emotions in the moment is to make sure children have the correct words for corresponding emotions. They then need to be able to sufficiently generalise in order to recognise that a wide variety of facial expressions can indicate a variety of differing, overlapping emotions. Children with a learning disability and/or ASC may struggle with this.

With regard to a child's own current emotional state, adults need to help them understand how an emotion feels physically for them. They may be able to say what happens in their body, such as butterflies or flutters in their tummy when they feel worried. If they are able to converse while feeling an emotion, or after the event if more appropriate, marking the physical sensations out on an image of a body (often referred to as 'body mapping') can help children identify what a particular emotion feels like for them. They can then begin to associate these sensations with this emotion and next time it arises, they can start to tune into the feeling more quickly.

Self-esteem and self-efficacy

Self-esteem reflects a person's overall subjective emotional evaluation of his or her own worth. It is related to the messages conveyed to them through their attachment relationships and their experiences. Self-esteem and self-efficacy are two related concepts, and yet they each have a distinct meaning. As discussed in ***Chapter 2: Ready to Learn***, self-efficacy (the belief in one's ability to succeed in a task) is predictive of academic performance (Salovey *et al*, 2002). All teachers are striving to facilitate academic performance for the children they teach. But performance requires not only acquiring new skills and knowledge, but also fostering a child's own belief in their abilities to perform (which is linked to motivation). Low self-efficacy results in increased anxiety and stress for both children and teachers (Salovey *et al*, 2002).

Supporting children's developing self-esteem may involve:

- **Avoiding self-fulfilling labels:** If negative behaviour is labelled, for example as lazy or disruptive, then there is an increased risk that a child (unconsciously) believes that he or she is actually like that and will therefore be more likely to behave in line with this developing self-concept.

- **Giving time for patient hearing:** Allowing children to share, tell their stories and give their opinions (despite the time that this can take), not only sets a precedent for them to develop good active listening skills, but also helps develop their confidence and enables them to feel more safe and secure in your company.

- **Identifying unique capabilities:** Find opportunities to give positive feedback regarding a range of skills and strengths within the classroom. Use positive re-framing – a child might have struggled with a task, but perhaps they completed every question. There is therefore still an opportunity to give positive feedback along with the corrective feedback. As we have previously discussed, focussing our attention on the process of learning and effort demonstrated increases the likelihood that the child will repeat this level of effort in the future.

- **Being aware of the unconscious messages being sent:** What might inadvertently give the message to a child that they are not good enough? Consider how you give constructive feedback. Does it convey disappointment? Is the child compared with others? Neither of these is helpful. Also consider whether behaviour and reward systems may be inducing the feeling of shame in a child (see discussion about behaviour policies in *Chapters 2 and 3* for further details).

- **Valuing and celebrating differences:** Some children may have some insight that they are different to their peers, perhaps due to a neurodevelopmental diagnosis. All children should be supported to have a positive narrative about difference and be able to recognise each other's unique strengths and capabilities. Peer-awareness sessions regarding certain neurodevelopmental conditions can be powerful in terms of promoting positive identities. For example, information can be shared about famous footballers, successful scientists and notable figures from history that have a diagnosis of ASC or ADHD. (See also discussion regarding building relationships and community in *Chapter 4*.)

Resilience

Resilience refers to an ability to cope with setbacks, respond flexibly and adapt to change. It is not simply our experiences that shape our emotional health; our response to them also counts. Challenges and 'stepping outside of one's comfort zone' can provoke uncomfortable and negative emotions. This is unavoidable – all of us encounter stress to a varying degree as we grow.

In the pursuit of building emotional resilience, the writings of John Gottman are insightful. He has outlined five clear steps of 'emotion coaching' (Gottman & DeClaire, 1998):

1. Be aware of a child's emotional response.

2. Recognise emotional times as opportunities for teaching and connection with a child.

3. Listen empathically and validate a child's feelings.

4. Help children verbally label their own emotions. This in itself can soothe the nervous system and support recovery.

5. Set appropriate limits and boundaries, while helping the child problem-solve.

Adults can help children to build resilience by confronting uncertainty and riding out difficult emotions with them. Negative emotions are normal and typically are transient. Children need to experience discomfort to a certain degree so that they learn that they can work through it and develop their own problem-solving skills. Providing children with opportunities to successfully solve problems independently and encounter new experiences contributes to developing emotional resilience. This could look like trying a new sport; participating in new experiences, such as a school play; appropriate scaffolding to enable success in a maths problem; or stepping out of a social comfort zone by speaking to a new member of the class. It is possible to narrate these experiences for children so that they build their awareness of what their comfort zone is, when they are leaving it and how that feels for them. Crucially, they also need to identify how they feel after the event in order to tune in to, and be comfortable with, feelings of pride and mastery. These feelings can then provide the motivation for them to take the next steps in their learning.

When children are learning about such a wide range of new subjects on a daily basis, it is to be expected that mistakes will be commonplace. Mistakes can be easily reframed as learning opportunities and celebrated within a class. As previously discussed, teaching staff can highlight the 'marvellous mistakes' made by children within a lesson. They can even make some themselves – deliberate or otherwise – and model how to respond with humour and grace. This further increases a child's insight into the process of learning and how to respond to setbacks with a positive attitude.

The concept of competition can be a controversial one in school. Of course, we do need to stay aware of those children who will find losing a challenge, and those for whom it may provoke behaviours that challenge. However, a balance needs to be achieved whereby children can still partake in competitive activities if they wish and if they are able. Even the action of trying and taking part can boost self-esteem and resilience. Be alert to those children who never wish to try for fear of failing. They will need support and encouragement to slowly engage in activities with unpredictable outcomes.

Building emotional intelligence in school

PSHE

High-quality PSHE teaching is a cornerstone of building emotional intelligence in school. As outlined in the **Introduction**, the new statutory guidance for Health Education and Relationships and Sex Education must be implemented from September 2020. Crucially, once this comes into effect, these elements of the PSHE curriculum will become compulsory for all schools. The inclusion of developing an understanding of emotions is a really significant step forward and will support all other efforts to boost wellbeing and mental health.

Most schools still teach PSHE in discrete lessons, following an overall plan for the year. But teachers know that PSHE is most successfully taught when it also responds to current circumstances and the ever changing needs of the class. Additional responsive discussions, at times of need, demonstrate that the significance of incidents and concerns is being acknowledged. This can have more impact than waiting until the next scheduled PSHE lesson. It is also helpful to widen the entire approach to PSHE. By embedding teaching throughout the school day, teaching staff can enable children to make links between concepts and strategies in the moment. Emotional and social skills can be modelled by adults constantly through every lesson and interaction. This can make the little moments count and they can feed back into the overall curriculum. Elements of health education are also promoted through many other curriculum subjects – through appropriate fiction and non-fiction texts in literacy, through science and through learning about different cultures in history.

Throughout all PSHE teaching, a wealth of real-life examples from school and home can be used. Teaching staff can tell relatable stories from their lives that will enable children to apply concepts to their own experiences. When teaching older children especially, it is important to stay as up-to-date as possible with current trends and language. Making teaching and conversations 'of the moment' can have even more impact. There are many excellent resources available to support the teaching of PSHE. See *Further Reading and Guidance* for details.

Strategies for self-reporting

Children who are becoming more aware of their emotional state need ways of alerting adults at times when they need support. It is necessary to develop various options for self-reporting and ensure that children understand when and how to use them. Consider these strategies and clearly explain to children the appropriate time to use each one:

- 'Chatter Time' – Children can be assigned (or choose) adults to whom they can speak about urgent concerns or ongoing concerns. If a concern is urgent, children need to be allowed to see their chosen adult as soon as is practically possible.

- A class 'Chat Book' – This can be used for less urgent concerns that children might feel uncomfortable saying out loud. They can write a message for the class teacher or TA at any time of the day and leave the book where they will notice it. Ensure the book is checked daily and that each message is removed once read to maintain confidentiality. Try to follow up concerns the same day if at all possible.

■ A whole-school 'Worry Box' – This can be used for the anonymous posting of non-urgent but ongoing worries, perhaps those that might affect more than one child. It can be kept in a central, accessible location such as the library. Have an agreed system for who will check the box and how often. Current issues can then be addressed without the need to identify children. Using a whole-school box also allows patterns to be noticed therefore it is helpful if children add their year group to the note). If, for example, it appears that many children are worrying about a similar news story, such as a kidnap, fire or natural disaster, this can be addressed within the class or key stage setting.

See *Chapter 1* for more detail on identifying children with specific mental health difficulties.

Frameworks for emotional literacy

It is very helpful to give children a specific framework for emotional literacy that will support their emerging understanding of emotions and emotional regulation. There are many recognised frameworks available, some of which are given in *Further Reading and Guidance*. A school can also design their own framework to fit with their overall school ethos, values and approaches to behaviour. The framework can be used throughout all classes and be integrated into personalised planning for children with specific mental health difficulties.

An emotional literacy framework needs to provide children with an opportunity to name their current emotion, enable recognition of where this emotion is within the range of emotions and facilitate emotional regulation from a state of dysregulation, if appropriate. Children should be encouraged to ask questions of themselves to identify how a particular emotion feels for them and what may have caused it. If the emotion is negative, they can then consider things that would help them to re-regulate. The resources and lesson plans relating to worry, sadness and anger in *Chapter 19* address these ideas in detail.

When a framework for emotional literacy is first introduced, expect that time will need to be spent addressing misconceptions. If children don't fully understand that all emotions are valid and welcomed, their anxiety may initially increase if they are not experiencing what they perceive to be the 'right' emotion. Be ready to reinforce the message that 'it is ok to not be ok'.

Interventions

Targeted interventions are invaluable to helping the most vulnerable children develop emotional intelligence and social skills. Two well-established examples are individual or group sessions with an emotional literacy support assistant (ELSA) and group sessions in a Nurture setting.

The ELSA role was developed by educational psychologists to provide emotional support for children, in order that they can learn more effectively and feel happier at school (ELSA Network). The support focuses on developing a respectful relationship in which the child is guided to think about their circumstances with an attitude of non-judgement. The sessions provide a focused, short-term intervention to help a child with a specific need and/or develop new skills and coping strategies. Concepts explored may include empathy, self-esteem and resilience.

Nurture groups also offer short-term, focused interventions for groups of 6–12 children. The groups commonly use the Boxall Profile (discussed in *Chapter 1*) to assess the learning, social and emotional needs of each child (Nurtureuk). Provision within the group places great emphasis on language and communication – narration, demonstration and role modelling are all essential. The sessions are run by two adults, who model a nurturing and supportive relationship for the children. If a male nurture leader is available, they can provide essential role modelling for children who may be missing this input at home. Demonstration of a positive male–female relationship between staff members is also hugely beneficial for all children. The inclusion of snack time, wherein children can practise good manners, learn to serve one another and experiment with different foods in a safe, low-pressure environment, is an essential part of a Nurture group.

Referrals for the interventions may come from teaching staff, from a parent or from the child themselves. Again, one of the many benefits of increasing awareness of emotions is that children can more easily realise that they may be struggling with something and they can ask for help. This should be welcomed and letting children know the options available to them is helpful.

Throughout all interventions, it is essential to maintain good communication with parents. Outline the purpose of the sessions, obtain initial consent (which is ideal and good practice, but not essential) and then keep them updated with progress. Remember to give positive feedback to parents and ask for it in return. Finding out how the child is getting on at home is useful, as is the opportunity to suggest follow-up activities for home that will support the work done in school.

Close liaison with teachers regarding planning, progress in sessions and feedback from the classroom is important. Carrying out repeat assessments and tracking progress is essential to measure the success of the interventions. Ideally, sessions will take place at a time of day when children will not miss key literacy and maths learning in class. It is also sensible to avoid taking them out of their favourite lesson. Consistency and predictability of session timing is needed too. If a session cannot take place for any reason, try to inform children well in advance and explain why.

As with the more formal therapies, establishing boundaries of confidentiality is important. Children need to know that they can share in confidence, but the adult should always make it clear that if there is concern for the child's safety then another adult must be informed of that concern. Disclosures may arise as children become more comfortable with the adults. Be alert to them and record appropriately.

The 'Thinking about…' box below explores some of the key features of interventions that aim to build emotional intelligence.

> ### ❓ Thinking about … interventions for building emotional intelligence
>
> Consider the following elements when planning group interventions for building emotional intelligence:
>
> - A calm transition in and out of the session. Lining up outside the room and entering when everyone is ready. Greet each child warmly by name.
> - A cosy, comfortable room, with appropriate spaces for group work and a calm area. Toys and resources should be well organised, labelled and rotated at intervals. Plenty of soft toys and puppets are needed.
> - A predictable routine for the session
>   - Creating safety for children in the intervention space is paramount. If the session structure keeps changing, children will not feel safe.
>   - The routine may include: a warm welcome, an opportunity for children to share how they are currently feeling, a reminder of personal targets, specific activities for building emotional and social skills, creative activities, game time, free play (which is structured so that adults can work on personal targets with specific children), snack time, a story, a closing ritual and a warm parting greeting.
> - Some curriculum links are possible at times. Following the seasons and acknowledging special holidays for each child is important.   →

- Planning can follow elements of specific programme but more importantly, it should respond to the needs of the children.

- Keep personal targets in child-friendly language e.g. *I can say something good I've heard about myself.*

- Make space for chatter and interruptions, but always model good manners and respectful communication. Keep everything slow and relaxed. Be patient with chattering and restlessness and allow movement breaks when needed.

- Activities:
  - Engaging, practical and creative activities that allow children to relax and talk while they take part. Adults should take part too – helping, playing and connecting.
  - These activities may include: clay, playdough, threading, craft, painting, sewing, mandalas, knitting, messy play and colouring, to name but a few. Try to link activities to the seasons and to their interests, where possible.

- Game time is a good opportunity to model having fun, within the boundaries of the rules. Explain to children that it doesn't matter if we win or lose, it is the playing that counts. Use games as an opportunity for developing good social skills – encourage children to wish each other luck, empathise if something doesn't go to plan and congratulate them at the end of their turn. If cheating is mentioned, try not to make a fuss. Simply comment that it is ok and we are all learning together.

- Give children special jobs around the room to help them feel valued and give them a sense of belonging to the group.

- Be attentive to children's attention spans and the length of time given to each part of the session. Getting the right balance for each child is very hard, so allow flexibility. If a child needs to move on, let them do a different quiet activity.

- If a child chooses to leave a session, do your best to encourage them to stay. However, if they really wish to return to class, allow this to happen (supported by the second adult) and follow up with them later.

- As a session finishes, reassure the children that even though you may not see them for a few days, you will still think of them.

- It can be helpful to explain that in the session the children are learning how to be role models. They can take the things they learn with you back to their own class and show other children.

- Adults should take opportunities to check in with children in a low-key way between sessions.

- Finishing the intervention can be difficult for some children. Giving children a 'goodbye' card with photos of the key adults and a message of praise and encouragement can help to ease this transition.

Mood-enhancing thinking

Thinking more positively and with gratitude is associated with feeling more positive. Ways to encourage and practise thinking positively about experiences can be embedded into each school day. These could include:

- Whole-school practices:
  - All members of the school community can nominate a staff member and a child for a 'Thank You of the Week'. These can be presented in assembly and names can be displayed in a prominent place for the following week.
  - Assemblies can begin or end with a gratitude reflection, to which children can contribute. This could focus on school events or events in the wider world.
- Class practices:
  - At the end of the day or week, children can suggest things that have gone well for the class. These can be recorded and displayed.
  - Create a 'Thank You Jar', in which children can place notes of gratitude for other children in the class throughout the week. Share these with the class at regular intervals.
- Individual practices:
  - End the day with a 'Thank You of the Day' for individual children – one from a teacher and one from a child. Display the names and reasons for the thank you in the window where parents can view it, if possible.
  - Create gratitude journals with the children. Encourage them to write personal positive reflections and things they are grateful for each day. Similarly (and these might be especially beneficial for children with low self-esteem or those who are highly critical), ask them to think of three things that they have done well that day or that they are proud of (however small).

Some children may find these practices very difficult at first. Effective modelling is essential to support them to gradually recognise the positive things in their lives and the kind words and actions of others.

Mindfulness

Mindfulness is concerned with being in the present moment, developing our awareness of what is happening now and remaining with that, rather than being constantly drawn to dwell on the past or worry about the future. We can experience mindfulness in many different ways: savouring a joyful moment, noticing details in the world around us and recognising, but not acting upon, a difficult emotion, to name but a few. Developing the ability to be mindful is a vital component of building emotional intelligence. As we have discussed, to become emotionally intelligent, children must learn to recognise their own emotions. This involves tuning into what they are feeling, naming the emotion and sitting with it until it passes, in spite of any discomfort that may be present.

Mindfulness is increasingly being used in a therapeutic setting to support individuals with stress and emotional difficulties. Anyone who has practised mindfulness regularly will likely attest to the various benefits that can be felt in relation to stress regulation, concentration and emotional stability. But importantly, research also suggests that mindfulness results in positive neurological changes in areas of the brain, including those relating to memory and attention (Goldin & Gross, 2010). Most mindfulness research currently relates to the benefits in adults; however, studies are beginning to emerge involving children and young people. The MYRIAD project is a large randomised controlled trial currently looking at the effectiveness of mindfulness training on mental health, wellbeing and social, emotional and behavioural functioning in adolescents (Kuyken *et al*, 2017).

Mindful activities encourage a sense of flow and engagement, but, crucially, not mastery. They need to encourage a child to engage with the process rather than the outcome. They allow a child to simply be and do things 'just because', with no agenda, rules or fixed steps to follow. Mindful activities can happen in the company of others, but ideally they are largely solitary pursuits, wherein children can lose themselves in the moment. They can help a child to re-regulate their emotions after a time of distress or dysregulation and they can allow the appropriate time and space needed to process something that has happened.

There are many opportunities for building mindfulness practices into the school day. Ideally, they will stem from a whole-school approach to wellbeing and integrate with the aforementioned frameworks for emotional literacy – a self-selected mindful activity can be the key to helping a child move from a negative emotional state to a positive one. As well as using mindful activities to support children who are distressed, we can plan them in for known trigger points in the day (see ***Chapter 16*** for a discussion of transitional trigger points) and we can use them as regular times of rest at the start or end of the day or between learning activities. Five to ten minutes may be all that is needed. The 'Thinking about ...' box overleaf suggests some ideas for the classroom and around the school. Obviously not all of these will be possible in a shorter slot of time, but perhaps once a week there might be a longer opportunity to set up messy play or visit the school garden. For those activities that can be fitted into the gaps in the day, have several accessible and ready to go each week so that little thought or organisation is needed in the moment.

Thinking about ... activities to encourage mindfulness

Examples of calming, mindful activities that could be accessible in the classroom or in other areas around school include:

- Jigsaw puzzles
- Colouring
- Creative activities – bead pictures, threading, painting or cutting and sticking
- Catching games with a squashy ball or soft toy
- Exploring sounds with soothing musical instruments
- Listening to audiobooks
- Listening to music
- Exploring sensory resources – lights, sounds and textures
- Gardening and looking after indoor plants
- Messy play with water, sand, paint, playdough, bubbles, rice, pasta or pulses
- Yoga
- Calming breathing practices
- Formal meditation

Meditation

The terms 'mindfulness' and 'meditation' are often used interchangeably, but there is a distinct difference. Mindfulness is centred on our moment-by-moment awareness and can be applied to any situation we encounter whereas, traditionally, meditation is a more formal sitting or lying practice of stillness and quiet, which concentrates on fostering a peaceful mind and a relaxed body. Meditation is an extension of mindfulness, with the focus being generally inward towards the self. However, increasing our awareness of the world around us is also key – especially by tuning into our sensory input. Meditation also emphasises the importance of the breath in creating calm in the body and mind and developing an awareness of thoughts – though, crucially, not trying to control them.

Like mindfulness, meditation helps to build emotional intelligence. In advanced practice, we may learn to recognise the emotions as they arise, sit with them and begin to regard them with non-judgement. For children, simply sitting still and quiet, while focusing solely on themselves, is a meditation. Slowing down to this degree is a huge challenge for many children, whether they have mental difficulties or not. The process of becoming calm in body and mind in this way is an exercise in emotional regulation, which will benefit all.

Many schools now create space and time for formal meditation practice each day. It is possible to do this with children of all ages. It doesn't need to be complicated. There are many excellent guided meditations for children available, but these are not essential. Simply talking through a slow breathing pattern for a few minutes while the children sit in their own space is enough. Once children are comfortable with this, it can be built upon. Of course, many children may find the whole practice rather silly to start with, and you may have a few sessions filled with fidgeting and giggles – but do persevere. Explain that we are learning to calm our minds and bodies. When our minds are calm, we can learn and grow. In his book *Wellbeing in the Primary Classroom*, Adrian Bethune suggests that is important to let children know that they cannot fail when practising mindfulness (Bethune, 2018). He helpfully explains:

'They may or may not get frustrated that their mind keeps wandering off. But each time they notice their mind has wandered off, that is the meditation. That's the point!' (Bethune, 2018)

There are many training courses available to help teaching staff develop their understanding of mindfulness and meditation. Details are given in ***Further Reading and Guidance***.

Summary

- Emotional intelligence involves the ability to recognise and name the emotions of oneself and others and use this information to guide thinking and behaviour.

- Good mental health requires us to be able to regulate our emotions appropriately.

- Children need to understand that all emotions are acceptable. We must support them to respond to emotions in appropriate ways.

- Adults in school need to be able to regulate their own emotions effectively, in order to support children to do the same.

- We need to support children to develop self-awareness, strong self-esteem and self-efficacy and good levels of resilience. These are all components of secure emotional intelligence.

- There are many ways to build emotional intelligence in school, including PSHE teaching, using strategies for children to self-report concerns, specific interventions, developing mood-enhancing thinking, mindfulness and meditation.

References

Bethune A (2018) *Wellbeing in the Primary Classroom: A practical guide to teaching happiness*. London: Bloomsbury Education. pp. 38.

Chen J (2016) Understanding teacher emotions: The development of a teacher emotion. *Teaching and Teacher Education* **55** 68–77.

Ciarrochi J, Chan AY & Bajgar J (2001) Measuring emotional intelligence in adolescents. *Personality and Individual Differences* **31** 1105–1119.

Ciarrochi J, Deane FP & Anderson S (2002) Emotional intelligence moderates the relationship between stress and mental health. *Personality and Individual Differences* **32** 197–209.

Cosnier J (2007) *The Psychology of Emotions and Feelings. Affections, emotions, feelings, passions*. Bucharest: Polirom.

ELSA Network (2017). *ELSA Network*. Available from www.elsanetwork.org/

Ekman P (2004) *Emotions Revealed. Understanding faces and feelings*. London: Times Books.

Erikson EH (1963) *Youth: Change and challenge*. New York: Basic Books.

Frenzel AC (2014) Teacher emotions. In: R Pekrun and EA Linnenbrink (Eds) *International Handbook of Emotions in Education* (pp494–519). New York: Routledge.

Ghanizadeh A & Jahedizadeh S (2015) Teacher burnout: A review of sources and ramifications. *British Journal of Education, Society, and Behavioural Sciences* **6** 24–39.

Goldin PR & Gross JJ (2010) Effects of mindfulness-based stress reduction (MBSR) on emotion regulation in social anxiety disorder. *Emotion* **10** (1) 83.

Goleman D (1996) *Emotional Intelligence: Why it can matter more than IQ*. London: Bloomsbury. pp. 43.

Gottman J & Declaire J (1997) *Raising an Emotionally Intelligent Child*. New York: Simon and Schuster.

Grandey AA (2003) When 'the show must go on': Surface acting and deep acting as determinants of emotional exhaustion and peer-related service delivery. *Academy of Management Journal* **46** 86–96.

Kimura Y (2010) Expressing emotions in teaching: Inducement, suppression, and disclosure as caring profession. *Educational Studies in Japan: International Yearbook* **5** 63–78.

Kuyken W, Nuthall E & Byford S (2017) The effectiveness and cost-effectiveness of a mindfulness training programme in schools compared with normal school provision (MYRIAD): Study protocol for a randomised controlled trial. *Trials* **18**; Article number 194.

Markham L (2012) *Peaceful Parents, Happy Kids: How to stop yelling and start connecting*. New York: Perigee Book. pp. 5-6.

Mayer JD & Salovey P (1997) What is emotional intelligence? In: P Salovey & D Sluyter (Eds) *Emotional Development and Emotional Intelligence: Implications for Educators* (pp3–31). New York: Basic Books.

Nurtureuk.org (2019) *An Inclusive Education for All*. Available from www.nurtureuk.org

Palomera R, Fernandez-Berrocal P & Brackett MA (2008) Emotional intelligence as a basic competency in pre-service teacher training: some evidence. *Electronic journal of Research in Educational Psychology* **15** (6:2) 437-454.

Rafaila E (2015) Primary school children's emotional intelligence. *Procedia Social and Behavioural Sciences* **203** 163–167.

Rodrigo-Ruiz, D (2016) Effect of teachers' emotions on their students: some evidence. *Journal of Education & Social Policy* **3** (4) 73-79.

Salovey P, Mayer JD & Caruso D (2002) The positive psychology of emotional intelligence. *Handbook of Positive Psychology* **159** 171.

Sutton RE & Wheatley KF (2003) Teachers' emotions and teaching: A review of the literature and directions for future research. *Educational Psychology Review* **15** (4) 327–358.

Wolff S (1995) The concept of resilience. *Australian and New Zealand Journal of Psychiatry* **29** (4) 565–574.

Chapter 6: Managing and Mastering Screens

A brief exploration of screens, social media and gaming

The development of digital technologies has meant that the role of screens, media and gaming in children's lives has changed dramatically. Media is no longer confined to television, radio, films and books. Instead, it is an ever-present part of their daily life. The current generation of children have been described as 'digital natives': 'native speakers' of the digital language of computers, video games and the internet (Prensky, 2001). Our children have known nothing else from an early age. This is their world. We need to find ways to help them manage it and use it for good, without damaging their mental health.

This engagement with screens and technology from such a young age is viewed by some as one big social experiment (Shifrin *et al*, 2015). We don't yet know what will be the long-term effects of various types of screen use on children's developing brains. Yet screens are unavoidable and can also be of benefit to our lives. 'Screen time' can mean so many different things and can be used in a number of ways – at its best, to aid and supplement a child's face-to-face learning; as a reward, or withheld as a punishment; or perhaps even simply used to keep children occupied.

The format and content of the media accessed plays an important part in how it impacts upon a child. For example, there is extensive evidence linking violent content, including playing violent video games (Media Violence Commission, 2012), to an increase in aggressive behaviour. However, there is also increasing research into how more interactive forms of media can facilitate and enhance learning and development (Roseberry *et al*, 2014). We also know that the extent of media and screens' effects on a child will be mediated by other factors such as their home life, self-esteem, overall health and temperament (Shriffin et al 2015).

The effect of screens on developing brains

Children's brains are constantly building neural connections while pruning away less used ones. They do this in response to the environments they interact with (both offline and online). What we need to know is: does excessive screen time have a negative impact on the developing brain? The first wave of data coming from the Adolescent Brain Cognitive Development (ABCD) Study, which is supported by the National Institute for Health, indicates a relationship between high screen use and premature thinning of the cortex (Paulus *et al*, 2019). The study has shown through magnetic resonance imaging (MRI) scans of 4500 9–10 year olds that the children that used smartphones, tablets and video games for more than seven hours a day had significant differences within their brains. These children tended to show earlier thinning of the cortex. As this occurs naturally over time, the exact impact of early cortex thinning is not yet established; although the study also found that children who spend more than two hours a day on screens got lower scores on language and thinking tests.

In another very recent, large study, involving 2441 mothers and their young children, higher levels of screen time for young children (2–3 years old) were associated with reduced performance on a measure assessing the child's achievement of developmental milestones at 3–5 years of age. The screening measure addressed how well the children had developed communication, problem-solving and social interaction skills (Madigan *et al*, 2019). The authors claim this association is evident even when other factors that influence children's development are taken into account e.g. parents' education and how physically active a child is. It also did not seem as though the children that had developmental challenges were more likely to be having more screen time. However, the study has been criticised: others looking at the data have put forward that the extent to which screen time explains the differences in scores in the development screening measure was not substantial. There is clearly a need for ongoing research in this area.

The benefits and risks of the digital world

Whatever one's view on the negative impact of screen use, it is hard to deny that the digital age has brought with it increased connectivity and new opportunities, to such an extent that those who don't embrace it risk being left behind. Many of the children in education today will go on to have careers based around digital technologies – careers which would not have existed only a decade or two ago. Social and peer relationships can be enhanced by the ease of access to online conversation and to like-minded people who may never have met without the internet. Children and adults alike enjoy the benefits of technology relating to entertainment and the simplification of busy modern life.

Alongside these positives, technology has created more risks for our children – the internet has increased the scale of child sex abuse, with offenders gaining increased access to children and having a platform for the sharing of indecent images. Some children are themselves using digital technology to share inappropriate images, engage in 'sexting' with peers and accessing pornography. Alongside this, cyberbullying means that some children can still be victimised even once at home. The longevity of hurtful photos and words online means they can linger and cause damage for years to come.

Like most things, balance is key. Depending on how they are used, digital technologies can either enhance or hinder a child's development. Media that distract from social interactions (e.g. background TV, parents' media overuse and excessive gaming) clearly impair learning, while other media (e.g. Skype, Facetime and online learning platforms) can promote social interactions and learning (Shifrin *et al*, 2015).

One risk that causes concern for parents is the potentially addictive nature of online games. Games are designed so that children come back to them time and time again and utilise elements of immediate gratification and built-in reward systems. The key neurotransmitter in the brain's reward system is dopamine and it is associated with pleasure. Dopamine and our tendency to seek pleasure have a strong impact on the activities we engage in. Parents should be alert to a child having significant difficulty (i.e. high emotional distress) coming away from screens even when time warnings and boundaries are in place. It is a concern if screens start to preoccupy a child's thoughts and interfere with daily functioning and relationships. (This may be more common for children with ASC, as certain online activities may be a preoccupation or special interest.)

Schools and parents should also be aware of the link between exposure to violent TV, films and video games and increased levels of aggressive behaviour. When a child's distress behaviour involves aggression to others, despite the knowledge that this is socially inappropriate, it is useful to have a discussion with the child's parents regarding what they are accessing online and what certificate it is. Research by Anderson *et al* (2001) indicates that exposure to violent video or online games increases physiological arousal and increases aggression-related thoughts and feelings. They also found that playing violent video games also decreases prosocial behaviours. Unpleasant and distressing images and scenes that are viewed online or on TV cannot be unseen. We need to be alert to the potential impact on children's mental health, in the short and the long-term. Research has found that 16% of children aged 8–11 years old and 31% of 12–15 year olds who go online have seen something that they found worrying or nasty (Ofcom, 2018). Although clearly this is too high and not something we should just accept, the study also found that a high proportion of these children would tell someone what they had seen or were aware of online reporting functions, although only 12% had actually reported it. Children who have seen distressing images may well wish to talk about this with an adult in school, or they may communicate it through other means, such as drawing, including ideas in their writing or through changes in their behaviour. All staff need to record concerns relating to inappropriate content that children may have viewed in accordance with the school's safeguarding procedures.

It is well known that a good night's sleep positively supports brain development and a child's ability to learn. Devices with screens emit blue light which suppresses the secretion of our sleep hormone, melatonin, disrupting sleep patterns and often making it harder to fall asleep. There is further discussion about the importance of sleep in *Chapter 4: Wellbeing for All*.

Finally, we would argue that one of the negative consequences of screens and digital technologies is that children rarely experience the feeling of boredom. Although long-term and high-level boredom is associated with negative outcomes for mental health, researchers have shown there can be benefits to boredom. In fact, experiences of boredom have been associated with increased creativity and use of imagination (Mann & Cadman, 2014). If children have protected time where their minds are left to wander and daydream, they might possibly come up with ideas and plans that have a significantly more positive impact on their mental health than their screens do.

Good practice in school

Teaching staff need to take opportunities to model mindful choices around screen use in school. This should underpin all good practice concerning online and screen safety, including whole-school policy. It is important to highlight to children that although screens and the internet hold great benefits for their learning, using them is not the ultimate goal. Learning is the ultimate goal. Devices are tools for learning and they must be used with intention.

The new guidance for health education, which becomes statutory in September 2020, lays out the requirements for schools in this area (DfE, 2019). This ensures that children understand the following:

- The benefits of the online world.
- The need to ration time spent online and the content viewed, in order to protect the mental and physical wellbeing of themselves and others.
- That actions online affect others.

- That personal information needs to be kept private.

- Why some online activities have age restrictions.

- The risks and dangers of the online world and the negative impact these have on our mental health.

- That we need to consider the validity of information we see online and be selective with regard to search results.

- How to report concerns and get support.

The guidance provides sensible direction for teaching regarding screens and the online world. Schools can then expand on this and target specific areas where needed. The 'Thinking about...' box below covers various considerations relating to how and when we allow children to access devices for learning purposes.

❓ Thinking about ... screen use in school

Before using a screen in school, always ask: *What is the purpose? Is it necessary? Could I do it another way?*

- Avoid becoming too reliant on screens. Make mindful choices about when they should be used for teaching and learning. Explain to children the benefits of using a screen for a particular activity and ensure you use analogue alternatives often.

- Ensure the correct controls are in place to restrict access online. If inappropriate content is accessed, on purpose or by accident, follow the guidance given in your school's online safety policy. Consider the impact of the content on the child and those around them. Always speak to parents as a priority.

- Using devices in class:

  - When children are using individual or paired tablets or laptops for learning, ensure you give a clear purpose for using them. Aside from the benefits of saving paper as a result of less photocopying, it is really useful for children to be able to access information right in front of them, removing the need for them to constantly look up at the board (this is especially beneficial for some children with particular mental health conditions e.g. ASC and ADHD). A photo of a text can be taken and sent to all iPads. The children are then able to highlight and make notes accordingly. Learning in this way encourages sharing, communication and cooperation.

  - Agree class rules for using devices e.g. 'My screen can always been seen by an adult'; 'I will only use my device for the purpose given by the adult'; 'If I see something I don't like, I will tell a teacher and not show it around the class'.

→

- Be aware that children may be able to use instant messaging to communicate with each other through the devices. Disable this if at all possible.
- It is immensely difficult when a child always wants to use a device – when they have screen use as their default activity. We do not recommend allowing a child to always complete learning activities using a device or using screen time as a reward. Try to gradually reduce children's dependence on screens by making other learning opportunities as appealing and interactive as possible. Perhaps the child can be allowed to use a device to complete a special learning project once the original learning activities are completed.
- Observe all school rules regarding phone use – for children and yourself. If older children are bringing phones to school, ensure these are locked away for the duration of the day, in line with the school's policy. Refrain from using your own phone when in areas of school used by children.
- Always follow the school's safeguarding procedures when a concern arises regarding screen use or online activity.

Helping children to become masters of their screens

So, how can we support the children in our schools to become masters of their screens, rather than letting them go down a path where their screens become *their* masters and their mental health is negatively impacted? They need our support to help them filter and process the sheer volume of information and digital stimulation that they bombarded with. It is not healthy for any of us to be constantly connected. As adults, we know the pressures felt from the repeated ping of notifications on our devices and the expectation that we must immediately respond. We have an opportunity to prevent our children from having to experience this too, but we must begin the conversations when they are young.

Questions from children about screens and the online world need to be welcomed. Teaching staff should avoid pushing it to one side because it feels too challenging or time consuming. Children need to trust that they can share their ideas and concerns in this area with adults – to trust that they will be listened to and helped to navigate the new digital world. To do this, we need to understand it ourselves. It is so difficult to keep up to date with the constant changes and advances in games, apps and phrases that children are using for elements of the digital world. Teaching staff need to tune in to this so they can support and advise them. We recommend keeping yourselves informed by using one of the many excellent online safety resources available (suggestions are given in **Further Reading and Guidance**).

Schools also need to support their staff to do this and circulate relevant advice and updates as necessary.

Teaching staff need to guide children to pause and reflect on their screen use, encouraging them to consider:

- which screens they are using and for how long
- why they are choosing a screen over an alternative activity
- how they feel before, during and after using a screen
- how they can put boundaries in place to protect their minds and bodies from the dangers of overuse.

It is so important to help children tune into the reasons behind their screen use and guide them to an understanding of whether it is appropriate or not. There may be positive reasons, for instance learning, entertainment or connection; or more concerning reasons, such as viewing of inappropriate content, a strong 'need' to continue playing a game, or boredom. As mentioned above, another essential lesson for children is the permanence and unpredictability of any information sent digitally or posted online. They need to understand that once something is shared it is no longer 'theirs' and they cannot control who sees it and what happens to it. Specific guidance should be given about social media account privacy and how to protect their passwords and content (regardless of age restrictions, it is safe to assume that some children will have their own social media accounts). Exploration of this can link in closely with learning in PSHE regarding friendships, trust and honesty.

The lesson plan and the frame 'Safe with my screens' in **Chapter 19** look at these areas in detail and suggest ways to begin the conversations about screens with children in school. However, so much screen use occurs outside of school – therefore we advocate making this area a priority for any parent education workshops each year, even for those with very young children. Reinforcing messages about safe screen use is important for all children, regardless of their age. The American Academy of Paediatrics (Shiffrin *et al*, 2015) has carried out extensive research into the effects of screens and media on children, and has made a number of evidence-based recommendations that may be helpful to share with parents:

- Co-viewing of television programmes by parents and children is preferred. This makes the experience more engaging and less passive, with adults able to point out interesting things which may contribute to learning and language skills.
- Eliminating electronic screens from bedrooms helps to improve sleep hygiene.

- Consider daily screen time limits.

- Discourage screen use in under-twos, as there is no evidence that this is beneficial to their development.

- Inform and educate families about media rating systems to ensure children are not accessing inappropriate material.

Overall, we need to be encouraging children to engage in, and modelling for them, mindful and intentional screen use. We need to empower them to know that they can be the master of the screen and that ultimately, there is so much more to life than that which they can experience in the online world.

Summary

- The current generation of children are known as 'digital natives' and screens are likely to be part of their lives from birth.

- High levels of screen use can affect brain development in younger children, and the long-term impacts are not yet known.

- Benefits of digital technologies include new connections and opportunities. The risks, however, include access to inappropriate material, increased vulnerability of children online and cyberbullying, along with the potentially addictive nature of some computer games.

- The new guidance for health education covers screens and the online world. Schools must also model mindful use of screens and avoid over-reliance on them.

- We need to help children to become masters of the screen and equip them with the skills to know when screens can help and when they may harm.

- Remember that this is changing all the time – faster than we can keep up with it.

References

Anderson CA & Bushman BJ (2001) Effects of violent video games on aggressive behaviour, aggression cognition, aggressive affect, physiological arousal and prosocial behaviour: A meta-analytic review of the scientific literature. *Psychological Science* **12** (5) 353–359.

Anderson CA, Shubuya A, Ihori N *et al* (2010) Violent video game effects on aggression, empathy, and prosocial behavior in Eastern and Western countries: A meta-analytic review. *Psychology Bulletin* **136** (2) 151–173.

Department for Education (2019) *Relationships Education, Relationships and Sex Education (RSE) and Health Education*. Available from www.gov.uk/government/publications/relationships-education-relationships-and-sex-education-rse-and-health-education

The Lancet Editorial 2018 Growing up in a digital world: Benefits and risks. *The Lancet Child & Adolescent Health* **2** (2) 79.

Madigan S, Browne D, Racine N *et al* (2019) Association between screen time and children's performance on a developmental screening test. *JAMA Pediatrics* **173** (3) 244–250.

Mann S & Cadman R (2014) Does being bored make us more creative? *Creativity Research Journal* **26** (2) 165–173.

Media Violence Commission, International Society for Research on Aggression (2012) Report of the Media Violence Commission. *Aggressive Behaviour* **38** 335–341. doi: 10.1002/ab.21443.

Ofcom (2019) *Children and Parents: Media Use and Attitudes Report, 2018*. Available from www.ofcom.org.uk/__data/assets/pdf_file/0024/134907/children-and-parents-media-use-and-attitudes-2018.pdf

Paulus MP, Squeglia LM, Bagot K *et al* (2019) Screen media activity and brain structure in youth: Evidence for diverse structural correlation networks from the ABCD study. *Neuroimage* **185** 140–153.

Prensky M (2001) Digital natives, digital immigrants. *On the Horizon* **9** (5) 1–6.

Roseberry S, Hirsh-Pasek K & Golinkoff RM (2014) Skype me! Socially contingent interactions help toddlers learn language. *Child Development* **85** (3) 956–970. doi: 10.1111/cdev.12166.

Shriffin D, Brown A, Hill D *et al* (2015) Growing up digital: Media research symposium. *American Academy of Paediatrics*. Available from www.aap.org/en-us/documents/digital_media_symposium_proceedings.pdf

Section 3: Mental Health Presentations and Conditions

Chapter 7: Anxiety, Panic and OCD

Anxiety

What is anxiety?

Anxiety is characterised by heightened autonomic arousal and it can have a positive effect on our behaviour. For example, it can motivate us to get things done and it can indicate the need to avoid danger. But too much anxiety can have a detrimental impact on performance (as demonstrated by the Yerkes–Dodson Law diagram below). Too much anxiety can tip you over the hill of 'peak performance' and into the realms of stress and distress.

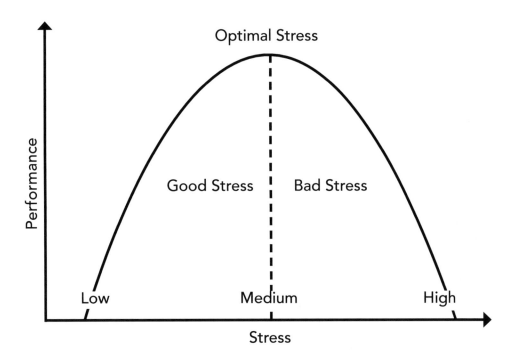

Figure 1: The Yerkes–Dodson Law (Yerkes & Dodson, 1908)

Anxiety is a normal human emotion and is most often transient. It is an emotion that alerts us to a problem and children may need support in order to work out a way through anxiety-provoking situations. Whilst 'worry' tends to refer to the repetitive negative thoughts in our heads, anxiety can affect our entire body in a physical way too (see below). Such transient challenges are a part of growing up and how adults respond to children's low-level worries can have an impact on their developing resilience. For example, teaching staff can helpfully:

- Work with the child to identify the specific cause of the worry. If they find it hard to identify, the frames 'Things that make me feel…' and 'All about school' (see **Chapter 19**) can help them begin to articulate the emotional impact of activities in school or events in their wider life.

- In partnership with parents, gently explore the 'why' behind a child's worries. This process can take some time and patience is needed. A child may find it hard to share the details of their worries with their parents.

A common analogy used to describe the situation when the demands placed upon us outweigh our emotional capacity to manage them is the overflowing bucket. We all have limitations to what we can manage – some people have a large bucket (and are therefore more emotionally resilient) and others have a smaller capacity to manage the accumulation of triggers, and therefore have a smaller bucket. The different stressors which are poured into our buckets on a daily basis are different for different people. In order for our bucket to not overflow we need to have strategies that enable the bucket to leak through a tap, allowing the triggers and stressors to empty out. Strategies that help modify the triggers and regulate us (for example, positive self-talk, engagement in activities that reduce our stress levels and positive self-care) reduce our levels of stress and anxiety.

Figure 2: The overflowing bucket

The exact nature of a child's worry or anxiety will determine the presentation. However, typical physical signs may be present for many children, but to a lesser or greater degree. These may include dizziness, trembling, sweating and a racing heart. The child may frequently mention other physical complaints, such as headaches, stomach aches, muscle pains or injuries. They may also experience frequent or excessive tiredness.

Significant anxiety can manifest in many ways, and health professionals may use a range of diagnoses all under the umbrella term 'anxiety disorders'. These include generalised anxiety disorder (GAD), panic disorder, obsessive compulsive disorder (OCD) and specific phobias. We all experience anxiety at times, as we have described – it is a normal human emotion, but if anxiety is causing a child to be significantly distressed, impacting on their daily functioning and/or stopping them from being able to take part in certain activities on a regular basis, they are likely to require some additional support to manage their difficulty.

If a child's anxiety reaches this level, they may meet the criteria for a diagnosis of an anxiety disorder. These disorders are characterised by anxiety at inappropriate times and/or to mildly aversive stimuli, and as such the level of anxiety is no longer adaptive, but maladaptive. The presence of anxiety disorders promotes mechanisms associated with harm avoidance across multiple levels of cognition, perception, attention, learning and executive function (Robinson *et al*, 2013). Specific anxiety disorders are explored later in the chapter.

How common are anxiety disorders

Anxiety disorders are amongst the common causes of mental health difficulties in young people. Between 5-19% of all children are estimated to be experiencing an anxiety disorder (NHS Inform, 2020). This figure covers the whole range of anxiety disorders including generalised anxiety, OCD and panic disorder. As many people experience more than one type of anxiety, it can be difficult to break these figures down further. We do know however that some anxiety disorders, such as separation anxiety, are more common in the under 12s (NHS Inform, 2020), but that generally other anxiety disorders are more prevalent in the over 12s (Public Health England, 2016).

Anxiety in school: What does it look like and how can we help?

Anxiety can present in a variety of different ways in the school environment. Each child will have different triggers and present with different signs. For some it may be very visible, e.g. crying, avoidance of triggers, trembling or constantly seeking reassurance. For some it may be well hidden, controlled and masked, with only subtle signs noticeable to those who are really tuned in to that child. In addition to the physical signs previously mentioned, there may be recurrent anxieties relating to specific situations, such as certain lessons, visiting the toilet, moving around school or close physical proximity to other children or adults.

Strategies

It is important to consider how anxiety presents with regard to various aspects of school life and how strategies can be used to help children manage their emotional responses and overcome the subsequent barriers to their engagement and learning. The sections below will explore anxiety in relation to the learning environment, emotional, behavioural and social regulation and the actual process of learning.

Learning environment

For a child with anxiety, having a stable, ordered and calm classroom environment is very important. Creating a calm area within the classroom can be very reassuring. This is explored further in *Chapter 8: Low Mood*. Teaching staff may notice a child presenting with anxiety in relation to a particular environment around school. A number of simple strategies can be employed to support children with specific triggers:

- Noise:
  - A child who finds assemblies difficult due to unpredictable, loud noises, such as clapping or cheering, can wear ear defenders or be seated at the end of a line and allowed to step out when needed. Have ear defenders always accessible for anyone to use. If they are normalised within the classroom, children who need them are more likely to access them. Even classroom chatter can be too much for children with noise sensitivities.
  - Specific noises may be triggers for distress, for example fire alarms, lockdown alarms or hand dryers. The unpredictable nature of these noises makes planning difficult, but warn the parents and child about planned fire drills if possible. Again, ensure ear defenders are always nearby for children who find these difficult.
- Close physical contact:
  - A child who becomes anxious when in close proximity to other children on the carpet or at a table can be allowed to move to an agreed quieter spot when needed.
  - Some children may find it difficult to move through narrow spaces and doorways with others. Allow them space to go first and support other children to show them understanding.
  - Consider the implications for assemblies. Allowing the child to sit on the end of a line is helpful.

- The playground:

    - Teaching staff may notice a child delaying moving out into the playground, always standing with the adult on duty or seeking frequent reassurance. Try to avoid telling them to 'go and play'. Relaxed conversation and distraction are best for putting the child at ease. If they are finding playtimes very difficult, consider how alternative provision can be made. See *Chapter 4: Wellbeing for All* for a full discussion of this.

    - If a child has been using alternative lunchtime provision for some time, consider how they can be helped to gradually transition back to the playground. Having a covered area where children can sit and enjoy games or mindful activities is ideal.

    - Have systems in place for ensuring all adults know the children that are struggling and how best to help them. This should include all teachers, TAs and lunchtime staff that may be on duty.

- Toilets:

    - For some children, frequent visits to the toilet may be related to anxiety. Speak to the parents and the child together to explore why this might be. Is it also happening at home?

    - It may be an avoidance strategy, in which case spend time addressing how you can support them with the original trigger activity.

    - If the anxiety is related to toileting itself, discuss with parents how best to support the child so that toilet visits are not disrupting their learning.

    - A child may be worried about going to the toilet at the wrong time and being told off. Explain to the class that although it is better for them to go in between lessons, if they are desperate to go, they may show teaching staff with a 'T' hand signal or use a 'toilet pass'.

Emotional, behavioural and social regulation

Supporting a child with anxiety with their emotional, behavioural and social regulation is crucial and should be embedded throughout all interactions. For a child experiencing intense distress, the action guide in *Chapter 9* considers how to support them through the process of de-escalation. Here we will consider specific emotional, behavioural and social considerations.

With regard to emotional regulation, children may:

- Be reluctant to discuss worries – teaching staff should not put pressure on a child to talk to them about their worries. Focus on creating a trusting and secure connection with the child. Always display patient hearing when they do speak and they are more likely to come and share further at a later time.

- Be unable to identify worries and feelings – support children to recognise and name the different emotions. Narrate their feelings and experiences for them and model how to name your own emotions.

■ Become upset or tearful frequently or easily – try not tell the child 'calm down' or 'stop crying', as this can escalate the situation. Greet these feelings with acceptance and allow space for them to pass naturally. Discuss the triggers in more detail after they are calm.

■ Take a long time to respond to comfort and reassurance – be patient and try to ensure an adult remains with the child if possible. Make use of calm areas in the classroom and around the school. Having a range of soft toys and puppets that a child can cuddle and talk to can be helpful.

Use the approaches given in **Chapter 5** and explore the corresponding resources in **Chapter 19** to gradually build a child's emotional intelligence and resilience.

With regard to behavioural regulation, children may:

■ Frequently seek reassurance from adults – always acknowledge children when they seek reassurance. Remain patient with repetitive questions and give gentle answers. Have set systems in place in the classroom for children to find out key information, for example a visual timetable (see **Chapter 16**).

■ Avoid certain activities, lessons or peers – when teaching staff notice avoidance behaviours, they should try not to address them in the moment but wait until the anxiety has passed. Use the frame 'All about school' in **Chapter 19** to support discussions about which parts of the school day cause worry for them. Once this is clear, you can develop specific strategies for each trigger.

■ Display anger, aggression and other behaviours that challenge (Karmin, 2016) – maintain your calm presence and consider using strategies from **Chapter 9**. Spend time trying to identify the exact cause of the behaviours with the child using the frame and lesson plan 'The bottle that wants to go pop!' in **Chapter 19**.

■ Present with hyperactivity – again, remain calm and patient with hyperactive behaviours and consider exploring relevant strategies from **Chapter 12**. Spend time exploring the anxiety behind the hyperactivity.

When a child is very distressed by anxiety, as well as using the action guide in Chapter 9, allow children to use a 'pass' or hand signal to self-direct to agreed 'calm areas'. This could be within the classroom, the next-door classroom, the library or the sensory room. Ensure the child knows to return when they are feeling calm or send an adult to check in with them regularly.

With regard to social regulation, children may:

- struggle to make friends
- experience frequent problems within a friendship group
- display over-reliance on a particular friend or group, perhaps using controlling behaviours.

Social anxieties can be addressed throughout all interactions adults have with children in school; however, some children will need more intensive support. Consider using strategies such as 'buddy systems', PSHE lessons, stories about friendship and social interaction and, if appropriate, interventions, such as a Nurture group (see *Chapter 5*).

Learning

Anxiety can present many barriers to the learning process. Some key areas to consider are:

- Concentration and attention:
  - At times of high anxiety, a child may find it very difficult to concentrate and become preoccupied with a particular worry. Tune into when this may be happening and offer understanding if learning activities are not completed. Keep a clear record of when it occurs. Consider using the strategies given in *Chapter 12*.

- Speaking and listening:
  - A child may demonstrate a generally quiet and shy demeanour or reluctance to contribute to class discussions or share work; have difficulties working in a group; or show a mismatch between verbal communication of understanding and written work.
  - Take opportunities to gradually build a child's confidence in small, low-pressure ways, perhaps sharing work with their previous teacher, or giving answers to a friend during paired discussion.
  - Be mindful of resistance to take part in group work and try to ensure an adult or peer can support them with this.
  - Offer consistent praise and encouragement of progress, however small.

- Difficulties in specific areas of learning:
  - Look for patterns in terms of non-attendance on days when particular lessons occur.
  - If it is observed that anxiety is related to one particular area of learning, for example maths or writing, find out which specific aspect is the problem and target support accordingly. Booster groups or low-pressure lunchtime clubs

can be helpful. Focus on designing inspiring lessons and activities in this area that may help the child to engage further. Linking planning to their interests and strengths can also be of benefit.

- Anxiety related to weight or appearance may be demonstrated by a reluctance to change for PE or take part in physical activity. See *Chapter 14* for strategies to address this.

- Memory:
  - Intense anxiety can impact on short-term working memory (Moran, 2016). This may present within a lesson with a child not recalling instructions or on a wider scale, in terms of remembering the activities of the week or things they need each day for school. Develop specific strategies for the exact presentation. Writing short instructions on a white board for the child to take their table or printing a copy of the success criteria may help in lessons. Always refer a child back to the visual timetable (see *Chapter 16*) and review this with the whole class at regular points during the day.

It is important to note that whole-school strategies embedded in the culture of the school can be helpful in reducing worries and anxiety for all children, and aid in their regulation.

Separation anxiety

Case example: Separation anxiety

Sam is in Year 2. Every morning he screams and cries when he has to leave his mum at the school gates. This has been happening every morning since he started school and it takes over an hour to calm him down. Once he is calm, he seems happy and engaged throughout the day.

What is separation anxiety?

Separation anxiety refers to the emotional response triggered by a person being separated from a specific person or persons. Separation anxiety is typical for all children at different stages within their development. When this anxiety is regularly overwhelming, intense or exceptionally prolonged, it may indicate other issues. Separation anxiety can be heightened in children with insecurities within their attachment relationships with their primary caregivers. It also tends to be heighted in children with ASC or with significant SEND, as these children rely heavily on their primary attachment figures to 'translate their world for them'. Without their attachment figures, the world is even more scary and unpredictable, so it makes sense that it is more of a challenge to separate from them to come into school. It is most helpful to resist the urge to have any negative judgements towards the parents whose child is struggling to separate from them. Instead, communicate with them about why the issue seems to have continued for longer than you would expect or why the child always seems particularly distressed over and above what you would expect for children of that age and at that time within the academic year.

Separation anxiety in school: What does it look like and how can we help?

When separation anxiety is becoming an issue, you may notice:

- low attendance overall
- refusal to attend school
- reluctance to come into class in the morning or re-enter after a break time.

Convincing a child who is in a heightened state of anxiety to enter the classroom can be very distressing for all involved. The child may be very upset and not want to separate from their parent at the door. The parent may also be upset at their child's reluctance to go into class. They may be embarrassed that other families are witnessing the situation unfold, they may feel powerless to help their child calm down and they may be anxious themselves about getting to work on time. Other children may also become unsettled while watching a peer struggle to leave their parent. And the teacher, of course, would very much like all children to enter their classroom happily and begin the day on time. Every party brings their own needs and feelings to the things that unfold at the classroom door.

How can teaching staff support a child in distress to transition into the classroom, re-regulate their emotions and still remain present with the rest of the class? How you decide to approach a situation like this will depend greatly on the school's morning routine. If time and circumstances allow, the following gentle routine can allow a teacher or TA to connect with a child and help them separate from their parent. Your aim is to transition the child into an attachment with a safe adult and set the conditions for them to re-regulate their emotions, so they can be ready for learning. The action guide below explores this further. See also the 'Thinking about...' box on school refusal later in this chapter.

⊚ Action guide: separation anxiety

In the moment

- If you have another adult, decide who will remain with the child and who will settle the other children.

- Remain calm and encourage the parent to remain calm. Ask them if they know what the trigger was for the anxiety today.

- Get down on the child's level and use a low but cheerful voice. Empathise with their distress and worry; reassure them that they are safe with you in school and that you will have a fun day together.

- Give them something to look forward to – what will a highlight of the day be for them?

- Explain that their parent is going to go now and that you are both going to go into the classroom together. Ask them what they would like to do when they get in. Be flexible – if at all possible allow them the freedom to choose their own settling activity.

- Give a cheerful goodbye to the parent and remind the child when they will see them next.

- Once through the door, encourage the child to move straight to the chosen settling activity. Remain with them for a few minutes and keep checking in with them once you return to the class.

- If the child continues to physically cling to the parent, allow the parent to come into the corridor if possible and gradually transition them out once the child is more settled.

- If the child still refuses to enter the classroom, or enters and then leaves again, assign an adult to remain with them at all times. Explain that you need to keep them safe at school and cannot let them leave. If they try to run or return home, the adult needs to stay close and keep chat light-hearted. Rather than continuing to persuade the child, distract and engage them with interesting conversation. Gradually allowing the child to re-regulate at their own pace will be more helpful than trying to rush them back into class.

What next

It is important to follow up situations of intense separation anxiety as soon as possible.

- Check in with the child throughout the day. How is their day going? What did they think of the highlight that you mentioned earlier? Provide a safe base for them to come back to. ➔

- Was it a first for this child or is a pattern forming?
- What was the trigger? Toward the end of the day, ask the child. Can they identify the cause?
- Speak to the parent at the end of the day. Let them know how the child has been during the day. Celebrate any successes. Give them something to look forward to tomorrow.

Big picture

In the longer term, work with the child and parents to create a plan for making the transition from home to school easier.

- Speak to child and parents to find out what is causing the anxiety (for example, is it general school anxiety, anxiety related to home or family life or a specific lesson or activity, peer-related or bullying?)
- Identify an assigned adult, who the child can get to know, to support them to enter the classroom, perhaps before or after the other children.
- Choose a settling activity with the child – what would make them feel comfortable and help them adjust? Agree a time frame for the activity and give them a signal or word for re-joining the class.
- Use a transitional object. This is a special item that is brought from home to school and vice versa. It may be something from home to show the teacher or something that they are asked to look after in school for their parents. It may be something they are asked to look after by their teacher and that they need to bring back in with them. It could be a sensory item that, when they stroke it, squish it or smell it, will help calm their difficult emotions.
- Having the same key person greeting the child and facilitate the 'handover' from the parent to a trusted adult (whom the child likes) can often be very effective. Maintaining this key person's availability can be a challenge but these small changes can have a significant impact on a child's sense of security.
- Start a 'one line a day story'. The child can add to this at home with the parent and at school with the teacher. Together, they can write a funny and entertaining story. When we use joint activities that model the positive relationship between home and school, children are more likely to feel safe with their teacher. Adding in the element of humour and distraction that engages the child in a creative activity can also support emotional regulation.

Generalised anxiety disorder

Case example: Generalised anxiety disorder

Jack's school attendance is poor. He has frequently been off school with headaches, tummy aches and unexplained pain all term. I have offered him the opportunity to work in a quieter area but he refuses. It's difficult to know how to support him if he doesn't manage to even get into school. He looks pale and tired and does not speak readily about what specifically it is that is worrying him. He rarely puts his hand up in class to contribute, even though I'm confident at times that he does know the answer as he demonstrates this later within his work. He's very quiet and seems to be struggling with friendships. I've spoken to his parents who report that he seems very anxious when he is at home too.

What is generalised anxiety disorder?

A child that is struggling to the extent that they would meet the criteria for a diagnosis of GAD would be experiencing anxiety that is both generalised and persistent, as demonstrated in the case example above. Their anxiety would not be restricted to, or dominated by, any particular circumstances. They would be experiencing worry and difficulty controlling this worry. Their symptoms might include persistent nervousness, trembling, sweating and dizziness. For a child to meet the criteria for this diagnosis, symptoms must be present on most days for a period of at least six months. Sadly, anxiety disorders that begin in childhood and adolescence frequently persist into later life (Ginsburg *et al*, 2018) and can negatively impact quality of life (Mendlowicz & Stein, 2000).

Anxiety related to a specific situation or event, for example exam stress, might be experienced as overwhelming and very difficult, but would not be viewed as indicative of GAD. In GAD, the focal point of anxiety tends to be transient, with worries shifting according to current life stressors and encounters with a range of triggers (Butler, 1994). GAD is associated with persistent attention to and hypervigilance to threat, which could be both real or perceived. It is also associated with inflated perceptions of the consequences or impact of threat (Mathews & Macleod, 1986; Butler & Mathews, 1983).

All of the strategies for supporting children with anxiety that are outlined above are suitable for use if a diagnosis of GAD is given.

When further help is needed for generalised anxiety disorder

Many children will go through phases of feeling worried or anxious. Noticing any patterns or triggers at these times and implementing some of the strategies listed above will often be all that is needed. Anxiety which is showing little improvement despite actions to help support the child to feel calm, and which is stopping the child from being able to access and participate in school activities, is likely to need further support. Treatment for GAD will usually be based around CBT, and for children of primary school age, sessions will often include parents, rather than being individual-only therapy. This therapy would usually be provided through CAMHS or local provision for school-based mental health support.

Panic disorder

Case example: Panic attacks

Freddie has become overwhelmed with distress and panic during lessons a few times. He seems to be hyperventilating and then gets very upset and leaves the classroom suddenly. There seem to be no warnings for these 'meltdowns' and afterwards it can be difficult for him to calm down. His school attendance has been impacted recently.

What is panic disorder?

Panic disorder is characterised by recurrent attacks of severe anxiety or panic, which are not restricted to a particular situation and often 'come out of the blue'. Symptoms of anxiety in this condition are intense as the body has been inadvertently triggered into 'fight or flight' mode despite there not being any imminent physical danger. Panic attacks start suddenly, peak in a few minutes and can include the sudden onset of physical symptoms such as palpitations, chest pain, sweating, shaking, choking sensations, shortness of breath and dizziness. Panic attacks usually last 5–20 minutes and can be accompanied by catastrophic thoughts e.g. thinking one is going to die or a feeling that something bad is going to happen.

Panic disorder in school: what does it look like and how can we help?

Panic can look different for different people. Take time to get to know what the child's triggers are and what panic looks like for them. Talk to them when they are calm and explore this with the parents too.

By definition, panic disorder involves multiple panic attacks which are random or unpredictable, but often situations such as public speaking or crowded assemblies are a trigger. If panic attacks are limited to one particular situation they may fall under a different diagnostic label e.g. panic attacks in crowded and busy places may be termed agoraphobia.

Strategies

It is important to consider how panic disorder presents with regard to various aspects of school life and how strategies can be used to help children manage their emotional responses and overcome the subsequent barriers to their engagement and learning. The sections below will explore panic disorder in relation to the learning environment, emotional and behavioural regulation and the actual process of learning.

Learning environment

If possible, encourage the child not to escape the situation completely and stay with them until the anxiety has subsided. This ensures that they are able to learn that nothing bad has happened as a result of the panic attack. However, this can be difficult in a school setting as there will also be a drive to protect a child's dignity. Additionally, many children experiencing panic within a busy group setting would remove themselves from that environment. Returning to the situation shortly after a panic attack can reduce the likelihood of the child starting to over-use avoidance strategies to prevent recurrent attacks.

When a child begins to show signs of panic, and it may become necessary for them to leave the demands of the classroom environment, a proactive exit strategy can be used. This could be a visual card or hand signal that they can use to communicate to the teacher simply and effectively that they need to leave. A visual contract might need to be put in place about how and when to use such an exit card. Informing all adults who work with the child that this system is in place is essential. The template for a 'I need you to know' card in **Chapter 19** can support with this.

Emotional and behavioural regulation

With regard to emotional regulation: hyperventilation is a symptom of a panic attack that can increase fear. Conversely, deep breathing can reduce symptoms of panic during an attack. Help the child focus on breathing deeply by breathing alongside them. Use a calm, reassuring voice and repeatedly encourage them to breathe out slowly, deeply and gently through the mouth. Some people find it helpful to count steadily from 1 to 5 on each in-breath and on each out-breath.

With regard to behavioural regulation: psychoeducation about panic attacks is likely to be helpful. In the moment, the child needs reassurance that it will pass and that although it is uncomfortable and frightening, the panic attack is not a sign that something harmful is happening. It may be helpful for the child to have strategies written down for them in advance (e.g. on a key ring) that remind them to breathe deeply, that they are perfectly safe and to focus on their surroundings in order to ground them in the here and now.

Learning

Children who experience any significant anxiety, including panic, can start to avoid the situation that they perceive to be the trigger. Of course, significant levels of avoidance can have an impact on a child's learning if this relates to a specific activity or subject. As with anxiety, work with the child to consider the exact nature of the worry linked to the learning area and develop ways to reduce pressure and expectations, without allowing the child to avoid the subject completely.

It is important that children are taught why avoidance feels easier, safer and calmer, but that it has major disadvantages. Crucially, the child reduces the ability to learn that nothing bad has happened and they reduce the likelihood of having positive experiences that could dispel their negative expectations. Spending time explaining this to the child and their parents can help, but it is a difficult concept to grasp for young children. Their fear of the moment may override the long-term benefits of exposure to the trigger.

When further help is needed for panic disorder

If the prospect of panic is causing avoidance of specific learning activities on a recurrent basis, and no improvement is seen despite efforts to reassure the child that a situation is safe, external support should be sought. A form of therapeutic intervention may be appropriate, such as CBT.

Obsessive compulsive disorder

Case example: Obsessive compulsive disorder

Amy is a quiet girl and recently she has seemed preoccupied in class. I've noticed her writing out the same word again and again, and also tapping on the table in a pattern repeatedly. Some of the other children have begun to notice too.

What is obsessive compulsive disorder?

OCD is a term used to describe difficulties with recurrent obsessional thoughts or compulsive actions, which are not pleasurable for the person experiencing them. It is not essential to experience both obsessions and compulsions for a diagnosis of OCD.

Obsessions are intrusive, unwanted thoughts. They may take the form of ideas, images or impulses to do something, that enter an individual's mind again and again. They often cause distress and are often resisted unsuccessfully. They are recognised as the person's own thoughts.

Compulsions are acts or rituals which are repeated again and again. These acts are not enjoyable and they do not result in the completion of useful tasks. Instead, the function is to reduce the obsessional thoughts and prevent some unlikely harmful event occurring, usually to the self or someone close to them. Attempts to resist completing compulsions often result in an increase in anxiety. Common themes include checking, ordering, counting and cleaning.

It is important to remember that some level of compulsive behaviour may be developmentally appropriate depending on the age of the child. For example, many children (and some adults) avoid standing on the cracks of the pavement or walking under ladders, and this is often driven by superstitious beliefs. They will usually lessen as the child gets older and are not associated with significant distress. Similarly, some obsessive traits relating to a need for order and cleanliness may persist into adulthood, but are often considered benign if they do not affect functioning or cause distress.

Obsessive compulsive disorder in school: what does it look like and how can we help?

OCD can impact on all areas of a child's life, including academic achievement, peer relationships and family life. Depending on a child's developmental level, they may not be able to clearly describe what they are experiencing. You may notice that they are performing actions repeatedly, such as hand-washing or tapping, or that they are needing to repeat parts of their work over and over again. There may be many reasons behind these behaviours, so further information is needed before considering if they may be experiencing OCD. For example, a child with ASC or sensory needs may perform tapping or touching rituals, which are not experienced as distressing or unwanted, and can in fact be quite soothing. Similarly, unwanted thoughts and images can also be experienced in other situations, such as following bereavement, trauma or abuse.

Obsessions and compulsions can impact on the whole family, with parents sometimes unwittingly accommodating the OCD in order to reduce a child's distress. This can involve parents repeatedly cleaning items or checking food labels for their child.

Keep in mind that children will feel powerless to resist the compulsions and obsessions of OCD. It can help if the adults around the child 'externalise' the condition and talk about it as something separate from the child. In this way teaching staff, the child and the child's parents work together to fight against the OCD. The adults around the child can also give a consistent message that nothing bad will happen if they do not carry out their compulsive actions. Evidence-based CBT should involve key components of externalising and behavioural experiments that test out the child's beliefs and teaching staff as well as parents can be key allies within this process.

Strategies

It is important to consider how OCD presents with regard to various aspects of school life and how strategies can be used to help children manage their emotional responses and overcome the subsequent barriers to their engagement and learning. The sections below will explore OCD in relation to the learning environment, emotional and behavioural regulation and the actual process of learning.

Learning environment

Compulsions may be observed in the classroom environment, or may be confined to other areas, such as toilets or sink areas, depending on their nature. A child may have a particular number of times they need to complete a compulsion or they may 'just know' when it they have done it enough times, usually when their anxiety is beginning to subside. Some behaviours may be disruptive to the whole class, but preventing a child from completing their compulsions can result in a significant increase in anxiety. If this is happening, it is important to address concerns by talking to the child and their parents to agree how this can be managed in the classroom. It may also be helpful, if the child is receiving treatment, that teaching staff are made aware of any strategies being used at home to ensure consistency in the school environment.

Emotional and behavioural regulation

A child experiencing unwanted intrusive thoughts may appear distracted or distressed. They may seek repeated reassurance if they are concerned about harm to themselves or others. You may see an increase in certain avoidance behaviours e.g. wanting to go to the toilet repeatedly, possibly to engage in repetitive behaviours without being watched. Rather than giving repeated reassurance (as reassurance seeking in itself can be a safety behaviour for some children), it is helpful to gently encourage solutions to come from the child themselves, e.g. by answering their question with a question which encourages them to think about the likelihood of their concern occurring.

Learning

In order to receive a diagnosis of OCD it is likely that a child will be experiencing some impairment of functioning, and this is likely to impact learning. For some children, obsessions and compulsions can interfere with completion of a task due to the overwhelming desire to carry out a necessary behaviour before they can proceed. These may be directly observable compulsions, such as tapping on the desk or rewriting words over and over, or could be mental compulsions such as counting the number of words on each line, which may be harder to stop. It may be necessary to gently redirect a child back to their learning task once they have carried out their compulsion. If a child is spending significant amounts of time on completing homework until it is perfect, this may have an impact on their sleep and general level of functioning. It is vital to work closely with parents to help support the child by putting boundaries in place around issues such as homework.

When further help is needed for obsessive compulsive disorder

As with all mental health conditions, NICE guidance for OCD suggests a stepped approach, with CBT being the first line treatment in most cases (NICE CG31, 2005). As part of the CBT, exposure and response prevention (ERP) is recommended. This involves exposure to a feared situation with a focus on reduction of 'safety behaviours', such as using hand gel or checking dates in germ-related OCD. Some children may also be prescribed medication such as SSRI antidepressants, which may help in reducing anxiety.

Thinking about ... school refusal

Some children will absolutely refuse to attend school, posing a dilemma for parents and teachers alike. Terms such as 'school phobia' and 'school refusal' are often used to describe this scenario, which could have many underlying causative factors. This is different to 'truancy', as parents will usually be aware that it is happening and the child is not motivated by a wish to engage in other pleasurable activities. It may be that a child is experiencing anxiety in the school setting or significant difficulties separating from their parents. There may be illness in the family and the child feels the need to stay close by. Or a child may feel overwhelmed by the social and academic expectations of school, or be experiencing bullying. School refusal often increases around the time of return to school after a break or transition.

It is important to tackle school refusal early on before it becomes more ingrained. Good teacher–parent communication is vital in understanding the reasons behind school refusal and also agreeing on a plan of action, which in some cases will require a phased return to school or a more flexible and personalised timetable. Not all children will be able to verbalise their worries, but giving them the opportunity to talk about what is worrying them and reassuring them that they are not in trouble is essential. Think about what may motivate or interest that child in attending school. In some cases, a peer 'buddy system' can help to ease their initial arrival into school. See the action guide on separation anxiety for further strategies to support a child's return to school.

Thinking about ... selective mutism

Selective mutism is a childhood anxiety disorder characterised by a child's inability to speak and communicate effectively within a specific social setting, such as at school. It usually starts in early childhood and is often first noticed when the child starts to interact with people outside their family, such as when they start nursery, pre-school or the EYFS. Children with this presentation are able to speak in settings where they feel comfortable and relaxed, such as at home. It is important to understand that a child with selective mutism does not choose not to speak and should not be thought of as simply refusing to speak. The expectation to talk to certain people triggers a freeze response, with feelings of panic, and they are literally unable to speak. Despite selective mutism being an anxiety disorder, it is normally assessed and diagnosed by speech and language therapists (SALT), who may or may not work within CAMHS. A referral should be sought by parents through the child's GP. Within schools, SENCOs should discuss the child's presentation with their parents and should be able to refer directly to SALT.

Summary

- The experiences of stress, worry and anxiety is normal for us all. We can develop ways of reducing these so we do not become overwhelmed.

- If a child is experiencing anxiety that is persistent and pervasive and which negatively impacts on their daily functioning, they may have a diagnosable anxiety disorder.

- Strategies for supporting children with anxiety can be embedded into a whole-school approach.

- Separation anxiety is distressing for all involved and can significantly impact learning. Strategies focus on creating safety within the school environment.

- A diagnosis of GAD may be given if symptoms are present on most days for a period of six months or more.

- Panic disorder involves recurrent attacks of severe anxiety, which often start without warning. The body responds to a known or unknown trigger by entering 'fight or flight' mode. Strategies used should try to prevent avoidance and encourage a child to recognise that nothing bad has happened as a result of the panic attack.

- OCD is a condition in which recurrent obsessional thoughts cause distress and subsequent compulsive acts attempt to prevent an unlikely harm from happening. Strategies should be developed in close partnership with the parents and child to ensure a consistent approach at home and school.

References

Butler G (1994) Treatment of worry in generalised anxiety disorder. In: GCL Davey & F Tallis (Eds) *Worrying: Perspectives in Theory, Assessment and Treatment* (pp35–59). New York: Wiley.

Butler G & Mathews A (1983) Cognitive processes in anxiety. *Advances in Behaviour Research and Therapy* **5** 51–62.

Ginsburg GS, Becker-Haimes EM, Keeton C *et al* (2018) Results from the Children/Adolescent Anxiety Multimodal Extended Long-Term Study (CAMELS): primary anxiety outcomes. *Journal of the American Academy of Child and Adolescent Psychiatry* **57** (7) 471–480.

Karmin A (2016) *Understanding Anger as a Secondary Emotion*. Psych Central [online]. Available from https://blogs.psychcentral.com/anger/2016/02/understanding-anger-as-a-secondary-emotion/

Mathews A & MacLeod C (1986) Discrimination of threat cues without awareness in anxiety states. *Journal of Abnormal Psychology* **95** 131–138.

Mendlowicz MV & Stein MB (2000) Quality of life in individuals with anxiety disorders. *American Journal of Psychiatry* **157** (5) 669–682.

Moran T (2016) Anxiety and working memory capacity: A meta-analysis and narrative review. *Psychological Bulletin* **142** (8) 831–864.

National Institute for Health and Care Excellence (2005) *NG31: Obsessive-Compulsive Disorder and Body Dysmorphic Disorder: Treatment*. Available from www.nice.org.uk/guidance/cg31

NHS Inform (2020) *Anxiety Disorders in Children*. Available from: https://www.nhsinform.scot/illnesses-and-conditions/mental-health/anxiety-disorders-in-children

Robinson OJ, Vyral K, Cornwell BR & Grilion C (2013) The impact of anxiety upon cognition: Perspectives from human threat of shock studies. *Frontiers of Human Neuroscience* **2** 2013.

Public Health England (2016) *The Mental Health of Children and Young People in England*. Available from: https://assets.publishing.service.gov.uk/government/uploads/system/uploads/attachment_data/file/575632/Mental_health_of_children_in_England.pdf

Yerkes RM & Dodson JD (1908) The relation of strength of stimulus to rapidity of habit-formation. *Journal of Comparative Neurology and Psychology* **18** (5) 459–482. doi:10.1002/cne.920180503.

Chapter 8: Low Mood

Low mood

> ### Case example: Low mood
>
> Mia is a Year 6 pupil who seems low in mood in the classroom. When I have observed her with her friends, she does not seem as engaged in the conversation as some of her peers and she does not readily smile. Her Year 5 teacher thinks this is a change from last year. Her parents have recently informed the school that she has been more withdrawn at home and spending a lot of time in her room. They have noticed some marks on her arms and are worried she may be harming herself but she has denied it. I wasn't aware of this ever happening in school, but now I don't know if I should allow her to go to the toilet on her own when she asks in class.

This chapter uses the term 'low mood' rather than depression because many children will experience episodes of low mood, but will never receive a diagnosis of depression. This may be because they do not access help or support; because they do access help but it is felt they do not meet the threshold for the diagnosis; or because the use of a diagnostic label is felt to be unhelpful and unnecessary for that child (see **Chapter 1** for a discussion regarding the pros and cons of diagnosis).

The term 'mood disorder' is often used to describe any significant and lasting change in mood, be that a lowering or an elevation. Many children can experience dysregulation of their mood, with rapid fluctuations and difficulty returning to baseline, but the term 'mood disorders' refers to longer-lasting, more pervasive changes in mood. As episodes of elevated mood (known as mania) are relatively rare in primary aged children, we are choosing to focus on low mood only here. There is a high rate of comorbidity (disorders which commonly occur together) between mood disorders and anxiety disorders, meaning that many of the strategies covered in **Chapter 7: Anxiety, Panic and OCD** are also applicable in this chapter.

The specific situations of self-harm and self-injury are considered at the end of the chapter in the 'Thinking about…' boxes.

Low mood or depression?

Changes in mood can be a common and normal part of life, but if these changes are lasting more than a couple of weeks and are interfering with functioning then additional support may be needed. There are many reasons why a child's mood may change, and you may notice this suddenly or over a period of time. Teaching staff may be aware of changes in a child's home situation, such as illness, bereavement or parental separation, which appear to coincide with the change. Low mood can affect concentration and interest in school work, and a child may refuse to attend school completely (see *Chapter 7*). Children who struggle to verbalise their emotions may instead describe various physical problems, such as aches and pains, as a way of letting people know that something doesn't feel right, much like with anxiety. A discussion with parents is an essential first step if there is concern about changes in a child's mood, especially if they have not raised their own concerns with school.

When the term 'depression' is used by health professionals to describe a period of low mood, it means that there has been a lowering of mood alongside other symptoms, such as changes in sleep and appetite, loss of enjoyment in usual fun activities and sometimes there may be thoughts around suicide and self-harming behaviours. Irritability can be a key feature of depression in young people and may be the thing that schools and parents notice, rather than low mood and sadness. The terms mild, moderate and severe depression relate to the number of symptoms a young person may be experiencing, along with the overall impact on their daily functioning.

How common are low mood and depression?

The prevalence of childhood depression has been estimated to be 1% in pre-pubertal children and around 3% in post-pubertal young people (NICE NG134).

Low mood in school: what does it look like and how can we help?

A child who is experiencing low mood may show some of the following changes in behaviour and emotions:

- 'Moody' and irritable behaviours – they may be increasingly sensitive to any perceived criticism.
- Negative thoughts about the world and the future – perhaps wondering 'what's the point?'
- Expressing thoughts about suicide or not wanting to be here.
- Low self-esteem or expressing critical feelings about themselves.

- Withdrawn behaviour and less interest in friendships.

- Change in appetite – this could be a loss of interest in food, or for some an increase in 'comfort eating'.

- Appearing tired and sleepy – the child may be sleeping more than usual or not sleeping enough.

- A loss of interest in or enjoyment of usual activities – the child may drop out of their usual clubs or hobbies.

- A reduction in usual level of functioning or sudden drop in academic achievement.

Strategies

It is important to consider how low mood presents with regard to various aspects of school life and how strategies can be used to help children manage their emotional responses and overcome the subsequent barriers to their engagement and learning. The sections below will explore low mood in relation to the learning environment, emotional, behavioural and social regulation and the actual process of learning.

Learning environment

A child with low mood may be struggling to concentrate for prolonged periods and may need a safe space to take some time away from the multiple sensory demands of the classroom. How and when this space is accessed will require some thought. Some children may struggle to voice their needs and feelings, and a card system or other non-verbal tool can be helpful (see template for 'I need you to know' card in **Chapter 19**). Equally, a child who is spending long periods of time out of the classroom may find that returning to their seat becomes increasingly difficult. A balance is needed between creating a safe space and always being complicit with a child's wish to opt out of class when things get tricky. Some theories around how low mood develop propose that avoidance of activities not only keeps the cycle of low mood going, but in fact may trigger low mood in the first place. This is the basis of 'behavioural activation', a type of therapy which seeks to gradually increase a person's activity levels and enable them to experience the feeling of accomplishing a goal, no matter how small (Cuijpers *et al*, 2007). It also aims to increase their exposure to activities that may help alleviate their low mood, such as hobbies and exercise.

Emotional, behavioural and social regulation

Low mood and depression in children can sometimes present as irritability rather than sadness. As described above, a child may benefit from having space to calm down and regulate. The 'Thinking about…' box below describes how to approach creating a calm, safe space within the classroom to support emotional and behavioural regulation. The lesson plan on sadness in **Chapter 19** can support a child to think about the things that can help them feel better when they are low in mood.

Thinking about ... creating a 'calm area'

A calm area is a place in every classroom or area of a school that a child can use when feeling anxious, dysregulated, low in mood or in need of rest. Use of this area is beneficial for all children at times, but especially for those experiencing low mood, anxiety or behavioural dysregulation, as well as those with attachment difficulties, ASC and ADHD. When thinking about how to use this strategy, consider the following:

■ Have a calm area set up and ready to go at the start of the school year. Explain its purpose to the class and explain that you will all play a part in looking after it.

■ Make the corner cosy – include rugs, blankets (some children will like to cover themselves completely in something soft), bean bags, cushions and fabrics with different texture. If you are tight on space, dividers can be used to section off small areas.

■ Include a small selection of carefully curated books, but remember this is not your book corner. Perhaps these could include special books from home, stories that are familiar and comforting or picture books without words.

■ Include some quiet sensory items, such as instruments or fiddle toys (for example: a rain stick, tiny bells, wooden frogs, a rubix cube, squishy balls and things that are nice to feel or mould). Avoid anything that can make loud or distracting noises.

■ Consider also more specific sensory resources (especially if a child has known sensory sensitivities) – perhaps a tent for a quiet and enclosed space, 'wobble seats' or textured cushions. Some schools may keep these in a central sensory room or area, but it is helpful for some to be available in every classroom as often they are required at short notice.

■ Consider the visual stimulation:

   ■ What will the children look at – calming or interesting photos and art work, perhaps?

   ■ Include visual reminders about what children can do in the calm area. Pictures and simple words that give clear instructions regarding breathing techniques, mindfulness or ways to tune into their senses can be helpful.

It is important to remember that for all conditions, the calm area should be offered as a choice and not a negative consequence. However, a child may choose to go there while they re-regulate after a difficult situation. The language used to support the use of the calm area can have different outcomes, e.g. try 'What do you think you need right now? Would you like to spend some time in the calm area?' rather than 'You need to visit the calm area now'. The idea will be less well received if a distressed child perceives that they are being forced to go there.

With regard to social regulation, children experiencing low mood may be actively avoiding social situations and withdrawing from friendships, which in turn may be a maintaining factor for their low mood. Active encouragement, providing support to nurture friendships and creating explicit social opportunities (such as the use of lunch time clubs), may increase the child's opportunities to access positive social feedback, enjoy themselves and have positive experiences.

Learning

Children with low mood may find it very hard to concentrate on their school work. It's possible the pace of work in class may need to be altered and that they will need a reduction in the amount of homework given. Breaking down tasks into chunks and encouraging small steps for increasing independence can foster feelings of achievement. A child with low mood may appear easily distracted, and may need extra support and encouragement with organisation and motivating themselves. Clear instructions and reminders are important. They may also have low self-esteem – therefore frequent praise and noticing what they do well is helpful. See *Chapter 5* for further discussion regarding building self-esteem.

When further help is needed for low mood

Many children referred for support with low mood to services such as CAMHS, will never receive a formal diagnosis of depression. Often, effective therapeutic support can be given without the need for this. Initially, the family and mental health professional may co-construct a formulation or joint understanding of why the low mood initially started, and how it is being maintained over time (see discussion of formulation in *Chapter 1*). However, if treatment options such as medications are being considered, it is likely that the child will be seen by a psychiatrist, who will use a diagnosis to enable evidence-based treatments to be used. Psychological therapies, namely CBT, should be the first-line treatment in all but severe cases. In addition, some children may be prescribed medication, although this is uncommon in pre-adolescents. The SSRI fluoxetine (also known as Prozac) is the only antidepressant licensed for use under the age of 18.

 Thinking about ... self-harm and self-injury

Although we acknowledge that self-harm is less common in primary than secondary school aged children, there are times that it may happen and this can be an understandable source of anxiety for both parents and teachers.

The terms 'self-harm' and 'self-injury' refer to behaviour which is an expression of distress. Although both terms are often used interchangeably, self-injury usually describes 'in the moment' actions which may cause harm to a person without ➔

clear intent to do so, such as head-banging and punching walls. The reasons for the self-harm or self-injury will vary from child to child, but may include anger and frustration and/or a desire to feel emotion when feeling numb, to let others know of their distress and unhappiness or to punish themselves if feeling worthless. In this regard, the behaviour is a form of communication, although in most cases it will occur in private. It is not necessarily linked to suicidal thoughts or a wish to die. It is important to be aware of any known triggers for a particular child, which can be modified to prevent behaviour escalating.

In addition to the above reasons, behaviours such as head-banging in children with a learning disability and/or neurodevelopmental disorders, such as ASC, may be linked to sensory overload or pain (though not exclusively). The child will not always wish to cause harm to themselves, as described above.

If a child has seriously injured themselves or reports feeling suicidal then an emergency response will be needed and there should be school procedures in place for this. On a practical level, first aid may be needed, and adults need to remain calm and non-judgemental. Ideally, every school will have their own local guidance for how to deal with self-harm, so that teaching staff feel empowered and confident in managing the situation with the appropriate support systems in place. This will usually be coordinated by the safeguarding lead. In most cases (unless there are safeguarding concerns related to the parents and their potential responses), parents should be informed immediately and a discussion had around the need for a referral for further support e.g. from CAMHS.

Other children may witness episodes of self-harm, which can be distressing. Detailed discussions about self-harm are not advised, but general discussion in PSHE about how people show distress and positive ways of coping with emotions can be helpful.

Summary

- Not all children who experience low mood will be given a formal diagnosis of depression, even if they are receiving support from CAMHS.

- Mood disorder describes a more lasting change in mood in all settings over a period of time, whereas dysregulation relates to frequent fluctuations in mood and difficulties returning to and maintaining a steady mood state.

- Depression can present as irritability in younger people. Young children without the skills to describe their emotions may also complain of physical symptoms.

- Evidence-based treatments for depression include CBT and SSRI medications.

- A child with low mood may be lacking in confidence and motivation, and as such may require additional support in voicing their needs. They will also need frequent praise and encouragement.

References

Cuijpers P, van Strate A & Warmerdam L (2007) Behavioural activation treatments of depression: A meta analysis. *Clinical Psychology Review* **27** 318–326.

NICE (2019) *NG134 Depression in Children and Young People: Identification and Management.*

Chapter 9: Behaviours That Challenge – Anger and Defiance

Behaviours that challenge

> ### Case example: Behaviours that challenge
> I have only taught Sara for a few weeks. I expect she is working below expected levels for her age, but her previous teacher was unable to get her to complete the end of year assessments. Sara has struggled with the change in teacher and new classroom and she finds unstructured break times hard. We have already had four incidences where she has been aggressive towards peers during playtime. It's difficult to know how these conflicts arise as I am not on the playground, but I expect that Sara gets angry with others if they are not following her agenda. She rarely initiates interaction with me and when I call on her to answer a question she can take a while to respond, as though she needs longer to process the question. She only gets the answer correct about half of the time. She gets angry and frustrated at times and has been banging her head on the desk.

What are behaviours that challenge?

'Behaviours that challenge' refers to a range of behaviours which are considered to be socially unacceptable and which are of sufficient frequency and/or intensity that they impact on a child's quality of life and often that of those around them. The most commonly encountered behaviours are anger and aggression projected towards others, self-injury and sexualised behaviours. These behaviours may prevent a child from being able to access the normal range of opportunities available to them, including mainstream education. It is therefore of vital importance that steps are taken to try to understand the function of the behaviour for a child, consider strategies which can reduce the frequency and intensity of such behaviour, and therefore help make sure they reach their full potential.

Traditionally, the term 'behaviours that challenge' has been used to refer to behaviours seen in the context of a learning disability and/or neurodevelopmental conditions such as ASC. It is estimated that the prevalence rate of challenging behaviour is around 5–15% in educational, health or social care services for people with a learning disability (NICE, 2015). For individuals with learning disabilities and ASC, difficulties with communication and/or social understanding are often thought to be the reason behind the increased levels of behaviours that challenge.

It is important to be aware that 'behaviours that challenge' is not in itself a diagnosis, and the emotional and/or cognitive reasons underlying the behaviour or the communicative element of the behaviour will be different for every child. Underlying triggers could include pain or an undiagnosed physical health problem, a change in routine or environment, boredom or a pre-existing mental health problem. All children use their behaviour as a form of communication, and this is even more evident when a child has not developed the skills to effectively communicate their needs effectively. Because the reasons for behaviours that challenge vary so much, it is important to consider why they may be happening for each child, what they may be trying to communicate and what may be keeping the behaviour going.

There will of course be children who display these behaviours and do not have a known learning disability or other diagnosed difficulty. Again, the reasons for this are varied and will depend on that child's particular circumstances.

Anger and defiance

Case example: Anger and defiance

Connor is an eight year old boy who moved to the school last year. He and his family have moved a few times and this is his third primary school. I understand that his biological father is currently in prison but I haven't been given any more details regarding this. Connor has struggled to make friends at school and has been in a few playground fights. In the classroom he refuses to follow the classroom rules and instructions and fails to complete tasks. He has thrown furniture and sworn at staff.

What do we mean by anger and defiance?

Anger refers to a completely normal emotion which is usually associated with a rise in adrenaline and other physical changes. External expressions of anger can include behaviours such as aggression, and it is these behaviours which tend to cause the most distress rather than the emotion itself.

Defiance is a refusal to follow rules or structures put in place by others. A child displaying defiant behaviour can present a real challenge in a busy classroom, especially if the behaviour is accompanied by anger. It may be that the behaviour is out of character for that child, and it needs to be seen in the context of other wider events such as a house move, family separation or a bereavement. These are events over which the child has little control. They may be displaying behaviour which enables them to feel more in control of what is happening to them. Some children will display more persistent patterns of defiant behaviour, and may be given a diagnosis of oppositional defiant disorder (ODD).

Oppositional defiant disorder

What is oppositional defiant disorder?

ODD is a condition occurring in younger children which is characterised by persistently defiant, disobedient and disruptive behaviour. As outlined in ICD-10, these behaviours include temper outbursts, arguing with adults, disobedience, deliberately annoying others, passing on blame and being easily annoyed, resentful, spiteful and vindictive. The behaviours are out of keeping with age appropriate expected social development, and go above and beyond mischievous or rebellious behaviours. The pattern of behaviour should be long-standing (at least six months) and not better explained by alternative difficulties or diagnoses. The behaviour is severe and frequent enough to have caused complaints from parents and teachers (ICD-10). A diagnosis of a behavioural disorder such as ODD ideally needs evidence of impairment in different settings – this is easier to achieve with accurate and detailed reports of incidents from parents and schools.

Where the behaviour is associated with persistent aggression or other antisocial acts such as vandalism, fire setting or harm to animals, then it is often termed conduct disorder. Conduct disorder (CD) is usually seen in the adolescent age group, whereas a diagnosis of ODD is generally reserved for younger children whose behaviour does not include violence or antisocial acts. CD and ODD in childhood have been found to predict the subsequent development of antisocial personality disorder, substance-related disorders, mood and anxiety disorders, and higher accident rates in adulthood (American Psychiatric Association, 2013; Theule *et al*, 2016).

How common are oppositional defiance disorder and conduct disorder?

Most data available refers to the prevalence of both disorders together, which is estimated to stand at around 6% of children aged 5-16 (Public Health England, 2016). It is important to remember that this is likely to be an underestimation as the conditions will often not be formally diagnosed.

Behaviours that challenge and oppositional defiant disorder in school: What do they look like and how can we help?

Children with ODD and those displaying other behaviours that challenge can find formal classroom teaching very difficult. The nature of ODD means that the child is often unwilling to cooperate and may seek to take control of a situation by pushing limits and testing boundaries. Children may often argue with authority figures, including teachers, and will not comply with school rules. Other behaviours for those with ODD may include:

■ running away from the classroom

■ persistently breaking school rules

■ telling lies or blaming others for their behaviour

■ difficulties in socialising and making friends.

More general difficulties that may occur in school for children displaying behaviours that challenge include:

■ patterns of particular activities, lessons or time of the day which appear to be more difficult for them

■ struggling to verbalise their emotions

■ struggling to regulate their emotions and return to baseline

■ showing behaviours which increase if physically unwell

■ showing behaviours which increase when tired or hungry

■ a low tolerance for frustration

■ reacting to perceived demands on them with an increase in anxiety, which may manifest as an increase in behaviours that challenge.

Functional analysis of behaviour

If a child is persistently presenting with distress and associated behaviour that challenges, it may not be immediately obvious as to what measures could be put in place to reduce their distress or indeed why they are struggling so much. An evidence-based approach to this would include a functional analysis of the behaviour. Functional analysis of behaviour refers to the examination of why a certain distress behaviour occurs. Aggressive or destructive behaviour can be thought of as the 'tip of the iceberg' and it is the unseen build-up of feelings underneath the surface that needs to be properly understood if we are going to be successful in supporting a child to regulate their emotions more successfully.

Many children are not able to tell us why they become so dysregulated. They may have limited insight into their own triggers. Triggers might be related to their attachment history or unseen challenges, such as sensory sensitivities. To analyse certain behaviours, it can help to take a scientific view and collect information over time. This involves examining the antecedents (what occurs just before an incident), the distress behaviours a child demonstrates (details of the incident itself) and what the consequences are (what occurs afterwards). A resource that can support this process is a STAR chart, which records details of the:

■ Situation – environmental factors, where the child is and where other people are

■ Trigger – what happened just before the incident

■ Action – what did the child do and say

■ Response – what did others do and say.

The more detailed the information recorded, the more useful this strategy will be. It is a good idea for this to be completed over a set period of time by different people. In this way the data is built up chronologically and patterns may emerge. This allows adults to understand when the child perceives a threat and what environmental or social factors can be modified to reduce the likelihood and frequency of the distress behaviours.

In theory, all human behaviour which repeats itself serves a function and is maintained over time due to the consequences of that behaviour. Understanding this can help us as we consider how to interrupt cycles of repeating behaviour. Examples include:

■ Sensory – A behaviour may give us positive sensory feedback.

■ Escape – A behaviour may enable escape or avoidance of undesired activities or people; this is especially relevant if anxiety is high and at the root of externalised anger.

- Attention – A behaviour may result in the attention we all need. A child's emotional needs for attention, connection and nurture may be higher than others, depending on their attachment history and life experiences.

- Tangible – A behaviour may lead to tangible gains or rewards.

Strategies

It is important to consider how behaviours that challenge and ODD present with regard to various aspects of school life and how strategies can be used to help children manage their emotional responses and overcome the subsequent barriers to their engagement and learning. The sections below will explore behaviours that challenge and ODD in relation to the learning environment, emotional, behavioural and social regulation and the actual process of learning.

Learning environment

If there are known risks associated with children using destructive behaviour, proactive risk assessments that reduce the likelihood of things getting broken can be helpful. Ensure the classroom environment is as safe as possible, with obvious breakable items, things that could be used as potential 'weapons' and other items associated with risk locked or hidden away.

Having consistent and easily accessible calm areas and appropriate resources in classrooms and around the school is essential. Further details about how to set these up are given in **Chapter 8**.

Emotional, behavioural and social regulation

Supporting an angry or defiant child with their emotional, behavioural and social regulation should be given high priority. Consistency from adults is crucial and all adults who come into contact with the child should be made aware of agreed strategies.

Emotional regulation

With regard to emotional regulation, use the ideas given in **Chapter 5: Building Emotional Intelligence** to gradually build a child's self-awareness and resilience.

When a child is experiencing anger, they may need to self-direct themselves to a calm area for a time (as described above). They can also be provided with appropriate safe avenues to allow them to release these feelings physically before they escalate. This could include:

- physical activity – running, jumping or kicking a ball
- squashing or pushing into cushions, bean bags or toys
- hammering activities with pegs or pins.

Once the intense feeling of anger begins to subside, the child will need space and quiet to fully re-regulate. Do not expect them to immediately reintegrate into class. It helps to have agreed spaces and processes for this. It is really important to ensure all staff and children are aware that any time out of class is not a reward. Explain that the child simply needs to get ready for their learning again. See the action guide below for a detailed discussion of de-escalation practices.

The ideas relating to anger and worry in *Chapter 19* will also support emotional and behavioural regulation. In particular, they encourage a child to think about the strategies they can self-select to help them with regulation. This information can be recorded on the 'I need you to know' frame, also in *Chapter 19*.

Behavioural regulation
With regard to behavioural regulation, there are many avenues to explore. Neurobiological studies indicate that for those children that reach the diagnostic threshold for ODD and CD, the ability to make associations between their behaviour and negative and positive consequences is compromised. Problem-solving is negatively affected due to differences in inhibition, attention, cognitive flexibility and decision making (Matthys *et al*, 2012). Reinforcing positive behaviour using a personalised reward system is often more helpful than punishment. By working towards small, realistic and achievable goals children with ODD can learn to succeed and experience the praise and pride that comes with this. Most children with ODD have very low self-esteem. Repeatedly getting into trouble and having negative, unwanted behaviours always highlighted can result in a negative internalised image of themselves and negative core beliefs that they are inherently 'bad'. See *Chapter 3* for a full discussion of how to avoid this occurring.

When difficult behaviours arise, it is important to always offer limited choices and ways out of every situation. Look for opportunities to make it easy for a child to walk away without 'losing face'. Ensure that recognition and praise is always given when a child is making progress with regulating their emotions and behaviour. Pass on positive messages to parents at the end of each day. This gives reassurance to the parent that things are going well and gives the child the message that they have key adults who are looking out for them consistently and want to celebrate with them when things go well. However if a child finds it difficult to hear positive messages, as many children with ODD do, share with parents in a low-key way. A simple smile and nod or thumbs up across the playground may be enough.

The following framework of redirecting, accepting, solution-focused and scaling strategies can help when we are striving to avoid confrontation with a child:

Redirecting: When a child refuses to follow an adult's request there is a clear danger that the interaction will escalate to a major confrontation. This in itself could result in the stimulation that the child is seeking. Redirecting is about trying to avoid being drawn into a power struggle. Instead, the adult has a number of activities that they can use to redirect the child towards some behaviours that are positive. For example, when a child refuses to go back to their seat, try saying 'Well, while you are out of your seat, could you go and collect something from the office for me?' or direct them to a prepared activity such as an interactive display or an area of the classroom that needs tidying.

Accepting: When a child expresses a negative viewpoint or gives a refusal, give immediate partial agreement to their comment. This sidesteps any confrontation and allows redirection of the behaviour, as described above.

Examples include:

Child: *I hate school.*
Adult: *Yes, there are times when you might hate school but I can help you with your learning so that you can enjoy it more. You can tell me about some things that you would like to do at school.*

Child: *'I don't like doing PE.'*
Adult: *'Yes, I can tell that you don't like PE. Is it getting changed that you don't like? Or is it the exercise that you find tricky?'*

Child: *'There is too much work to do.'*

Adult: *'Yes, it can seem like there is too much work to do, but let's get this part done and then we might be able to find time for some other things you enjoy – perhaps you could tell me what they are?'*

Solution-focused: This involves focusing on enabling desired behaviours. Offer solutions and support to enable them to become reality. Solution-focused approaches are positive and brief. For example:

'For this week I am going to be watching for all those times when you get it right, when your behaviour is helping you to learn. These will be times when you are listening to instructions. I am going to write those times down and if you want me to, I will give you a note to take home explaining how hard you've been trying. I want you to also notice those times when you are working well.'

Scaling: Support the child to rate their problem on a scale of 1–5, where number 1 is no problem and 5 reflects the problem at its worst. Consider this interaction:

Adult: *'On a scale of 1 to 5, how do you think you are doing with staying in your seat and not disturbing others in the class?'*

Child: *'About 2.'*

Adult: *'Okay, what do you think you are doing right to put your mark at 2?'*

Child: *'Well sometimes when we are drawing I don't leave my seat at all.'*

Adult: *'If you moved your score to 3 or 4, what do you think you would be doing more of?'*

Child: *'I would be putting my hand up when I got stuck and needed help.'*

Adult: *'Ok. Let's work together to see if we can do that.'*

Notice the problem is not analysed and the conversation between the adult and the child is positive. They focus on what the child needs to do more of rather than drawing attention to what they are not doing or their negative behaviour. If a child is able to understand this technique it can be helpful. Most of the time children do not know why they behave the way that they do. Teaching staff do not need to get drawn into analysing the issue at hand, but instead they can use their energy to discover and understand those times when the problem was less severe.

@ A guide: Supporting children in distress to de-escalate

In the moment

For children demonstrating distress behaviour or extreme 'meltdowns', which often include destructive behaviour and anger projected towards others, the following suggestions are designed to support the reduction of risk and de-escalation. The same principles can be adapted for use in situations of extreme anxiety and panic.

■ **Tune in to what is happening for the child**

  ■ Tuning in to the first signs of anxiety and stress becoming overwhelming is important. There may be sudden changes of body language or tone in conversation, or an increase in pacing or fidgeting. Once a child's autonomic arousal system is in a state of 'fight or flight', proactive preventative measures are always going to be more effective than reactive measures. It is important that the adults around the child focus on regulating the child and not on the content of what is being said (inappropriate laguage and verbally aggressive behaviour can be addressed at a later time). Knowing the specific child well is very helpful.

■ **Adapt your communication and avoid making demands**

  ■ Keep your voice at a lower pitch and volume. It is important that a child does not feel intimidated by an adult's presence when they are stressed. This may be more likely if a child has attachment difficulties or social and emotional difficulties. Some children may be able to calm more quickly if we avoid direct eye contact, use fewer words (especially if they have learning difficulties), simple gestures and a relaxed body posture. It is common for adults to expect a child to describe how they are feeling, but emotional literacy skills develop with age (and may be delayed if a child has ASC or learning difficulties). Naming emotions is often a high-demand task that children are unable to do in the moment.

■ **Show empathy for the emotions**

  ■ Remember all feelings should be allowed and accepted. Stay calm, show that you understand how a child is feeling and join up the child's emotion with their thoughts and behaviour – this will support a child's developing emotional intelligence. Don't tell a child who is distressed or angry to calm down as this can make a child escalate further in an attempt to feel heard and validated. Instead try 'You must be really angry to speak to me in that way. Tell me what's happened' or 'I can see you are really upset, that must feel really difficult. Is there anything you want to talk about?'

  ■ Allowing feelings does not mean an acceptance of aggressive and destructive actions. Hurting another person is always unacceptable. Remember however that giving consequences at a time of distress is counterproductive. The child will not be able to process and engage with them and it may escalate the situation further. ➔

■ **Keep yourself calm**

  ■ Some people find it helpful to repeat a self-soothing statement to themselves or remind themselves 'I can pretend to be calm' or 'I am able to regulate myself'. Continue to take deep breaths during the interaction with a distressed child. Noticing the contrast between the child's out of control manner and your own calm demeanour can support your confidence in your ability to manage a challenging situation. See ***Chapter 5*** for a more detailed discussion of adult emotional regulation.

What next?

■ **A calm body doesn't always mean a calm mind**

  ■ A child who has calmed their body down and who may seem calm may still be experiencing incredibly difficult emotions such as shame, embarrassment or remorse. Stress hormones such as adrenaline can stay in our systems for up to 90 minutes, meaning that children often need a significant length of (reflection) time to calm following an occurrence of the 'fight or flight' stress response. Try 'time in' with an adult after an episode of distress rather than time out, so that the adult can continue to support the child's emotional regulation.

■ **Positive feedback for calming down (reflection)**

  ■ As a child is calming down, it's helpful to narrate this and support their increasing awareness of what it feels like to be 'calming down'. It might feel counterintuitive after a 'meltdown', but reflecting back the emotions you observe and making best guesses again supports children's developing emotional intelligence.

■ **Making amends (restoration and reconciliation)**

  ■ Once an incident is over and sufficient time has passed, discuss with the child how to make amends. This can include ideas about how the child can make it right, cleaning up anything that was destroyed or damaged and apologising to anyone that was hurt or scared by their actions. When the child is ready, they can consider how they can express their stress more safely and appropriately next time. Ensure that any consequences put in place are in line with your school's behaviour policy.

Big picture

■ **De-briefing**

  ■ If other children have witnessed the incident or distress, it is necessary to spend some time de-briefing them and answering their questions. Children may have felt scared or distressed by the behaviour they saw. If possible, give an explanation as to what happened and why. It is also important to let them know a plan of action for any potential future incidents, once this has been agreed with the child. The class needs to know that the adults in school will keep them safe. Ensure that the child in question is not present for this conversation. None of this is easy, but it is absolutely vital.　　➔

■ **Recording**

- ■ Use your school's agreed recording system for incidents of difficult behaviours. Do this as soon as possible after the incident so that all relevant staff members are alerted and you do not forget any crucial information.

- ■ Incidents relating to anxiety and panic also need to be recorded carefully so that patterns can be identified.

■ **Communicating**

- ■ Parents should be contacted as soon as possible, ideally before the end of the day. Follow-up meetings may need to be arranged so a full discussion of triggers, the incident and the consequences can happen.

- ■ If another child has been hurt during the incident, contact their parents as an absolute priority. This should not be left until the end of the day.

- ■ In collaboration with the SENCO and parents, take time to look at the bigger picture surrounding incidents of distress behaviours. Consider whether external support needs to be sought going forward. See **Chapter 1** for a full discussion of this.

See also discussions about managing difficult behaviours in **Chapter 3**.

Social regulation

With regard to social regulation, children displaying behaviours that challenge and those with ODD can often struggle in social situations. Additionally, they may not be receptive to receiving help with this. The reduced sensitivity to reward and punishment discussed above affects the learning of socially appropriate behaviour and also the ability to refrain from inappropriate behaviour (Matthys *et al*, 2012). The 'Thinking about…' box below explores a specific way in which we can support social interactions for children with ODD, and also those with ASC and anxiety. We can also use formal social skills training to support children, which often incorporates explicit social instructions, modelling, role-play activities and behavioural rehearsal (Elliott & Gresham, 1993). Explicit teaching of emotional regulation skills will complement this work. All of this can take place within the safe setting of a Nurture group (discussed in **Chapter 5**).

❓ Thinking about ... supporting social interactions for children with mental health difficulties

When a child finds social interaction difficult, whether that be due to their own challenging behaviour or not understanding how to relate to others, they can become isolated from their peer group. At times it will be necessary to gently explain the effect of their behaviour on others, e.g. 'The other children are scared when you get angry' or 'They get fed up when you want to run all the games'.

One method of supporting a child to gain confidence in their social interactions and move away from using behaviours that challenge is to encourage them to work with peers from a younger year group. This gives them a sense of responsibility and a chance to model positive behaviours. Possibilities for this include:

■ reading to younger children

■ peer mentoring schemes for specific subjects

■ playground buddy systems

■ play leader opportunities

■ assembly monitors

■ prefects

■ wet play monitors.

Consider the following when implementing this strategy:

■ Think about the needs of the child and which activity and year group would work best. Avoid siblings working together if this is likely to cause friction.

■ Give responsibility, but not too much. Let them know that you and other adults will be there to help them.

■ If they struggle with challenging behaviours while with peers from their own age group, explain why it is important to be a role model for younger children. If they are keen to try, trust them but ensure adults are on hand in case support is needed. Only use this strategy if you are confident that the child can cope with the responsibility and that all children will be safe and fully supervised. It may take time to reach this point for some children.

■ Allow the child a chance to discuss how things went afterwards. What went well? Were there any challenges? What surprised them?

■ Seek out positive feedback for them on their behaviour from other adults and children. If they find it difficult to receive positive feedback, support them to gradually accept that they are making a positive difference to the school community.

Learning

Children with ODD can miss out on significant amounts of learning time. This may be because they refuse to take part, because they wish to do work of their own choice or because their behaviour leads to them having to spend time away from the classroom. The impact of this on their academic development and chances of achieving their potential are huge. Crucially though, a child who is angry and dysregulated cannot learn. Depending on how dysregulated they are, it may be possible to use diversion strategies to avoid potential conflict and escalation, as described above. Moving towards visual prompts can be useful when children are too distressed to listen and process verbal instructions. Even when learning interventions are put in place to support these children, some can be very reluctant to receive any individual help. There can be many reasons for this: it may be continued defiance and control-seeking behaviour as part of the ODD-profile, perhaps they do not wish to appear different from the rest of their class or perhaps they are worried about not being able to complete tasks. Diverting the focus away from them as an individual and working in a group situation can be beneficial. The adult can be seen to be helping all children on a table and the child in question may feel less singled out and more receptive to support.

We must also consider the impact on the learning of the other children in the class. Disruptive behaviour affects all who witness it (and hear it). Teaching staff must endeavour to reduce the impact on the class as much as possible, but it must be acknowledged that this is one of the most difficult aspects of teaching. If learning is being interrupted on a regular basis, ensure that you seek the support of your SENCO and senior leadership as soon as possible so that a plan that benefits all can be made.

When further help is needed for oppositional defiant disorder

The evidence base for supporting young people with ODD suggests that strategies to help develop positive parenting skills relating to setting boundaries and giving praise are of most benefit. There is little evidence to support any specific individual therapy, but support for developing social skills and building self-esteem is often helpful. There is no medication licensed to help specifically with the difficulties seen in ODD.

Children with ODD often have other, co-occurring conditions, such as ADHD or mood disorders (Loeber et al, 2000). In this case, they may receive support for the features of ODD alongside these other conditions through CAMHS. A young person with ODD alone may receive support from a number of agencies, for example children's social care often run evidence-based parenting courses, which can help parents to develop the skills they need.

It should be noted that many more children who would meet the criteria for ODD will never receive specialist assessment or get this diagnosis. Whether the presentation should come under the remit of CAMHS or not remains a controversial issue. The arguments against labelling a child with a diagnosis such as ODD include the idea that this places focus (or blame) for the difficulties solely on the child, whereas often they are a reflection of wider difficulties within a family and the system around the child. On the other hand, acknowledging that a child is experiencing difficulties around their behaviour can enable a plan of intervention to be put in place. The evidence base for managing children with oppositional behaviour who present clinically remains firmly in favour of parenting support for under twelves (NICE, 2013). This reflects our understanding of the necessity for consistent approaches at home in managing behavioural problems, and the need to work together closely with parents and families.

Summary

- Behaviour that challenges often has a function and has a communicative element.

- Functional analysis of behaviour enables exploration of the reasons of why a certain distress behaviour occurs.

- ODD is a condition occurring in younger children which is characterised by persistently defiant, and disruptive behaviour.

- Supporting an angry or defiant child with their emotional, behavioural and social regulation should be given high priority.

- Children that reach the clinical threshold for a diagnosis of ODD and CD have difficulties making associations between their behaviour and negative and positive consequences. Problem-solving is negatively affected due to differences in inhibition, attention, cognitive flexibility and decision making.

- Increased positive praise for prosocial behaviour, redirecting, accepting, solution-focused conversations and scaling can be beneficial proactive strategies.

- De-escalation techniques may be necessary strategies for teaching staff to be aware of.

References

Elliott SN & Gresham FM (1993) Social skills interventions in children. *Behaviour Modification* **17** (3) 287–313.

Loeber R, Burke JD, Lahey BB, Winters A & Zera M (2000) Oppositional defiant and conduct disorder: A review of the past 10 years, part I. *Journal of the American Academy of Child & Adolescent Psychiatry* **39** (12) 1468–1484.

Mattheys W, Vanderschuren LJ, Shutter DJ & Lochman JE (2012) Impaired neurocognitive functions affect social learning processes in oppositional defiant disorder and conduct disorder: implications for interventions. *Clinical Child and Family Psychological Review* **15** (3) 234–246.

NICE (2013) CG158 *Antisocial Behaviour and Conduct Disorders in Children and Young People: Recognition and Management. London: NICE.*

NICE (2015) NG11 *Challenging Behaviour and Learning Disabilities: Prevention and Interventions for People with Learning Disabilities Whose Behaviour Challenges. London: NICE.*

Public Health England (2016) *The Mental Health of Children and Young People in England.* Available from: https://assets.publishing.service.gov.uk/government/uploads/system/uploads/attachment_data/file/575632/Mental_health_of_children_in_England.pdf

Stratton CW, Reid J & Hammond M (2001) Social skills and problem solving training for children with early-onset conduct problems: Who benefits? *Journal of Child Psychology and Psychiatry* **42** 943–952.

Theule J, Germain SM, Cheung K, Hurl KE & Markel C (2016) Conduct disorder/oppositional defiant disorder and attachment: A meta-analysis. *Journal of Developmental and Life-Course Criminology* **2** (2) 232–255.

World Health Organisation (2016) *International Classification of Diseases for Mortality and Morbidity Statistics* (10th Revision). Available from www.who.int/classifications/icd/icdonlineversions/en/

Chapter 10: Attachment Difficulties and Trauma

Attachment difficulties and disorders

> ### Case example: Attachment difficulties
>
> Laura came to us from a different school and is struggling to make friendships. She can be overfamiliar, disregard other people's needs for personal space and actively seek out others. At other times she lashes out and rejects others that are trying to be her friend. Her behaviour seems quite chaotic and she gets upset very easily. Sometimes I have no idea why she is upset, and she does not seem able to explain either, which is very frustrating for both of us. She struggles to remain concentrated on her work, but so wants to please me and she comes to show me her work constantly.

What are attachment difficulties and disorders?

It has long been accepted that the attachment relationships we have with our primary caregivers influence our brain development. Children develop internal working models of themselves, others and the world based on their early attachment experiences and their environment (Bowlby, 1990). Research and observations clearly indicate that secure attachment between a child and their parent is linked with more successful engagement in school (Golding *et al*, 2013). Children who experience insecurity within their early attachment relationships are more likely to experience continued difficulties within their developing relationships with themselves, others and the world around them. Children with significant attachment difficulties struggle to interact with others, displaying a range of atypical social behaviours, from inappropriate friendliness and lack of inhibition towards everyone they meet, to highly withdrawn behaviour and hypervigilance. These behaviours occur across situations and with many people. Although particular types of attachment classification (especially disorganised attachment) may indicate a risk of later problems, these classifications do not represent a disorder. In extreme cases, as a result of early trauma and/or neglect in the early years of crucial brain development a child may meet the criteria for a diagnosis of an attachment disorder (such as reactive attachment disorder or disinhibited social engagement disorder).

How common are attachment difficulties?

It is estimated that approximately 35% of infant-parent attachment relationships in the general population are insecure (Lewis-Morrarty *et al*, 2015).

There is limited evidence available about the prevalence of attachment difficulties within the general population. It is estimated that approximately 35% of infant-parent attachment relationships in the general population are insecure (Lewis-Morrarty *et al*, 2015). The limited evidence available about the attachment classification and/or prevalence of attachment disorders in looked-after children and young people and those adopted from care suggests that only 10% are securely attached to their biological parents. Around 80% of children who suffer maltreatment can be classified as having a disorganised attachment style (NICE 2015). A disorganised classification is strongly predictive of later social and cognitive problems and mental health difficulties. Some children who have a disorganised attachment style might also meet the criteria for a diagnosis of reactive attachment disorder but these categories are not the same.

How are attachment disorders diagnosed?

Psychiatrists might diagnose reactive attachment disorder which can only be caused by inadequate caregiving (neglect) during childhood. The DSM-5 details the following diagnostic criteria:

- A consistent pattern of inhibited, emotionally withdrawn behavior toward adult caregivers, manifested by both of the following:
  - The child rarely or minimally seeks comfort when distressed.
  - The child rarely or minimally responds to comfort when distressed.
- A persistent social and emotional disturbance characterised by at least two of the following:
  - Minimal social and emotional responsiveness to others.
  - Limited positive affect.
  - Episodes of unexplained irritability, sadness, or fearfulness that are evident even during non-threatening interaction with adult caregivers.
- The child has experienced a pattern of extremes of insufficient care as evidenced by at least one of the following:
  - Social neglect or deprivation in the form of persistent lack of having basic emotional needs for comfort, stimulation and affection met by caregiving adults.
  - Repeated changes of primary caregivers that limit opportunities to form stable attachments (e.g. frequent changes in foster care arrangements).

■ Rearing in unusual settings that severely limit opportunities to form
  selective attachments (e.g. institutions with low child-to-caregiver ratios).

■ The inadequate care is presumed to be responsible for the disturbed behavior
  detailed above.

■ The criteria are not met for ASC.

■ The disturbance is evident before age 5 years.

■ The child has a developmental age of at least 9 months.

In clinical practice, this does not appear to be a frequently used diagnosis,
although there are likely to be differences across services (and depending on
commissioning arrangements). Psychologists however, frequently take into account
a child's likely attachment style and the relationships that they have within their
families. A child's attachment style is likely to have an influence on their mental
health, their relationship with themselves, with the therapist and the therapeutic
process.

Co-occurring disorders

The impact that a child's attachment style has on their ability to make
relationships and their mental health is important. Children with disordered
attachment styles are likely to experience emotion regulation difficulties and
the way they interact with others and their world could contribute to elevated
symptoms of anxiety and/or low mood. If a child is struggling with school
attendance, sleeping well and eating adequately, it is likely that a referral for
mental health support is warranted.

Attachment difficulties in school: What do they look like and how we can help?

All humans are designed to start making relationships with their caregivers from
the moment they are born. Through the 'dance' of interaction between the baby's
attachment cues and the primary caregiver's attunement and responsiveness
to these cues, psychological security, trust and attachment style will develop.
Through the extensive early work of John Bowlby and Mary Ainsworth, four
distinct styles of attachment have been conceptualised and researched: secure
attachment, insecure-avoidant attachment, ambivalent attachment and
disorganised attachment. Kim Golding and colleagues have carried out detailed
research regarding different attachment styles and how these play out within
the classroom setting (Golding *et al*, 2013). All types of insecure attachment are
associated with increased anxiety and under-achievement in the classroom. It is

important to consider how attachment styles present with regard to various aspects of school life and how strategies can be used to help children manage their emotional responses and overcome the subsequent barriers to their engagement and learning. The sections below will explore the different types of attachment styles in relation to the learning environment, emotional, behavioural and social regulation and the actual process of learning.

Secure attachment

A child develops a secure attachment with their caregivers if the parent's responsiveness to the child's signals and needs are relatively quick, sensitive and consistent. Children with a secure attachment style are those children more able to demonstrate resilience and confidence. They have a positive internal working model of themselves and therefore present as more confident and with positive self-esteem. As they have experienced a consistent safe base they have developed curiosity and independent exploration. Secure attachment is associated with greater emotional regulation, social competence and willingness to take on challenges (Bergin & Bergin, 2009).

Insecure-avoidant attachment style ('I will do it myself. I fear closeness')

Children who have experienced emotionally unresponsive caregiving or caregiving that is emotionally distant and disengaged are likely to develop an avoidant attachment style. A child with an avoidant style of attachment is more likely to present as indifferent towards others and may be withdrawn and quiet. They can appear more isolated or their friendships may lack depth, as they avoid close connection with others. They may have a strong desire to be autonomous and deny that they need the support of their teacher, which can contribute to under-achievement. They may have developed defence strategies to keep others at a psychological and physical distance from them, such as hostility. Golding and colleagues (2013) have also discussed the three-way relationship between the student, the teacher and the academic task or activity. The child with an avoidant attachment style may overly rely on the task as it is perceived to be a safer area of engagement than the relationship with the teacher.

Strategies

The following strategies may support or increase engagement in the classroom for children with insecure-avoidant attachment.

Learning environment

■ Have the child work in pairs or small groups with an adult.

■ Use visuals in their environment that might promote a sense of security and safety are those that increase predictability e.g. visual timetables.

Emotional, behavioural and social regulation

■ Ask the child to help you with specific tasks.

■ Gently, but overtly, encourage the child to seek help from the adults in the room.

■ Demonstrate to the child that they are held in mind (for example: 'I was thinking about you when…').

■ Gradually develop their ability to trust adults and express themselves.

Learning

■ Get the child to participate in highly structured games but avoid those that are very competitive, such as team games.

■ Use structured writing tasks, mind-mapping and enable fast access to resources.

■ Use concrete structured activities.

■ Use metaphors to describe emotions.

Ambivalent attachment style ('You will attend to me. I fear abandonment')

Children who have experienced a significantly inconsistent level of caregiving (for instance, when the caregiver has been at times sensitive and at other times neglectful) have learnt that they cannot rely on their needs being met. They therefore experience insecurity, anxiety, frustration and anger. Children with an ambivalent attachment style are more likely to present with high attention-needing behaviour and be over-dependent on the support of teaching staff. They could be unable to focus on the task for fear of losing your attention and engagement. They may have developed hypervigilance to actions and behaviours of adults and also a fear of separation from trusted adults. They may talk excessively, or act as a 'clown' in order to keep your attention.

A child with an ambivalent attachment style may lack confidence and self-esteem and struggle more in relatively unsupervised settings, such as the playground or transitions between the events of the day. They are more likely to reject tasks or any educational challenge for fear of failing or not knowing.

Strategies
The following strategies may increase attention and concentration and reduce anxiety in the classroom for children with ambivalent attachment.

Learning environment

■ Allow access to special objects to support transitions and to provide reassurance.

■ As above, visuals in their environment that might promote a sense of security and safety are those that increase predictability e.g. visual timetables.

Emotional, behavioural and social regulation

- Plan for and prepare the child for beginnings, separations and endings, especially involving adults they have managed to develop a relationship with.

- Identify a consistent (trusted) adult to support them with any worries and anxieties.

- Involve the parent in the child's learning as much as possible.

- Gently teach the child explicit emotional literacy skills (see *Chapter 5: Building Emotional Intelligence* for further details).

- Increase responsibilities and opportunities for self-esteem building jobs.

- Use supported small group work to improve social awareness and provide opportunities to develop social skills.

Learning

- Break tasks into smaller, more manageable steps.

- Use visual sand timers to delineate tasks, increase motivation and aid concentration.

- Use board games to help develop shared control and enjoyment.

Disorganised attachment style ('I am powerful. I am scared. I fear')

If a child's primary attachment figure has been abusive, the child has learnt through maltreatment that the world is unsafe and unpredictable. Disorganised attachment is associated with a cluster of parenting behaviours referred to as 'frightening/frightened' (Cyr *et al*, 2010; van Ijzendoorn *et al,* 1999). This style of parenting often co-occurs with other known risk factors, including paternal mental health difficulties, parental alcohol and drug use and domestic violence (commonly known as the 'toxic triad'), socioeconomic deprivation and poverty, and single parenthood. Strategies that the child has employed to either approach or withdraw from their parent/s may have involved risk for the child. Therefore, they have been unable to organise their attachment style in a way that consistently reduces risk to self.

Reviews of research have found no increase, or a modest increase, in prevalence of all kinds of mental health difficulties associated with avoidant and ambivalent attachment patterns. In contrast, significant and greater increases in mental health difficulties (particularly externalising difficulties, such as problems with aggression) have been found among children displaying disorganised attachment patterns (Solomon & George, 2011). Sadly, at one year of age, disorganised attachment is a good predictor of psychopathology at seventeen years of age (Stroufe, 2005).

Maltreated children tend to be more aggressive than other children, show less empathy with other children's distress and struggle significantly more within peer relationships. Teaching staff are more likely to feel frightened in response to their behaviour. They may have developed a powerful way of being with others, characterised by control, distrust and rejection of authority and noncompliance. Meta-analysis suggests that children who meet the clinical criteria for ODD or conduct disorder (see *Chapter 9*) are four times more likely to have a disorganised attachment style (Solomon & George, 2011). Children who have been psychologically deprived are more likely to reject the help they badly need. They may be unable to accept being taught, and/or unable to 'permit' others to know more than they do as this triggers overwhelming feelings of humiliation.

Strategies

The following strategies can support children with disorganised attachment to manage the above difficulties:

Learning environment

■ Use explicit classroom contracts explaining how to maintain safe classrooms.

■ Maintain a high level of predictability and consistency within the classroom. Clear and visual timetables, written rules and routines and consistent boundaries can help with this.

■ Ensure all adults in school (and supply staff) are aware of the child's individual needs, triggers and agreed procedures as much as possible by having these recorded visually.

■ The 'I need you to know' frame in *Resources and Lesson Plans* can support this process.

■ Reduce physical proximity of other people in crisis situations.

Emotional, behavioural and social regulation

■ Tune in to the emotional development of the child (potentially younger than their chronological age), as this will help you design the most effective individualised strategies for support.

■ Building trust is paramount. These children need to know that an adult will do what they say they are going to do. They might really struggle with plans changing, things that are spontaneous or surprises.

■ There is a high need for an assigned adult to check in with the child at regular predictable intervals within the day. Despite this being a hard strategy to put in place within a busy working day, it could have a very significant grounding effect, increase the predictability and enable opportunities for emotional regulation. In this way, the child is given the opportunity to develop a trusting relationship with an adult.

- Provide time and space for regular emotional regulation activities (for example, music, gross motor exercise, relaxation techniques and meditation).

- Develop emotional literacy skills by teaching emotions in more concrete terms. Scale emotions using colours and numbers (typically 1–5, with 5 being high stress or 'meltdown'). See *Chapter 9* for more details.

- Through interactions, create opportunities for modelling of the conscious ability to change our emotional state from one to another.

- Provide frequent positive feedback in class and around the school (assuming that the child is able to accept and process praise).

- Contain the child's emotions calmly and predictably as they may be triggered or exacerbated by adults' stress levels.

- Make sure all staff are aware of how to effectively manage the individual child's distress behaviour through developed de-escalation techniques (see *Chapter 9*).

- Reframing 'attention-seeking' as 'attachment-seeking' can help in understanding the function of some difficult behaviours and help staff remain calm and empathic.

- Try to avoid anything that the child may perceive as a threat to their safety, self-image or kudos with peers.

- Manage endings sensitively, especially when staff are absent or leave their role. Children with attachment difficulties (and/or ASC) might significantly struggle with teachers leaving the school. How the ending of relationships is addressed is likely to have a powerful impact on how well they cope with this experience.

- Facilitate extra provision, such as nurture groups and other interventions that focus on developing knowledge and skills regarding relationships. This can include exploring the concept of friendship, developing specific special skills and self-esteem building exercises.

Learning
- Give closed choices regarding learning activities to allow for the perception of control, within clear boundaries.

- Use concrete and mechanical activities in between learning tasks if the child struggles with unstructured time.

- Avoid power struggles, in relation to learning and in all regards (see *Chapter 9* for more details). Power struggles evolve when a child is asked to do something, they refuse or are openly defiant, and the adult then engages in a back-and-forth struggle to get them to comply with the request. Avoid this by making their specific choices very clear. Don't leave it open-ended or give them the option to not do what you want them to.

■ When giving the perception of control through choice, ensure that all of the responses are acceptable choices to you, e.g. 'You need to start on this task. You can either do it now, or you can wait a little bit, but you have to have made a start before break time'. Crucially, the option of not doing it is not given – only the option of when to start. These choices can be given in positive ways, being mindful of tone of voice and non-verbal communication. Always use a playful emotional tone for the interaction. In this way, you are promoting the child's ability to be successful and not leading them to feel overly controlled or dominated by adults (which they may have previously experienced). See **Chapter 3** for a detailed discussion of approaches to language and communication.

When further help is needed for attachment difficulties

If a child's style of interacting with others, their world and their sense of self is characterised by significant difficulties, extreme insecurities and feelings of being unsafe, it is likely to have a significant impact on their mental health and a referral to CAMHS may be warranted. Commonly, the CAMHS approach would involve managing the impact of the attachment difficulties, for instance, on their emotional regulation. Therapeutic approaches may include Theraplay® or dyadic developmental psychotherapy (DDP) which both involve the child and their primary caregiver and aim to increase parental/caregiver responsiveness, sensitivity and attunement.

❓ Thinking about ... when the adults change

Children with significant attachment difficulties (and also children with ASC) are much more likely to struggle with unplanned changes. If a new adult is going to be present in class, e.g. a supply teacher, a quick email or phone call home is warranted as soon as possible (definitely before the adult enters the classroom). This can be effective in reducing the impact of this known trigger. The change may be perceived completely differently if the child hears through one-to-one interaction or from parents when compared with finding this out in a group setting. If you are personally sharing this news, give the child the message that it is known and understood that this change is a challenge for them to cope with. Allow time for them to process this information and perhaps access a time-limited calming activity. This can be beneficial in reducing the likelihood of a child perceiving abandonment, rejection and loss, and in reducing subsequent distress behaviours. In general, the more planned an ending can be (for example, when a staff member goes on maternity leave), the more able a child with attachment difficulties may be able to cope with this ending.

Trauma

Case example: Trauma

Jake is a looked after child who lives with foster carers. I am aware that he has had two previous foster care placements that have broken down due to his behaviour, which people find extremely challenging and stressful. Jake appears stressed every day and this is usually projected towards his peers at playtime. He can be very controlling and will not always comply with what the rest of the class are doing. He is working below the expected level for his age, but it is incredibly difficult to get him to remain seated for the whole lesson. I have noticed that he is hypervigilant about what is going on around him and a couple of times I have seen him have a startle response when the school bell goes.

What is trauma?

If a child has experienced a 'trauma', this refers to an experience that our typical psychological defences cannot protect us against. It is emotionally overwhelming. Both abuse and neglect can have a traumatic effect. Importantly, though, an event could be traumatic for one child but not for another. Teaching staff may have limited information regarding whether a child has had traumatic experiences in the past.

Early stress and trauma cause changes in brain circuitry and hormonal systems – 'states become traits' (Perry *et al*, 1995), meaning that repeated emotional states affect the development of who we are and become expressed within our personalities. However, even if trauma affects the very structure of our brains, these same brains can later be influenced by positive experiences and interactions.

Children can experience a wide range of traumatic events that can impact their functioning in school, such as assaults, serious accidents, or community or domestic violence. Brief distress following a trauma without significant impairment in functioning may be characterised as a normal reaction to the event. In some cases, a child might develop some signs and symptoms of post-traumatic stress disorder (PTSD). Within the first month after a traumatic event, a child might start re-experiencing the event or showing signs of hyperarousal. However, in a minority of cases there might be a delay of months or even years before symptoms might appear.

Following a traumatic event, some children may be more likely to develop PTSD than others. Risk factors for PTSD include characteristics of the trauma exposure (greater trauma severity, proximity to the event), individual factors (female gender, history of psychopathology), and parent characteristics (parental psychopathology including PTSD and other trauma-related symptoms and lack of parental support following the trauma). Those children who have had multiple traumatic events and those who have experienced interpersonal trauma such as an assault can also be at an increased risk of developing PTSD (Kataoka *et al*, 2012).

How common are trauma and PTSD?

Not every child who goes through a trauma will develop symptoms of PTSD. For those that develop symptoms of PTSD, these usually start within 3 months of the traumatic event. The British National Survey of Mental Health, surveyed over 10,000 children and young people and reported that at the time of the survey 0.4% of children aged 11-15 yrs had a diagnosis of PTSD (Meltzer *et al*, 2000). Below the age of ten PTSD was scarcely registered, but the survey was not a PTSD specific screening measure. Estimates of the incidences of PTSD vary significantly following natural disasters and acts of terrorism. It has been reported that refugees are approximately ten times more likely to have PTSD than the general population in the countries of resettlement (Fazel *et al*, 2019). Children of refugees exposed to parental PTSD are at increased risk of developing mental health difficulties (Neilson *et al*, 2019).

How are trauma and PTSD diagnosed?

PTSD may be diagnosed if symptoms reoccur for more than a month and there is evidence that the symptoms are negatively affecting a child's functioning. The main signs and symptoms are:

■ Exposure to a traumatic or stressful event (this can be either direct or indirect e.g. witnessing domestic violence, but not being directly physically hurt). It does not include events witnessed only in electronic media, television or films. It can include learning that a traumatic event occurred to a parent or primary caregiver.

■ Intrusion symptoms, such as re-experiencing, flashbacks or nightmares. Re-experiencing refers to when a person involuntarily and vividly re-lives a traumatic event. The most extreme re-experiencing involves a complete loss of awareness of present surroundings. Trauma specific re-enactments may occur in play. Flashbacks can include being troubled by repetitive and distressing images or sensations. They could also be accompanied by physical sensations associated with high anxiety and panic (sweating, feeling sick, trembling and pain). Children may also start experiencing nightmares and sleep difficulties following a traumatic event.

- Avoidance of trauma-related stimuli, such as avoidance of certain places or activities, or even avoidance of thoughts or feelings that are related to the trauma.

- Negative thoughts or feelings that began or worsened as a result of the traumatic experience. These can include an inability to recall key features of the trauma, overly negative thoughts or assumptions about oneself or the world, exaggerated blame of self or others for causing the trauma, negative emotions, decreased interest in activities, feeling isolated or a difficulty experiencing positive affect.

- Trauma related arousal and reactivity that began or worsened after the trauma. This may include irritability or aggression, risky or destructive behaviour, hypervigilance, heightened startle reaction, difficulty concentrating and difficulty sleeping.

Trauma in school: what does it look like and how can we help?

Children who have experienced trauma may appear constantly on high alert, a state known as hyperarousal. Hyperarousal refers to difficulties with relaxing which can lead to irritability, anger outbursts and difficulty concentrating. Survival mechanisms of fight, flight and freeze tend to be more easily triggered. Related to hyperarousal, children may become hypervigilant and appear in a state of increased alertness, demonstrating a high level of sensitivity to the environment. In addition, the following features may be noticed by teaching staff:

- High stress levels.

- Higher levels of aggression than peers.

- Reduced empathy to other children when they are upset.

- Significant problems with emotional regulation – children may struggle to manage strong emotions and take a while to calm down once distressed.

- Multiple interpersonal difficulties.

- Dissociation – an extreme form of psychic numbing or detaching from reality in which a child appears cut off.

- Rejection of help.

- Difficulty focusing and concentrating (related to hyperarousal).

- Difficulties in executive functioning.

- Increased avoidance of places, people and activities.

- Re-enacting traumatic events through their play.

Strategies

It is important to consider how the effects of trauma can present with regard to various aspects of school life and how strategies can be used to help children manage their emotional responses and overcome the subsequent barriers to their engagement and learning. The sections below will explore the impacts of trauma in relation to the learning environment, emotional and behavioural regulation and the actual process of learning. Additionally, all of the strategies suggested for children with a disorganised style of attachment are likely to be of use with children that have experienced trauma or abuse.

Learning environment

- If a child presents with hypervigilance, ask them about their position in the classroom. Some children may feel safer positioned near the door; others may feel better with a wall behind them and/or closer to the teacher.

- If a child is experiencing flashbacks (and associated physical symptoms), it is understandable (and should be permitted) that they may need to leave the classroom. 'Exit passes' that enable them to leave without the need for verbal communication are helpful. Ideally an assigned adult should be able to go with them. The 'I need you to know' card frame in *Chapter 19* can support this.

- There might be certain things within a child's environment that may trigger flashbacks. If these are known by the child or parents it is important that they are shared with teaching staff so that the risk of encounters with triggers can be minimised. Re-experiencing is incredibly distressing and can lead to other difficult emotions such as embarrassment, shame and more fear.

Emotional and behavioural regulation

- Children who have experienced significant trauma (and who struggle with significant anxiety) are likely to benefit from being taught explicit relaxation techniques such as deep breathing, progressive muscle relaxation, positive visual imagery and mindfulness. Such techniques can benefit all children – it can be helpful to the child concerned if they are taught and practised in groups. Relaxation techniques can be transferred to different settings. They can be taught at home and at school. It is helpful to allow children to practise them regularly when they are calm, before they are expected to begin to try and use them at times when they feel anxious, frustrated, irritable or angry. See *Chapter 5* for a full discussion of mindfulness and meditation.

- Use of a feelings thermometer (a scale of 0–10, where 0 is feeling OK and content and 10 is feeling very upset, anxious or scared) can help children rate how they feel before and after using a specific relaxation technique.

Learning

- Following a specific traumatic experience, a child's learning is likely to be affected significantly.

- They may need to have time off school to recover or to attend appointments.

- Their capacity for attention and concentration may also be affected. Hypervigilance will often impact on a child's ability to focus and complete work in class and at home.

When further help is needed for trauma

If a school or parents think that a child is struggling with symptoms of PTSD or mental health difficulties associated with trauma, a CAMHS referral is certainly warranted. NICE guidelines suggest CBT as the most appropriate evidence-based intervention, which should include direct exploration of the trauma, stress management techniques and correction of any cognitive distortions (NICE, 2018). It is important to note that pharmacological agents should not be used as a first line treatment for PTSD in young people (Strawn *et al*, 2010).

Summary

- Children develop internal working models of themselves, others and the world based on their early attachment experiences and their environment.

- Four distinct styles of attachment have been conceptualised and researched: secure attachment, avoidant attachment, ambivalent attachment and disorganised attachment.

- Children with attachment difficulties experience difficulties within their relationships with themselves, others and the world around them.

- Children can experience a wide range of traumatic events that can impact their functioning in school, such as assaults, serious accidents, or community or domestic violence.

- Children might be developing signs and symptoms of PTSD if they are re-experiencing the event (through flashbacks and/or nightmares) and/or showing hypervigilance or hyperarousal and/or numbing or avoidance.

- The strategies suggested in this chapter are intended to help increase a child's sense of feeling safe and secure, and to reduce their levels of anxiety and arousal.

References

American Psychiatric Association (2000) DSM-IV-TR. Diagnostic and Statistical Manual of Mental Disorders, Text Revision.

Bergin C & Bergin D (2009) Attachment in the classroom. *Educational Psychology Review* **21** 141–170.

Bowlby J (1990) *Attachment: Attachment and Loss. Trilogy: Attachment and Loss.* (Vol 1, 2nd ed.) Bookstore Martins Fontes.

Center for Family Development (2007) *An Overview of Reactive Attachment Disorder for Teachers* [online]. Available from www.center4familydevelop.com/helpteachrad.htm

Cozolino L (2013) *The Social Neuroscience of Education.* New York: Norton.

Cyr C, Euser E, Bakermans-Kranenburg M & van IJzendoorn M (2010) Attachment security and disorganization in maltreating and high-risk families: a series of meta-analyses. *Development and Psychopathology* **22** (1) 87–108. doi: 10.1017/S0954579409990289

Department of Health (2015) *Statutory Guidance on Promoting Health and Wellbeing of Looked after Children.* London: DoH.

Golding K, Fain J, Frost A *et al* (2013) *Observing Children with Attachment Difficulties in School: A Tool for Identifying and supporting Emotional and Social Difficulties in Children ages 5–11.* London: Jessica Kingsley.

Lewis-Morrarty E, Degnan K & Chronis-Tuscano A (2015) Infant attachment security and early childhood behavioral inhibition interact to predict adolescent social anxiety symptoms. *Child Development* **86** (2) 598-613.

Kataoka S, Langley A, Wong M *et al* (2012) Responding to students with PTSD in schools. *Child and Adolescent Psychiatric Clinics of North America* **21** (1) 119–133.

Meltzer H, Gatward, R & Goodman R (2003) Mental Health of children and adolescents in Great Britain. *International Review of Psychiatry* **15** (1-2); 185-187.

National Institute for Health and Care Excellence (2015) *Children's Attachment: Attachment in Children and Young People Who Are Adopted from Care, in Care or at High Risk of Going into Care.* NICE guideline. www.nice.org.uk/guidance/ng26.

National Institute for Health and Care Excellence (2018) *Post Traumatic Stress Disorder.* NICE guideline. https://www.nice.org.uk/guidance/ng116.

Neilsen MB, Carlsson J, Rimvall MK, Peterson JH & Norredam M (2019) Risk of childhood psychiatric disorders in children of refugee parents with post-traumatic stress disorder: a nationwide register-based cohort study. *The Lancet* **4** (7) 353-359.

Perry BD (2001) The neurodevelopmental impact of violence in childhood. In: D Schetky & EP Benedek (Eds) *Textbook of Child and Adolescent Forensic Psychiatry* (pp221–238). Washington, DC: American Psychiatric Press.

Solomon J & George C (2011) Disorganization of maternal caregiving across two generations: The origins of caregiving helplessness. In: J Solomon & C George (Eds) *Disorganization of Attachment and Caregiving: Research and Clinical Advances.* New York: Guilford Press.

Stroufe LA (2005) Attachment and development: A prospective, longitudinal study from birth to adulthood. *Attachment & Human Development* **7** 349–367.

Strawn JR, Keeshin BR, DelBello MP *et al* (2010) Psychopharmacologic treatment of posttraumatic stress disorder in children and adolescents: A review. *Journal of Clinical Psychiatry* **71** 932.

van IJzendoorn MH, Schuengel C & Bakermans-Kranenburg MJ (1999) Disorganized attachment in early childhood: Meta-analysis of precursors, concomitants, and sequelae. *Development and Psychopathology* **11** (2) 225–249.

Chapter 11: Autism Spectrum Condition

Children may present with a range of social, emotional and communication differences for a wide variety of reasons. However, parents and teaching staff might become concerned that a child is developing differently and may actually be 'hard wired' differently, rather than these differences being the result of their experiences. When parents' concerns are discussed, it might be found that they have had worries since the child was very young, there may be evidence of differences in the child's play, language development and social interaction style since before they started school. In these situations, a diagnosis of ASC may be considered.

Autism spectrum condition

Case example: Autism spectrum condition

Chloe is very difficult to engage in a to-and-fro conversation. The only things that she ever talks about are things that she seems to have an intense interest in, such as animals and anime. At those times, she seems to talk 'at me'. I tend to find myself prompting her to give me eye contact and she struggles to follow group instructions, particularly if she is not interested in the subject. She has significant long-term difficulties with friendships. There was a phase where she was incredibly intense with one other girl and could not tolerate the other girl having other friends. She rarely plays within the group and prefers being on her own or on a 1:1 basis. I've noticed that she does things in the same order at lunchtime every day and that she eats exactly the same thing and the same amount every day. Her memory for long-term details is amazing and she is intelligent. However, she can frequently be non-compliant. She often does not do her work and it is incredibly difficult for her to evidence what she knows in assessments. She is particularly struggling with creative writing and coming up with new concepts and ideas. She also finds the actual process of writing really difficult and clearly dislikes it, preferring to give her answers verbally, despite her reading ability being advanced for her age.

What is autism spectrum condition?

Autism is a spectrum condition. All people diagnosed as being on the autism spectrum share certain difficulties, but all people on the spectrum will present in different ways. Symptoms and characteristics are expressed in many different combinations and degrees of severity (Mash & Wolfe, 2005). ASC refers to a neurodevelopmental difference resulting in difficulties within social communication and interaction, the presence of restricted or stereotyped behaviours, interests and activities, and also sensory challenges. Symptoms can include differences in language, difficulties relating to other people, unusual forms of play, difficulty with changes in routine, and repetitive movements or behaviour patterns. Individuals along the spectrum exhibit a full range of intellectual, functioning and language abilities.

Why does ASC occur?

Research indicates that ASC develops from a combination of genetic and environmental influences and there is not one identifiable single cause. The difficulty in establishing gene involvement is compounded by the interaction of genes and their interactions with environmental factors. It is known that certain factors increase the likelihood of a child meeting the criteria for a diagnosis of ASC. These are factors which affect early brain development including: pregnancy and birth complications (e.g. born before 26 weeks, low birth weight and multiple pregnancies), advanced parental age, and pregnancies spaced less than a year apart. For some families, their concerns about their child's development, and potentially a diagnosis, has coincided with the timings of childhood vaccinations. Extensive research over the last two decades has established there is no link between childhood vaccinations and ASC.

How common is ASC?

The latest prevalence studies indicate that 1.1% of the population in the UK may be on the autism spectrum. This means that more than 695,000 people in the UK may have ASC, an estimate derived from the above prevalence rate and applied to the 2011 UK census figures (National Autistic Society).

How is ASC diagnosed?

Under the 2009 Autism Act, local authorities and NHS organisations gained new responsibilities to develop services to support people with ASC and their families and carers. Since then, NICE has developed guidelines on recognising and diagnosing ASC in children and young people (2011) and on how best to support and manage it in childhood (2013).

The ICD-10 is the most commonly used diagnostic tool for ASC within the UK. As stated earlier, the ICD-11 was published in 2018 and is due to come into clinical use in 2022. This highlights that there is expected to be a 'functional impairment' in at least one of the following areas before the age of 3 years old:

- **Receptive or expressive language as used in social interaction** – A child may have a language delay or develop unusual aspects of their language (e.g. unusual volume, intonation or accent). Children with ASC tend to have more advanced expressive language compared to their receptive language, meaning they may be using language that they do not fully understand themselves.

- **Atypical or impaired development of reciprocal social interaction and selective social attachments** – Typically by three years of age, children are showing preferences for some peers over others and starting to develop friendships and play with others rather than simply alongside them (parallel play). A child with ASC may show reduced interest in social interaction, actively avoid others or show a marked preference for adults over peers.

- **Atypical or impaired functional or symbolic play** – Typically by three years of age, a child is able to play with a range of toys or objects according to their intended function. Children also demonstrate the use of objects symbolically and show imaginative skills through pretend play and role play. A child with ASC may demonstrate repetitive rigid play e.g. lining things up or simply categorising play items. They may demonstrate a lack of play overall, especially a lack of creative and imaginative play. They might also show preferences for 'part objects' rather than the whole of the toy e.g. spinning the wheels of a toy car or preferring to deconstruct toys into parts rather than playing with the item in a way it was intended.

The ICD-10 stipulates that at least two of the following symptoms within social interaction needs to be present for a child to receive a diagnosis of ASC:

- They may struggle to use eye contact and the full range of facial expressions, gestures and body posture in order to regulate social interaction.

- They may be unable to develop (in a manner appropriate for their mental age, and despite sufficient opportunities) mutual peer relationships that involve reciprocal sharing of interests, activities and emotions.

■ They may demonstrate either a lack of, or unusual responses to, others' emotions. They may show a lack of modification of behaviour according to different social contexts or social, emotional and communicative factors.

■ They may show a lack of spontaneous seeking to share enjoyment, interests or achievements with other people (e.g. a lack of showing, bringing or pointing out objects of interest).

The ICD-10 also stipulates that at least one of the following symptoms a child's communication needs to be present for a child to receive a diagnosis of ASC:

■ A delay in or a total lack of development of spoken language (with no compensation for this by increased use of gestures).

■ A relative failure to initiate or sustain conversational interchange (at whatever level of language skills are present) in which there is reciprocal responsiveness to the communications of the other person.

■ Use of stereotyped and repetitive language or idiosyncratic use of words or phrases.

■ A lack of varied spontaneous make-believe or (when young) social imitative play.

Finally, the ICD-10 stipulates that restricted, repetitive and stereotyped patterns of behaviour, interests and activities must be manifest in at least one of the following areas for a child to receive a diagnosis of ASC:

■ They may have an all-encompassing preoccupation with one or more stereotyped and restricted patterns of interest that are abnormal in content or focus; or one or more interests that are abnormal in their intensity and circumscribed nature, though not in their content or focus.

■ They have an apparently compulsive adherence to specific, non-functional routines or rituals.

■ They have stereotyped and repetitive motor mannerisms that involve either hand or finger flapping or twisting, or complex whole-body movements.

■ They have preoccupations with 'part objects' or non-functional elements of play materials (such as their odour, the feel of their surface or the noise or vibration that they generate).

Co-occurring disorders

Co-occurring conditions are common. The conditions that overlap with ASC generally fall into four groups:

■ Medical problems, such as epilepsy, gastrointestinal issues or sleep disorders.

■ Genetic conditions, including Fragile X Syndrome and Tuberous Sclerosis Complex.

■ Mental health conditions, such as ADHD, anxiety disorders (e.g GAD and OCD) or depression.

■ Developmental diagnoses, such as language delay or intellectual disability.

A significant proportion of people with ASC may also be classed as having a learning disability (IQ less than 70). Research studies regarding the prevalence of learning disabilities within the autistic population vary immensely.

Autism spectrum condition in school: what does it look like and how can we help?

As is evident from the wide range of possible symptoms described above, a child with ASC can present in many different ways in school. As stated earlier, no two children on the autism spectrum are the same, just as no two neurotypical children are the same. Some of the many presentations in school include:

■ A child with ASC is likely to show differences in terms of socio-emotional reciprocity. They are likely to have difficulty reading and responding appropriately to the emotions of others.

■ They might demonstrate socially inappropriate behaviour as they are struggling to naturally and implicitly learn the social norms and cues. This behaviour should not be perceived as rude or disrespectful, but instead indicative of the underlying social skills that they are struggling to learn.

■ There may also be delayed theory of mind, which means a child will struggle in understanding and making best guesses about the thoughts and feelings of other people. They might actually be working really hard to compensate for this all of the time, which makes social interactions, and particularly being in large groups, emotionally exhausting.

■ Compliance is often reduced, as the motivation to do as others ask simply to please others is often reduced. They are often described as being 'on their own agenda', but this of course relates to the reduced information their brain is giving them regarding other people's agendas!

- Significant differences may be observed in a child's communication skills. Speech and language difficulties are common and they may need specialist input from a speech and language therapist.

- Some children will dominate conversations and have a tendency to speak in monologues, which impacts on the reciprocal nature of a typical conversation. A child with ASC might not be able to maintain a reciprocal conversation when their conversational partner is using statements or comments. It may be better to use closed questions for some children. What a child talks about might also be dominated by any intense special interests they have.

- There may also be unusual features of speech, such as differences in intonation, pitch, accent or speed of speech.

- Repetition of speech may occur, with a child saying the same things over and over again.

- They might also use overly formal speech and unusual idiosyncratic words not commonly used in their age group.

Children with ASC can experience a high 'base level' of anxiety every day and are therefore vulnerable to experiencing high levels of stress (Attwood, 2000). Anxiety can have a further impact on the ability to focus on instruction, ability to participate in classroom activities, learning and social relationships (Laugeson & Frankel, 2010). A detailed and accurate understanding of all the different stressors or triggers that go into an individual child's 'stress bucket' (based on information from both home and school) is required in order to know which individualised strategies and techniques are likely to be effective for that child. This sounds potentially time consuming – but often using a stepped, time-line approach to look at the child's routines and navigation through the school day can highlight trigger factors that might be able to be modified. It is helpful to do this in partnership with a parent. Knowing a child's individual stress triggers can significantly aid regulation and, in turn, aid the child's capacity to learn.

Teaching staff are well placed to collect information regarding a child's imagination skills, which are affected in ASC. Such skills are typically observed through play and activities such as creative writing. We also use our imaginations in order to think of our future selves when we are planning and organising, and also in problem-solving. Difficulties with imagination in ASC may also include struggling to differentiate between fact and fiction, which can trigger heightened emotional reactions to films and books.

Many neurotypical children have intense hobbies or interests that change over time and are most frequently in line with what their peers like. A child with ASC may have a highly unusual interest (e.g. electricity pylons) or their interests may be more typical, but the intensity of this interest is unusual. It preoccupies their thoughts and behaviours and is linked with a high level of repetitive behaviours and even possible distress if they are prevented from engaging in an activity in line with this interest. Teaching staff may be aware of a child that only talks about their area of interest and has a high degree of specialist knowledge about a specific topic.

Strategies

It is important to consider in detail how ASC can present with regard to various aspects of school life and how strategies can be used to help children manage their emotional responses and overcome the subsequent barriers to their engagement and learning. The sections below will explore ASC in relation to the learning environment, emotional, behavioural and social regulation and the actual process of learning.

A diagnosis of ASC falls within the remit of the Equality Act (2010), which means that schools are required to make reasonable adjustments. Many of the strategies suggested below will be suitable for a child struggling with social and communication difficulties, even if they have not received a diagnosis, or a diagnosis is not being sought.

Learning environment

- Simple environmental changes e.g. facing a wall with no displays on it or having a divide between them and peers, or specific workstations, help to reduce sensory overload and aid concentration. Some children may prefer a divider that is covered with pictures of their specialist interest to aid motivation and improve their mood.

- Processing visual information in ASC is easier than processing verbal information, so typically an increase in the use of visuals is helpful. A personal and portable visual timetable will allow them to know exactly what they are doing and when. They can check this off as they go through the day (see **Chapter 16: Daily Transitions** for further discussion of visual timetables). It might seem like this is not necessary if children are able to follow a class timetable, but such strategies have been found to reduce anxiety (Hoffman, 2013).

- Reminders and lists can help a child who has organisation and planning difficulties and support their developing independence skills. This could look like a list of things they need for their school bag each day of the week.

- Sensory stimuli:

- Over or under-sensitivity to sounds, touch, light, visual stimuli and temperature within the classroom environment can contribute to difficulties. Children with heightened senses are constantly taking in more sensory information than others and this can cause sensory overload and overwhelm. If sensory differences impact on daily functioning, a child may require sensory assessments through occupational therapy.

- It is important for those supporting a child with ASC to be aware of their sensory sensitivities and do as much as possible to help the child make reasonable adjustments in order to cope. If a child has a known noise sensitivity, they can wear ear defenders when necessary or be allowed to undertake a different activity when there is a noisy assembly or event taking place.

- Other simple adjustments such as allowing a child to use a different door to enter and leave the school or being the first one to collect their belongings can have a significant impact on reducing the sensory demands associated with busy corridors, crowded spaces and groups of noisy children.

Emotional, behavioural and social regulation

Emotional regulation

- Explicitly teaching emotions to children with ASC (what they look like, what they feel like, what activities you can do to change your emotions and what other people can do to help you move from one emotion to another) can be hugely beneficial (see *Chapter 5* for further details).

- Emotions need to be taught in a very concrete and visual way. The Incredible 5 Point Scale (Baron & Curtis, 2004) is a clear simple visual tool that helps with this. Some children with ASC may be able to identify their feelings using a scale like this (using colours or numbers or both). They may be able to use this to communicate to others how they are feeling using a scale on a keyring or lanyard. This can be a helpful way to allow children to communicate when they need a break.

- There are four types of break which can be of benefit for a child with ASC: quiet breaks, movement breaks, special interest breaks and sensory breaks. If a child is demonstrating significant emotional dysregulation or parents are reporting that they are coming out of school extremely distressed, actual modification of their timetable might have a significant impact. However some children might not want to be perceived as different and they may be working very hard to seem as though they are doing the same as everyone else. For this reason, different breaks might need to be embedded into their daily routine more creatively e.g. their movement break may consist of doing a job for an adult on the other side of the school.

■ Children with ASC should have opportunities to meet their sensory needs within their daily routines in school. Access to sensory activities at different points in the day (within lessons and at break times) can have a calming effect and could potentially aid attention and emotional regulation. A grab bag of different items that they can access in line with their needs, or a specific area they are able to visit (e.g. a pop up tent in a corner of the library or a sound-proofed pod), can be beneficial.

■ Ensuring a child has access to special objects in line with their preoccupations or special interest can also have a regulatory impact (Bryan & Gast, 2000).

■ Remember that many children may be able to hold it together emotionally at school and then let out all their emotions at home. Due to this social masking, this can make it especially challenging for teachers to gain a full understanding of the individual child or gather evidence that techniques and strategies being tried are indeed effective.

Behavioural regulation

■ Children with ASC may engage in repetitive behaviours. They will often *need* to carry out these behaviours – they are commonly ways of externally regulating themselves. Teaching staff should not prevent them from engaging in these behaviours but they can instead help them find alternative ways of meeting the need, in a manner that does not significantly impact their learning or social development.

■ Eye contact:

■ It is often noted that children with ASC have different or reduced eye contact. Eye contact is an important non-verbal social skill. People tend to naturally prompt a child to look at them when they are talking to them as this tends to indicate to neurotypical people that a child is listening and attending. This is a helpful strategy if we are sure that for that individual child, eye contact does increase attentiveness. However, a child with ASC might find eye contact physically uncomfortable and/or a source of stress, so it might therefore not improve their ability to process what is being said to them.

■ However, eye contact remains an important social skill that we use to indicate not only that we are listening, but also that we want to initiate interaction with someone else or show an interest in what they are saying. If a child finds eye contact too challenging, they might be able to learn alternative ways to show their interest e.g. fully facing the person, staying within a conversational distance and remaining until the person has finished what they are saying.

■ It might be also helpful for a child to learn some socially appropriate comments they can use to indicate attention when the other person pauses e.g. 'yes' or 'okay' or even 'mm-hmm'. Ideally, a child will get to the point where they can communicate: 'I'm the kind of person who can pay attention better when I'm not looking directly at someone' or 'I know I'm not looking at you but I am listening'. Until that time, the child can use an 'I need you to know…' card to share this information with adults and children (see ***Chapter 19***).

Social regulation

- In general, social relationships are likely to be sources of stress for children with ASC and will need more support and scaffolding. Any developing peer relationships need to be nurtured.

- Some children will demonstrate a high level of social avoidance, but both neurotypical children and children with ASC need to be encouraged to develop connections with others (and this becomes especially important by the adolescent years, when it is peers who contribute even more to our emotional regulation).

- Children who are struggling socially may need some specific support regarding friendships. They may really want to develop friendships but not know how to. Ask if the child can identify what is going wrong and pair this with your own detailed observations over time. The child may be struggling with not understanding group rules, or a lack of greeting or initiating behaviours. All of these skills are typically learned implicitly, but children with ASC benefit from more explicit teaching of these social norms and being taught the advantages of certain responses.

- Children with ASC may display persistent difficulties with specific social skills such as sharing, turn taking, winning and losing, even when most children in the class have developed these key social skills. These are skills that can be explicitly taught through social skills training.

- When a difficult situation arises, for example with turn taking, take a moment to coach the children through it. Ask for all sides of the story and refer to established class rules as you support the child to understand why they must wait for their turn: 'Everyone needs to have a go. It can be fun to watch the other children as well as taking your turn.' Acknowledge the frustrations of the other children who are following rules, but ensure you empathise with the child who is finding it hard.

- Some schools have had incredible success with designing interest groups around highly specific interests of children with ASC e.g. computer coding or Pokémon. These groups often enable a child to shine alongside neurotypical children. They create the opportunity for them to be socially successful as the amount of information they might know about a particular topic (especially if it is a preoccupation) is likely to be high.

- Many children with ASC struggle with unstructured time, such as playtime and lunchtime. This is due to the social demands within these times and also potentially because imagination differences make it harder to think of how to spend the time. Increased break and lunchtime support can be highly effective in reducing stress, reducing incidences of distress behaviour and reducing the level of experienced negative social interactions. Some schools utilise small group play with play leaders, 1:1 support for these times or indoor lunch clubs. These can offer opportunities for a child to interact in calmer and potentially quieter areas, taking part in activities they enjoy. See **Chapter 4** for a full discussion of alternative lunchtime provision.

■ Carol Gray's Social Stories can be used to teach children about everyday situations that they may find confusing or stressful (Gray, 2010). They can be used for teaching social and life skills and preparing for transitions or new events. They need to be written in a specific way and they are best individualised for a child with pictures in order to teach through narrative and visuals. See the link in **Chapter 19** for more details.

Learning

■ An adapted curriculum, in terms of how it is presented and the length and nature of the learning activities, can improve on-task behaviours and academic output (Bryan & Gast, 2000; Myers *et al*, 2007).

■ A child with ASC may need tangible positive reinforcement (due to decreased reinforcement from social reinforcers and pleasing others) in order to stay motivated e.g. a token economy system or increased access to their special interest following a targeted pro-social behaviour.

■ Looking at information on a large white board at the front of the class is not suited to all children with ASC. Furthermore, they may not be able to express how they feel about accessing information in this way. Always provide essential learning information in a portable visual form e.g. on a printed sheet, small white board or iPad. A child can hold this on the carpet or use it at their table. This will also support them with any attention or concentration difficulties.

■ Aim to increase the number of visuals used in teaching and decrease the amount of complex verbal instructions. Use of accessible checklists, timetables, written expectations and contracts can be individualised and designed specifically to increase the predictability of the child's experiences.

■ Keep special interests in mind at all times – this can be helpful when attempting to engage a child who is avoidant of demands (often due to high anxiety). They may be more likely to participate in a learning task if it is linked to their interests. A skills-based learning objective can still be accessed and met by the child even if they are not writing about the same subject matter as the rest of the class.

■ Children with ASC can find competitive activities very difficult. There will be times when it is important to allow competition and children do need to experience the highs and lows of winning and losing. However, if you know that a child is particularly sensitive to losing it is very important to create a culture of cooperation, rather than competition, in your classroom. At times it can be very tempting to motivate children with the promise of a prize for the winner. But sometimes swapping the instinctive 'The first table ready for lunch wins an extra point' for 'Once your table is ready, today you need to go and help the table next to you – then you will both win an extra point' can be less stressful for those children who find it hard to cope with competition. This is true for all children, not just those with a diagnosis of ASC.

■ Children with ASC are often very literal thinkers and struggle to understand speech that is not logical, such as the use of sarcasm, idioms and metaphors. Although it is easier said than done, it is helpful if people around them avoid using speech that could be taken literally, such as 'pull your socks up' and 'rule of thumb'.

❓ Thinking about…Pathological demand avoidance

Pathological demand avoidance (PDA) is a term first coined by Professor Elizabeth Newson and refers to what her research indicates as a distinct subset of children within the umbrella of pervasive developmental differences. These children present with an extreme obsessional avoidance of the ordinary demands of life. These children are therefore deeply threatened by educational demands and organisational rules. However challenging the behaviour and extreme the noncompliance, the child is not wilfully being naughty and cannot easily behave differently (Newson *et al*, 2003). Children with PDA may demonstrate comparable levels of autistic traits and peer relationship problems with those children with a diagnosis of ASC, and a similar level of anti-social traits like those seen in children with conduct problems; but higher levels of emotional symptoms than in both of these groups (O'Nions *et al*, 2014).

The defining criteria for diagnosis of PDA syndrome according to Newson and colleagues are:

■ passive early history

■ long term avoidance and resistance of ordinary demands (and socially manipulative avoidance)

■ surface sociability, but lack of sense of identity, pride or shame

■ lability of mood, impulsivity and the child is led by a high need to control (generally due to underlying anxiety)

■ comfortable in role play and pretending

- language delay (seems to be as a result of passivity)
- obsessional behaviour.

Despite these criteria being available, there are relatively few services nationally commissioned to assess and diagnose PDA, so many may have a diagnosis of ASC but have a PDA-profile. What is important to note is that the guidelines that are successful with children with ASC need major adaptations for children with a PDA-profile. Here are some suggestions for these adaptations:

- Disguise demands in order to reduce the child's anxieties. Avoid using demand words like should, must or need and instead use indirect language e.g. 'Let's see if we can…' or 'Maybe we could…'.
- A flexible approach is likely to be more effective than a highly structured approach. Monitor the child's stress levels and scale back demands proactively.
- Use choices and options within interactions.
- Use visual supports to de-personalise demands and give the child more opportunity for control, spontaneity, choice and ordering different activities.
- Re-word demands creatively to give the opportunity for them to perceive being in control or use their initiative e.g. 'What does everyone have to do next to get ready to learn?' instead of 'Get your book out'.
- Create games (e.g. using pretend skills or races: 'Let's see who's the first one to get their shoes on') to give indirect demands.
- Use a child's special interests embedded within their curriculum and daily activities.
- Use humour and distraction.
- Set absolute boundaries using reference to a 'higher power' – there will always need to be non-negotiable boundaries in place at home and school for safety reasons. These can be taught in a planned way e.g. by giving information about health and safety laws.

When further help is needed for ASC

If teaching staff have concerns that a child may have undiagnosed ASC, the SENCO will need to make an analysis of need, including evidence of the child's academic progress, social relationship skills and behaviour. The concerns must be discussed with parents. Depending on local services, a parent may be able to self-refer to CAMHS for an ASC assessment or they may need to visit the child's GP to discuss this referral. The school may be able to refer directly (with parental consent) and it is likely that they will be asked to complete screening questionnaires. These should ideally be completed by a staff member who knows the child well and can document any concerns and observations in detail. Unfortunately, there are long waiting lists nationally for ASC assessments within the NHS.

Further support may be sought from CAMHS for children with a diagnosis of ASC who are presenting with signs and symptoms of mental health difficulties or behaviours which are challenging at home or at school. If the child's emotional and behavioural presentation is potentially harmful to either themselves or those around them, and if there is evidence that their behaviour is affecting their level of functioning and impacting on their daily life, a referral to CAMHS would be warranted.

Positives of ASC

The differences seen in ASC may indeed lead to difficulties, but with sufficient understanding and appropriate support in place, differences can often be utilised as strengths and skills. It is crucial for the strengths and skills of a child with a diagnosis of ASC to be noted and maximised as much as possible, especially in light of the significant challenges they face, over and above those of neurotypical children. Many of these challenges come from the expectation that people with ASC should conform to the expectations and environments designed by neurotypical people.

Obviously, no two children on the autism spectrum are the same and it is always helpful to be on the lookout for individual strengths that a child might present with and ways in which they may be able to demonstrate their intelligence. They might show a high ability to decode language and be reading at a very young age (hyperlexia), though their reading ability might be significantly better than their comprehension skills. Many children with ASC have a heightened consideration of details and are very precise. They may be very skilled in playing games that involve quick identification of visual information, when compared to neurotypical children. They may also have a determination to seek the truth and have an interest in rules and fairness. Related to this, they might be incredibly reliable, honest and punctual and have the ability to keep to routines and schedules over time.

Children with ASC may be more likely to be independent thinkers (perhaps less concerned with what others think of them), think things through in a visual way and show alternative problem solving skills. Many may have an extraordinarily good long-term memory and be able to remember facts for a very long period of time (compared to neurotypical people). This, coupled with a tendency to have intense special interests and preoccupations, means that many children with ASC are able to remain focused on a topic and gain a high level of specialist knowledge through deep study of a topic. As with all children, the more they practise their skills and build on their strengths, the happier and more successful a child with ASC will become. Autism spectrum intelligence is atypical (a distinctly uneven profile is often a feature), but it is also genuine, general and often underestimated (Soulieres *et al*, 2011).

It is important to remember that children with ASC are often (potentially both consciously and unconsciously) trying to fit into the neurotypical world and trying to both say and do the things that others will judge as being appropriate. This social masking can be exhausting and stressful. Some children will be troubled by a constant feeling that they are different from others and are not fitting in. Others may have no or limited insight into their differences. Either way, it is essential to keep in mind the fact that children with ASC can face seemingly endless challenges within school. However, teaching staff, peers and parents can do much to model celebration of a child's differences and strengths. Creating a culture of openness and narration of events in the classroom and in the wider school community is very helpful. If a child is comfortable with the attention, recognising and sharing their talents and positive learning experiences can help to foster feelings of belonging and community, making them feel less different from their peers.

Summary

- Autism is a spectrum condition, which means that symptoms and characteristics are expressed in many different combinations and degrees of severity.

- A diagnosis of ASC indicates neurodevelopmental differences resulting in difficulties within social communication and interaction, the presence of restricted or stereotyped behaviours, interests and activities and also sensory sensitivities.

- There are a wide range of strategies and techniques that should be put in place to support a child on the spectrum with their cognitive, social and emotional development.

- Most strategies involve using visuals to increase the level of consistency and predictability in the child's everyday life (e.g. timetables, contracts, checklists lists, schedules etc) as well as explicit teaching of social skills in areas of need (e.g. turn taking or sharing).

- Many children with ASC have strengths and skills that neurotypical children may not have.

References

Attwood T (2000) Strategies for improving the social integration of children with Asperger Syndrome. *Autism* **4** (1) 85–100.

Bryan LC & Gast DL (2000) Teaching on-task and on-schedule behaviours to high-functioning children with autism via picture activity schedules. *Journal of Autism and Developmental Disorders* **30** 553–567.

Baron KD & Curtis M (2004) *The Incredible 5-point Scale: Assisting students with autism spectrum disorders in understanding social interactions and controlling their emotional responses*. Shwanee, KS: Autism Asperger Publishing Co.

Emerson E & Baines S (2010) *The Estimated Prevalence of Autism among Adults with Learning Disabilities in England*. Stockton-on-Tees: Improving Health and Lives.

Fombonne E, Quirke S & Hagen A (2011) Epidemiology of pervasive developmental disorders. In: DG Amaral, G Dawson & DH Geschwind (Eds) *Autism Spectrum Disorders* (pp90–111). New York: Oxford University Press,

Gray C (2010) *The New Social Story Book*. Jenison Public Schools. Arlington, TX: Future Horizons Inc.

Hoffman F (2013) Evidence-based classroom strategies for reducing anxiety in primary aged children with high-functioning autism. *New Zealand Journal of Teachers' Work* **10** (1) 25–43.

Laugeson E & Frankel F (2010) *Social Skills for Teenagers with Developmental and Autism Spectrum Disorders: The Peers Treatment Manual*. New York: Routledge.

Mash E & Wolfe D (2005) *Abnormal Child Psychology*. Belmont: Thompson Wadsworth.

Myles B, Hudson J, Lee H, Smith S, Tien Y & Swanson T (2007) A large scale study of the characteristics of Asperger Syndrome. *Education and Training in Developmental Disabilities* **42** (4) 448–459.

National Autistic Society. Available from www.autism.org.uk/about.aspx

National Institute of Clinical Excellence (2011) *Autism Spectrum Disorder in Under 19s: Recognition, Referral and Diagnosis*. Available from www.nice.org.uk/guidance/CG128

National Institute of Clinical Excellence (2013) [online]. *Autism Spectrum Disorder in Under 19s: Support and Management*. Available from www.nice.org.uk/guidance/cg170

Newson E, Le Marechal K, David C (2003) Pathological demand avoidance syndrome: A necessary distinction within the pervasive developmental disorders. *Archives of Disease in Childhood* **88** 595-600.

O'Nions E, Christi P, Gould J, Viding E & Happe F (2014) Development of the 'Extreme Demand Avoidance Questionnaire' (EDAQ). Reliminary observayion on a trait measure for Pathological Demand Avoidance. *Journal of Child Psychology and Psychiatry* **55** 758-768.

Soulieres L, Dawson M, Gernsbacker MA & Mottron L (2011) The level and nature of autistic intelligence II: What about Asperger Syndrome. *PLoS ONE* **6** (9).

World Health Organisation (2016) *ICD-10*. Available from www.who.int/classifications/icd/icdonlineversions/en/

Chapter 12: Difficulties with Attention, Hyperactivity, Impulsivity and Tics

Children vary in their ability to stay on task and concentrate, and some will struggle with particular types of activities and ways of learning. With the frontal lobe of the brain (the part which helps in regulating emotions, being organised and problem solving) being the last to develop – and often not until we are in our mid-twenties – it is unsurprising that a classroom environment can present a challenge for some children.

Difficulties with attention, hyperactivity and impulsivity

Case example: Difficulties with attention, hyperactivity and impulsivity

Callum is in Year 3 and is often disruptive in class – not staying in his seat, making funny noises and fidgeting with pens. He can't seem to follow instructions as he is staring around the room and so easily distracted. In assembly, he fidgets constantly and often has to leave. In class, we've used some fidget aids to help him stay in his seat. As his teacher, I find myself repeating instructions to him and needing to give him multiple prompts to stay on task. There have been a couple of incidents in the playground where he seems to have impulsively hit other children, and he's also climbed on the school roof a couple of times.

Many children struggle with maintaining attention and concentration, particularly in the school setting. When this is combined with issues around impulsivity, such as shouting out, interrupting or running off into the road, it may be part of a condition called attention deficit hyperactivity disorder (ADHD). However, these difficulties are best viewed as lying along a spectrum. At the most severe end, a diagnosis may be given, but it is still possible to have significant difficulties without meeting the threshold for this.

Attention deficit hyperactivity disorder (ADHD)

What is ADHD?

ADHD is a neurodevelopmental disorder, meaning it is related to how the brain develops, and is present from birth. It is thought that development of the frontal cortex is primarily affected in ADHD – the area responsible for planning, organisation and impulse control. Children with ADHD will have difficulties in three main areas: attention and concentration, hyperactivity, and impulsivity, all of which are described in more detail later in this chapter. For some young people with ADHD the difficulties will lessen with age as the brain develops and the frontal lobe matures. However, a significant proportion will continue to have difficulties into adulthood.

These difficulties are usually seen before the age of six, and must be present for over six months and in more than one setting for a diagnosis of ADHD. There are many other reasons why a child may display these difficulties, especially if they are only seen in certain settings, which is why a full assessment by a specialist paediatric or mental health team is required for diagnosis. Recently there has been more recognition that exposure to alcohol in-utero can lead to ADHD-type symptoms that are less responsive to treatment with medication, as part of foetal alcohol spectrum disorder (FASD).

Why does ADHD occur?

There is no single cause or gene that results in ADHD. It does however seem to be more common in certain groups, including children born preterm (before 37 weeks of pregnancy), looked after children (LAC), children with a learning disability and children who have a family history of ADHD (NICE, 2018). The difficulties are thought in part to be related to levels of dopamine in the brain, a chemical that helps us to pay attention, and many medications for ADHD seek to increase dopamine levels.

How common is ADHD?

Research suggests that global prevalence of ADHD is between 2% and 7%, with the average being at around 5% of children. At least a further 5% of children have substantial difficulties with overactivity, inattention and impulsivity that are just under the threshold to meet full diagnostic criteria for ADHD (Sayal *et al*, 2018). Recent official statistics in England found that rates of hyperactivity disorders were lower in children aged 17–19 (0.8%) compared to children aged 11–16 (2%), suggesting some improvement in difficulties with age (NHS Digital, 2017).

How is ADHD diagnosed?

Mental health services in the UK will usually use the ICD-10 or DSM-5 criteria to help them in diagnosing ADHD. You may also hear the term 'hyperkinetic disorder', which is another term used to describe ADHD. Attention deficit disorder (ADD) can also be used to describe a child who has difficulties with attention and concentration which are impairing their function, but without the associated 'H' of hyperactivity seen in ADHD; this tends to be used more in the US than in the UK.

An assessment for ADHD will usually include observation of the child in the school setting. The teacher may also be asked to complete a Conner's questionnaire using observations from the classroom and break times. This is a tool used to assess if the child is having difficulties in the area of attention, concentration, overactivity and/or conduct. In order for a diagnosis to be given there needs to be evidence of impairment in three main areas, in several different settings (NICE, 2018):

- **Impaired attention** – This may include being easily distracted, making careless mistakes, struggling to follow instructions, being forgetful and appearing not to listen.

- **Hyperactivity** – This may include a child who finds it difficult to stay in their seat, who fidgets or moves about excessively, who struggles to queue and who may climb a lot.

- **Impulsivity** – Shouting out answers in class, interrupting others, difficulty in taking turns or running out into the road without looking can all be features of impulsivity.

Co-occurring disorders

A high percentage of children with ADHD will also have an additional diagnosis, such as a learning difficulty, ODD and/or sleep problems. There is also an increased prevalence of other neurodevelopmental difficulties including ASC, tics and Tourette's, as well as OCD. It is estimated that only a third of young people with ADHD will not have an additional diagnosis (Reale *et al*, 2017). Many children with ADHD can also struggle with executive functioning in general, which encompasses the skills we need to plan, stay on task, regulate our emotions and understand different points of view. This means that, in addition to the three core features outlined above, a child with ADHD may also have other associated difficulties such as poor memory, problems planning ahead and following what they have done during a task and they may struggle to manage their emotions (Biederman *et al*, 2004).

Difficulties with attention, hyperactivity and impulsivity in school: what do they look like and how can we help?

School can be a particularly difficult place for a child with ADHD, as they are expected to conform and sit still for long periods of time in class. Difficulties in following instructions and completing tasks may mean the child doesn't achieve their academic potential. Additionally, many children with ADHD also have difficulties with reading and writing, which further compounds their problems. A child who is struggling with attention, hyperactivity and/or impulsivity may display the following difficulties:

- Appears to not be listening.

- Struggles to follow instructions.

- Can become distracted and fail to finish a task.

- May make careless errors or mistakes in class.

- Often loses or forgets things.

- Often fidgets or squirms in their seat.

- May run or climb excessively.

- May struggle to keep quiet, perhaps humming or make odd noises.

- Blurts out answers.

- Interrupts others.

- Struggles to queue or wait their turn.

- Talks excessively regardless of the situation.

Strategies

It is important to consider in detail how ADHD can present with regard to various aspects of school life and how strategies can be used to help children manage their emotional responses and overcome the subsequent barriers to their engagement and learning. The sections below will explore ADHD in relation to the learning environment, emotional, behavioural and social regulation and the actual process of learning. A diagnosis of ADHD falls within the remit of the Equality Act (2010) which means that schools are required to make reasonable adjustments. Many of the strategies suggested below will be suitable for a child struggling with attention, hyperactivity and impulsivity, even if they have not received a diagnosis, or a diagnosis is not being sought.

Learning environment

At times the classroom and the wider school environment can overwhelm a child who has inattention, hyperactivity and impulsivity difficulties. Consider these small ways in which the environment can be designed to support a child with such difficulties:

- Seating:
  - Whenever carpet seating is used, arrange seating so that the child has a learning or talk partner who will support and encourage learning. Involve them in this decision if possible, which will make cooperation more likely.
  - Place them in a position that allows them good eye contact with you and an optimum view of the board.
  - It may help to display seating plans so the child knows when they are sitting.
  - For younger children names may need to be taped on desks.
  - Explain to the class that seats have been chosen to help everyone with their learning, but ensure there are times during the week/day when children can choose their own spaces.
  - With all this said, enforcing a rigid seating system which causes distress to a child is not beneficial. Remember the aim is to support learning. A distressed child will not be able to learn effectively.

- Consider distractions from doors and windows, the phone ringing and other adults and children entering the classroom. How can these be minimised?

- Give permission for movement, but in a way that doesn't disturb learning. Allow fiddle toys to increase a child's chances of sitting still. Children can be allowed to wiggle their legs or feet under the table, or use wobble cushions. Make their coping strategies acceptable and normalise them for their peers.

- Allow children to work standing up with a desk of an appropriate height so that they can move their legs more easily while they concentrate.

- Consider movement and sensory breaks in response to periods of high distraction.

Emotional, behavioural and social regulation

Emotional regulation

- Children with ADHD or similar difficulties may struggle to regulate their emotions and can become easily frustrated. Helping children to recognise the changes in their body and voice when they are becoming frustrated can be a helpful strategy.

- See *Chapters 3* and *9* for advice and strategies for supporting a child who is emotionally dysregulated.

Behavioural regulation

- Impulsivity can lead to some unwanted behaviours in the classroom. Low-level 'silly' behaviour is best ignored, as it may not progress to more concerning or unsafe behaviour. If it does, this should be handled in line with the school's behaviour policy.

- As we have discussed, in the longer term, positive feedback is generally more successful than punishments in managing difficult behaviours and motivating future good behaviour. Using educational consequences in response to difficult behaviours tends to be accepted better and hence is more helpful in the long run than punishments unrelated to the 'offence' (see **Chapter 3**).

- For some children, being able to self-direct to a calm area in the classroom or around the school can be a great support if a difficult situation is developing (see **Chapter 8**).

- If a situation escalates and the child becomes angry and their behaviour dysregulated, having a plan in place to support them to re-regulate is essential (see **Chapter 9**).

- Constant calling out or challenging, even in a polite manner, can be an issue – sometimes the child may think they are just having a dialogue with an adult, and they may be unaware of the rest of the class. Making time for the conversation at a more appropriate time, such as at the end of the lesson, can be helpful.

- To support children who find it hard to wait for their turn to speak, consider:
  - Praise wanted behaviour, such as putting a hand up and waiting.
  - Give calm reminders to all and always phrase in the positive e.g. 'I want to hear what you have to say. Please remember to put up your hand first'.
  - Give firm and consistent boundaries. Develop a class culture in which everyone deserves to be heard and valued, but explain that rules are needed so each person gets their turn to speak.

- Unstructured times, such as playtimes or choosing times, can be difficult for some children. Strategies which may help include:
  - Ensuring staff on duty are aware of the difficulties.
  - Supporting the child in their development of friendships.
  - Providing access to games and activities, particularly during the longer lunch break (see **Chapter 4: Wellbeing for All** for discussion regarding alternative lunchtime provision).

Social regulation

- Children with ADHD may struggle to learn social rules and pick up on social cues. They may frequently interrupt others, push in line and become easily frustrated. They may therefore struggle to maintain relationships with their peers and often require support in this area.

■ Get to know the child and their friends by observing the dynamics and looking for patterns.

■ Work to find ways of reducing a child's triggers and avoid situations where the child needs to take turns unsupervised.

■ It can help to have agreed systems in class for turn taking. Ensure children know that these are class rules, not just rules for that particular child.

■ Have a class system in place for talking about problems and address specific friendship issues during PSHE.

■ Some children may also display over-familiarity with adults and be socially disinhibited. It is important to have a whole-school culture around what is expected for all, behaviour-wise. Gently remind children of boundaries. However, remember that there may be times when a child just needs reassurance and support from an adult.

■ If social difficulties seem to be a particular problem for a child, consider referring them to a group nurturing intervention within school, where they can receive personalised support. See **Chapter 5** for more information.

Learning

Children with ADHD or similar difficulties may experience problems with learning relating to the core features of the condition: inattention, concentration and impulsivity. They may also find it difficult to switch between tasks, and re-focusing attention after a break may be particularly difficult. In addition, there may be some overlap with learning difficulties relating to the following areas:

■ Working memory – there may be difficulties in retaining information and needing instructions to be repeated multiple times.

■ Executive functioning – planning, organising and higher-level cognitive tasks.

■ Fine motor skills – evident in handwriting.

■ Specific learning areas e.g. reading, writing and mathematical processing.

Strategies that may support a child with their learning include:

■ Breaking down work into shorter chunks can help them keep focused.

■ Making frequent eye contact and saying the child's name before talking may help in sustaining attention.

- Presenting information visually in addition to verbally can help with information processing. An instruction card on the table may help if following information on the board is difficult.

- Use simple language, and as few words as possible, to give a clear message.

- Having a clear routine and schedule to lessons can be helpful.

- Give a short, personalised summary at the end of a lesson.

- An individual portable visual timetable can have a grounding effect for children with attention difficulties – after each small chunk of the day they can take the symbol off and see what's next (and it might reduce the need for repetitive questioning). See *Chapter 16* for further details.

- Use a variety of learning methods and activities across the day.

- Encourage a child to be involved in the lesson, for example by giving them a specific task.

When further help is needed for ADHD

Left untreated, ADHD can have a severe impact on a child's functioning, socially, academically and in their family life. If a child is displaying the types of difficulties listed above, talk to their parents to see if they are seeing similar behaviours at home. If the difficulties have been present in more than one setting for over six months, and are affecting their functioning, it would be appropriate for a referral to specialist services to be made. Depending on the area, an assessment for ADHD may be carried by a CAMHS team or by community paediatrics. The child's GP is usually best placed to make this referral, but many CAMHS teams now also accept self-referrals from families.

Initial management of ADHD involves education and support for the child themselves, their family and the education professionals supporting them. Many services which diagnose ADHD offer support groups for parents and teaching staff which include psychoeducation around the condition and strategies which may help at home and at school. If a child continues to experience difficulties that are affecting their functioning, they may be offered medication to help improve their attention and concentration, particularly in the school setting. Medication is only licensed for use above the age of five.

The most commonly used medications are stimulants such as methylphenidate, also known as Ritalin. These drugs work to increase the levels of dopamine in the brain, which can improve attention and concentration. Children may experience a number of side effects, including reduced appetite, growth restriction, sleep disturbance, headaches and tummy aches. These side effects often limit the doses that can be used, and children will be reviewed frequently to ensure that the risks do not outweigh the benefits.

There are different forms of methylphenidate, including immediate release, which lasts for around four hours, and longer acting slow-release forms, which can last up to ten hours. It is also possible to 'top up' long-acting versions with an extra dose of short-acting methylphenidate after school to help with homework and after school activities when needed. However, it is important that the medication has worn off by early evening to reduce the impact on a child's sleep (see **Chapter 4** for further discussion regarding sleep in children with neurodevelopmental conditions). Some children will only take these medications on school days and not at weekends and/or during school holidays, which may minimise unwanted side effects.

These stimulant drugs are classed as 'controlled' drugs, due to their potential for misuse in the wrong hands. This means that usually only a short supply is given at a time. A number of non-stimulant options are now available to help treat ADHD (such as atomoxetine and guanfacine), which may have fewer side effects. These tend to be used as a second-line treatment, as the evidence base remains firmly in favour of stimulant medication initially.

Looking to the future, once a young person with ADHD leaves school, they can choose to study or work in a setting that better suits their strengths. In this way, ADHD may cause less impairment in functioning in adulthood. It is also common for the symptoms of ADHD to lessen with age as the frontal lobe matures.

Tics and Tourette's syndrome

Tics and Tourette's syndrome are covered in this chapter as there is some overlap with ADHD. Around 20% of children with chronic tics have ADHD. Other conditions frequently seen in children with tics include ASC, OCD and difficulties with anger and emotional regulation. It is important to note that many children experience tics at some point and if these are not causing distress or interfering with functioning there is often no need for any specific intervention.

Case example: Tics and Tourette's

I've known Tom for a few months now, and his previous teacher mentioned to me that he sometimes makes odd humming and grunting sounds, which I've also noticed. He also seems to jerk his head to one side, and the other children in class have noticed this too.

What are tics?

Tics are often classified as motor (movement related) or vocal (noise related). A motor tic is an involuntary, fast, repeated twitching movement which begins quite suddenly and doesn't appear to serve a purpose. Common motor tics include eye blinking, shoulder shrugging and tongue movements. Complex motor tics include more elaborate movements such as touching things, facial grimacing or making obscene gestures. A vocal tic is a noise which is made involuntarily and repetitively. They may include sounds such as growling, animal sounds, humming or coughing. Complex vocal tics are vocal tics which include clear words or phrases, which are sometimes swear words or obscene words (this is known as coprolalia). Despite media fascination, coprolalia is actually quite uncommon and only occurs in around 10% of people with Tourette's.

What is Tourette's syndrome?

Tourette's syndrome may be diagnosed when both vocal and motor tics are seen over a period greater than one year, and they are causing distress and/or functional impairment for a child. Although Tourette's syndrome is considered to be a lifelong condition, tics often lessen in frequency and severity with age (Bagheri *et al*, 1999).

Why do tics and Tourette's syndrome occur?

For many children with tics, they are more likely to occur at times of stress, tiredness or worry. Some medications may also worsen tics. It can sometimes be difficult to tell tics apart from 'silly' behaviour, particularly if a child is shouting out words. There are of course many reasons why a child may be doing this, but one reason is tic disorder or Tourette's syndrome. Tourette's syndrome is a hereditary condition and a person with the condition has around a 50% chance of passing it on to their child.

How common are tics and Tourette's syndrome?

Tic disorder is more common in boys than girls (around 1.6% of boys, compared to 0.6% of girls aged 5–10), with tic disorder being far more common than Tourette's syndrome. Transient tics – that is, tics which come and go – are fairly common. They occur more often in boys than girls, with a peak onset around 7–8 years of age.

How are tics and Tourette's diagnosed?

If tics last for longer than a year, a diagnosis of tic disorder may be given. As there are no particular tests, diagnosis is made from observation and gathering history from the child and family. This is usually done by a child psychiatrist or a community paediatrician. Often no specific treatment is needed, but getting the diagnosis right and educating people about what this means is often very beneficial for a child.

Tics and Tourette's syndrome in school: what do they look like and how can we help?

Tics can vary greatly in their presentation and some will be more obvious than others. Remember that a child may not always be aware that the tic is happening.

Common motor tics include:

■ nose wrinkling

■ head twitching

■ blinking

■ facial grimaces

■ lip smacking

■ shoulder shrugging.

Common vocal tics include:

■ coughing

■ throat clearing

■ grunting

■ barking

■ sniffing

■ hissing.

Strategies

It is important to consider how tics and Tourette's can present with regard to various aspects of school life and how strategies can be used to help children manage their emotional responses and overcome the subsequent barriers to their engagement and learning. The sections below will explore tics and Tourette's in relation to the learning environment, emotional, behavioural and social regulation and the actual process of learning.

Learning environment

Teaching staff and peers should not try to prevent a child from carrying out a tic. Providing a safe space where a child can release their tics at school can help prevent a build-up of tension. It may be helpful to consider where a child with tics is seated in class – a child at the front of the class is more visible to others when tics occur. A child with motor tics may require greater physical space around the desk.

Emotional, behavioural and social regulation

Some children will be able to suppress their tics in school (although this may take a lot of mental energy) and teaching staff may be surprised to hear a parent's description of their child's frequent tics at home. Home may feel like a safe place to let out their tics, but a child may also experience distress and upset at this time. This could impact on their ability to complete homework in the evenings.

It is helpful to agree approaches with parents. Generally, not reacting or responding to tics is the preferred approach, as drawing further attention to it often heightens anxiety and worsens the tic. This can also be damaging to a child's self-esteem. It is possible that if a child is embarrassed by their tic they may pretend that it was intentional in order to cover this up, particularly if they are causing disruption in the classroom. Children with tics may be vulnerable to bullying and teasing. It is important to be alert to this and manage any bullying which occurs as result of tics in line with school policy.

Learning

The exact nature of a child's tic will determine the impact on learning. A motor tic involving the arm or hand may lead to physical difficulties with handwriting. Distraction from learning tasks may occur due to the frequency of tics or the effort of trying to supress tics, particularly in front of peers. Children may require more time to complete tasks, and may benefit from additional written instructions if their attention and concentration has been impaired during initial teaching. It is important to be aware that conditions which commonly occur with tics, such as ADHD, may also impact on a child's attention and concentration.

When further help is needed for tics or Tourette's

Whilst the majority of tics do not require any specific treatment, those that are impacting on functioning, such as academically or socially may require specialist assessment. Some particularly vigorous or frequent motor tics may cause pain or muscle injury, which can also prompt a need for further help.

Summary

- The core features of ADHD include impulsivity, inattention and hyperactivity.

- Many more children may have difficulties in these areas than those receiving a formal diagnosis of ADHD.

- Children with these difficulties can benefit from some simple modifications relating to how work is presented and classroom seating arrangements.

- Transient, short-lived tics can be quite common and often do not need any intervention if they are not bothering the child.

- At least 20% of children with chronic tics will also have ADHD.

- Tics and ADHD can affect social confidence and self-esteem, and lead to an increase in negative emotions.

- It is helpful to know the impact a child's difficulties are having on them individually and agree approaches with parents.

- Generally, not reacting or responding to tics is the preferred approach, as drawing further attention to it often heightens anxiety and worsens the tic.

References

Bagheri M, Kerneshia J & Burd L (1999) Recognition and management of Tourette's syndrome and tic disorders. *American Family Physician* **59** (8) 2263–2272.

Biederman J, Monuteaux M, Doyle A et al (2004) Impact of executive function deficits and attention-deficit/hyperactivity disorder (ADHD) on academic outcomes in children. *Journal of Consulting and Clinical Psychology* **72** (5) 757–766.

Elia J, Ambrosini P & Berrettini W (2008) ADHD characteristics: I. Concurrent co-morbidity patterns in children & adolescents. *Child and Adolescent Psychiatry and Mental Health* **2** (1) 15.

Ford T, Goodman R & Meltzer H (2003) The British Child and Adolescent Mental Health Survey 1999: The prevalence of DSM-IV disorders. *Journal of the American Academy of Child Psychiatry* **42** 1203–1211.

NHS Digital (2017) *Mental Health of Children and Young People in England*. Available from https://dera.ioe.ac.uk/32622/1/MHCYP%202017%20Summary.pdf

NICE (2018) *Attention Deficit Hyperactivity Disorder: Diagnosis and Management*. NG87.

Reale L, Bartoli B, Cartabia M et al (2017) Comorbidity prevalence and treatment outcome in children and adolescents with ADHD. *European Journal of Child and Adolescent Psychiatry* **26** (12) 1443–1457.

Sayal K, Prasad V, Daley D et al (2017) ADHD in children and young people: Prevalence, care pathways, and service provision. *The Lancet Psychiatry* **5** (2) 175–186.

Chapter 13: Onset of Puberty and Gender Identity

Children naturally become aware of the differences between genders at an early age, assigning themselves to a particular sex by the age of four in most cases (Martin & Ruble, 2010). In the years that follow many children will gravitate towards friendship groups composed of the same gender, and will choose to express their gender through their choice of clothing, hairstyle, activities and interests. As children approach the later years of primary education they are likely to become more aware of their bodies, and some may begin puberty. This brings with it some practical issues to consider in a school setting, such as access to sanitary products and facilities for changing for PE lessons.

Onset of puberty

Case example: Onset of puberty

I've taught Charlotte for around six months in my Year 5 class, and her mum let me know that she started her period over the weekend. She is feeling quite embarrassed about it and doesn't want to do PE today.

Talking about puberty and periods

Puberty tends to occur earlier in girls than boys, with the first changes being breast development and vaginal discharge, often followed around a year later by menarche – the onset of periods (Tanner, 1962). Children will vary in how they handle the changes. Ideally, they will be well aware of what to expect ahead of time, and feel prepared and supported.

RSE lessons are the ideal place to begin exploring the concepts of these changes in the body; but the science curriculum also covers changes from birth to old age, including puberty. Generally, it is advised that children aged 9–11 are educated about the changing adolescent body, including physical and emotional changes (DfE, 2019). As the transition to secondary education and adolescence approaches, it is important that children are equipped with the knowledge to keep themselves safe and feel prepared.

Onset of puberty in school: what does this look like and how can we help?

As puberty approaches, children may display the following developmentally normal changes in behaviour:

- An increased desire for privacy when getting changed for PE.
- Some anxiety around PE or swimming lessons for girls who are beginning their periods.
- Changes in physical appearance for both sexes.
- Some secrecy, giggling and possible embarrassment in relation to conversations about sex.

Strategies

It is important to consider how the onset of puberty can present with regard to various aspects of school life and how strategies can be used to help children manage their emotional responses and overcome the subsequent barriers to their engagement and learning. The sections below will explore puberty in relation to the learning environment, emotional, behavioural and social regulation and learning related to this area.

Learning environment

From Year 5 onwards, if not sooner, it is important to ensure that different spaces are available when changing clothing. Some schools hang a curtain across the classroom from this age when children are changing for PE. In two-form entry schools this may be easier, as boys can change in one room and girls in another. If that is not possible other strategies may be trialled, such as small groups taking it in turns to change in the cloakroom, if this is out of sight.

Regarding periods, it is important to ensure that girls know who they can speak to if their period starts when at school and they need sanitary wear or support. This is especially relevant when approaching school journeys in Year 5 and 6. Discuss this with the girls in the class well in advance (informing the parents first). Ideally, there will be sanitary bins in all toilet cubicles from Year 3 upwards, rather than these being placed in specific areas such as disabled toilets, which children may feel reluctant to use.

Emotional, behavioural and social regulation

A whole-school and whole-class culture of respect and care for others is vital. The classroom must be a safe space for discussion and questions. This can help children feel they can be open and honest when it comes to issues that some may regard as sensitive, such as sex and puberty. Within a class group there is likely to be a range in levels of maturity, and there may be some differences between the genders. For some classes that are finding it difficult to remain sensible and focused on topics, teaching small groups separated by gender or otherwise can work best. However, it can be helpful to come together afterwards to share learning with the whole class.

Learning

At primary level, children may have questions about sex and sexuality that go beyond the scope of what is taught. While these questions should be handled in line with school policy, be aware that unanswered questions may result in online searches and access to potentially harmful and inaccurate sources of information. It is recommended by the Department for Education that schools consult with parents about the content of their sex education. Head teachers must comply with parents' wishes to remove their child from sex education lessons which go beyond the level of the science curriculum (DfE, 2019). Schools are also advised to ensure that their teaching and materials consider the age and religious background of the children.

It is important that education around topics such as periods is provided to all students, not simply girls. This enables boys to be aware of the changes that may be happening to their peers and also helps in removing the historic shame or stigma around menstruation.

❓ Thinking about ... sexual orientation

Children need age appropriate information about sex and sexuality. As part of RSE children should learn that relationships should be a source of mutual love and support between two people. It is important that children know that families and relationships come in different forms, but all have love at their core. Some children may have two mums or two dads. It is important to model acceptance and celebration of difference, which is likely to come from everyday routine conversations rather than one big 'talk'.

Gender identity

> ### Case example 2: Gender identity
>
> Daniel is an eight-year-old boy who has always tended to play only with the girls from his class. There have been incidents of the other boys in his class laughing at Daniel because he doesn't like football or other sports, and likes to play with dolls. His parents have told me that at home he wears a dress, and has been talking about wanting to be a girl from the age of three.

What is gender identity?

Most children develop a sense of their identified gender between the ages of two and four, when gendered behaviours and interests become more evident. However, it is common (and normal) for children to show an interest and enjoy playing with toys and games traditionally associated with either gender, and it is often societal norms and expectations that influence a child's preference.

Some children, even from a young age, will feel that their gender is different from the sex they were assigned at birth. They may express this in a range of ways through clothing and play and may also inform adults and peers around them that they feel they are the opposite gender. If this is met with a negative response or rejection they may internalise this unacceptance and become ashamed of how they feel. This could then lead on to problems such as depression and anxiety (Budge *et al*, 2013).

What is gender dysphoria?

'Gender dysphoria' is a term used to describe a conflict between a person's assigned, physical gender and the gender they identify themselves with. 'Transgender' is an umbrella term used to describe an individual with a gender identity which does not match their gender assigned at birth. The conflict experienced by someone with gender dysphoria can lead to significant distress and unhappiness, and can interfere with daily functioning. It often presents in childhood, although not all children who meet the criteria for gender dysphoria will continue to meet them in adulthood (Steensma *et al*, 2013). Research has suggested that children who display more intense symptoms and persistent distress, and those who use more declarative statements (e.g. 'I am a boy/girl' rather than 'I want to be a boy/girl'), are more likely to become transgender adults (Steensma *et al*, 2013).

Why does gender dysphoria occur?

It is not fully understood why a young person may develop feelings of gender dysphoria. The exact reasons are likely to vary between each individual and may include biological, social and psychological factors. There are many theories around why gender dysphoria develops, including the suggestion that it is something a child is 'born with', placing more emphasis on the biological factors. Another suggestion is that a child's experiences of different genders and how they relate to them, or difficult experiences in a child's life, may play more of a role than biology alone.

How common is gender dysphoria?

Whilst it is difficult to get an exact figure, a survey of 10,000 people in 2012 found that 1% were gender variant. Many more people may experiences these feelings but never tell anyone or seek help (Equality and Human Rights Commission, 2012).

Gender dysphoria in school: What does it look like and how can we help?

It is important to consider how gender dysphoria can impact on various aspects of a child's life in school. Schools are required to publish equality information and equality objectives. It is important to ensure that details of the school's approach to gender dysphoria is included in the equality policy. Additionally, there should be a whole-school approach to zero tolerance around bullying and discrimination, including issues around gender and sexuality.

It is helpful to try to agree with the child what they would like to be called and what pronouns will be used. Close communication with the child and parents regarding this will be important. Give the child the choice and control over this – your role will often be to just listen and be available for support. Some transgender and gender non-conforming people may prefer gender-neutral or gender-inclusive pronouns when talking to or about them. 'They' and 'their' are sometimes used as gender-neutral singular pronouns. Allow time for ongoing communication throughout the school year regarding the child's wishes. Once the child's wishes are known, there is a real need to ensure a consistent approach from all relevant adults in school, in order to avoid any inadvertent upset. If a child has chosen to dress differently or have different hair from a young age, this will likely be accepted by other children without question. Their peers have grown up with them. However, there will be times when children have questions; if appropriate, a small group discussion may be helpful. This may involve a child choosing a group of peers they feel comfortable talking to about their gender identity.

The following areas should also be addressed when planning how best to support children with gender dysphoria (Lancashire County Council, 2014):

- **Clothing**
  - School uniform policy should be followed as for any other child, and this should include providing a choice of approved items which will allow a fit with the child's gender identity. Ideally, an inclusive uniform policy will list all accepted items of clothing without defining these as 'male' and 'female'.
  - Choosing to dress in the uniform associated with a gender different to that assigned at birth is a big step, and can mark a child out as different from their peers.
  - Children will require support during this time. Teaching staff should be trained to ensure understanding of what this means to a child and why they may wish to do this. Allowing a child to dress in the clothes that they feel comfortable in can be empowering and gives a message of support and acceptance from the school.
  - On a non-uniform day, if a child chooses to wear clothes usually worn by the opposite assigned sex, this should be viewed as a positive choice. It shows they are comfortable in doing this, they feel ok to express themselves in this way and a positive environment has been created for them.
- **Toilets**
  - Toilet arrangements are a sensitive area. There may be concerns that children will be open to the risk of bullying when accessing the toilets for the opposite sex, but on the other hand transgender children want to be seen and treated as their true gender. Ideally, transgender children should be able to use the facilities of their preferred gender. If they do not feel comfortable doing this, then an accessible toilet or changing area should be offered.
- **Physical education**
  - It is important to ensure equal access to PE for all children. For children with gender dysphoria, there may be some specific issues which should be identified and discussed openly and honestly. Access to a separate changing area may be needed. As puberty begins, some female-to-male transgender young people choose to bind their chests. These children will require increased observation during physical activity to ensure that they don't overheat or that the binding isn't too tight, as this may impair breathing.

When further help is needed with gender identity

A diagnosis of gender dysphoria is usually made by a specialist service, although most children are initially seen by CAMHS. The Gender Identity Development

Service (GIDS), which has clinics in London and Leeds, is the only service of its kind in the UK and offers support for children and young people, and their families, who experience difficulties in the development of their gender identity. GIDS will usually ask for CAMHS to remain involved in supporting a child therapeutically. Not all people with gender dysphoria will come in contact with services, and this decision must be driven by the child and their family.

Summary

- Puberty typically occurs earlier in girls than boys.

- Practical considerations in the school environment include access to sanitary products and private changing areas.

- Children need age appropriate information on sex and relationships. Avoidance of questions may lead to them accessing potentially inaccurate information from peers or online.

- Some children may have a gender identity which does not match their assigned sex at birth.

- It is recommended that schools have an equality policy which includes consideration of the needs of transgender children.

References

Budge S, Adelson J & Howard K (2013) Anxiety and depression in transgender individuals: The roles of transition status, loss, social support, and coping. *Journal of Consulting and Clinical Psychology* **81** (3) 545–557.

Department for Education (2019) *Relationships Education, Relationships and Sex Education (RSE) and Health Education*. Available from https://assets.publishing.service.gov.uk/government/uploads/system/uploads/attachment_data/file/781150/Draft_guidance_Relationships_Education__Relationships_and_Sex_Education__RSE__and_Health_Education2.pdf

Equality and Human Rights Commission (2012) *Technical Note: Measuring Gender Identity*. Available from https://www.equalityhumanrights.com/en/publication-download/technical-note-measuring-gender-identity

Gender Identity Service (GIDS) (2019) *Guidance for Schools*. Available from http://gids.nhs.uk/professionals#guidance-for-schools

Lancashire Children and Young People's Trust (2014) *Transgender Guidance*. Available from https://www.blackpoolsafeguarding.org.uk/assets/uploads/resources/Children/Trans%20Guidance%20Finalmarch1714_2_nowmark%5B1%5D%5B1%5D.pdf

Martin C & Ruble D (2010) Patterns of gender development. *Annual Review of Psychology* **61** 353–381.

Sherer I *et al* (2015) Affirming gender: Caring for gender-atypical children and adolescents. *Contemporary Pediatrics*. Available from www.contemporarypediatrics.com/article/affirming-gender-caring-gender-atypical-children-and-adolescents

Steensma T *et al* (2013) Factors associated with desistence and persistence of childhood gender dysphoria: A quantitative follow-up study. *Journal of American Academy of Child and Adolescent Psychiatry* **52** (6) 582–590.

Tanner J (1962) *Growth of Adolescents*. Oxford: Blackwell Scientific Publications.

Chapter 14: Eating Disorders

Eating disorders

What are eating disorders?

All children have their own likes and dislikes regarding food, with a smaller number showing more extreme avoidance of certain food groups or textures. There may be a number of reasons for this, such as sensory aversions (as sometimes seen in ASC), a dislike of new foods or anxiety around particular foods, including fears of choking or vomiting. Sometimes the difficulties are so severe that they impair a child's growth and may be given the diagnostic label of 'avoidant and restrictive food intake disorder (ARFID). A child who is low in mood or experiencing other mental health difficulties may also find that their appetite is impaired.

The types of eating and feeding difficulties in children described above are usually not related to a wish to lose weight or concerns about body shape and image. They are therefore considered as quite separate to eating disorders such as anorexia nervosa and bulimia nervosa, which centre on overvalued ideas[3] and a preoccupation with weight and body shape. There may be a range of difficulties underlying an eating disorder, including attachment difficulties or issues within the whole family, over-valuing of competitive sporting activities and other mental health difficulties.

With this in mind, it is easy to see that there may be a number of reasons why a child is avoiding foods, and uncovering these reasons may take some time. The primary concern is to ensure that a child is physically well, particularly if they have lost a large amount of weight over a short time period. Exploration of the reasons behind the avoidance is less urgent.

The most commonly known eating disorders are anorexia nervosa and bulimia nervosa. Although there are specific criteria for the diagnosis of these conditions, which are discussed below, children struggling with their weight and eating will

---

3   A belief which a person is preoccupied with and which dominates their life. They are usually less fixed and less bizarre in nature than a delusion.

require support regardless of whether or not they receive a formal diagnosis. The sooner this support is accessed, the better the outcomes. Younger children in particular seem vulnerable to the physical effects of rapid weight loss.

Case example part 1: Unknown eating disorder

Lillian is ten years old. She brings her own packed lunch to school but I saw her throw her sandwich in the bin one day, and then again later in the week. The other day I overheard her talking to her friends about 'needing to go on a diet'. Her mum also told me that she's wanting to get more exercise, so she's begun walking the mile to school instead of getting the bus.

Developing an interest in health and appearance can be completely normal, particularly as a child approaches puberty. Wanting to eat the right food and look after your body is not in itself a cause for concern. Distinguishing between a wish for a healthier lifestyle and the onset of an eating disorder such as anorexia nervosa can be difficult – initially many people will see a child wishing to eat more vegetables and exercise more as a positive thing. It can take experienced clinicians some time to fully complete an assessment and schools should not be expected to identify an eating disorder, but rather to notice change and escalate this if there are concerns.

The most recent data in the UK suggested that around 6% of adults displayed features of an eating disorder (Adult Psychiatric Morbidity Survey, 2007) but data for children is lacking, particularly pre-adolescents. Although classically the onset of eating disorders is around the time of puberty, it is thought that the number of pre-pubertal onset cases is rising. In one study up to 60% of girls aged 6-12 were said to be concerned about their weight or about becoming too fat (Smolak, 2011).

If you are concerned about a child showing signs of a possible eating disorder then early discussion with parents is vital. Younger onset of eating disorders can result in greater risks to physical health as young children are more vulnerable to the effects of rapid weight loss and may require admission to a paediatric ward. One study found that half of all cases involving under thirteen year olds required admission (Nicholls, 2011). Earlier onset can also be linked to a poorer prognosis and treatment outcome, making early detection and treatment even more important.

Anorexia nervosa

Case example part 2: Anorexia nervosa

Lillian is now visibly losing weight – I've noticed that her school uniform looks baggy and she appears to be struggling to concentrate in lessons. At lunchtime, rather than sitting with her friends, she is walking laps around the playground.

In the case above it seems that many classic features of an eating disorder are developing, and although there could be other reasons behind the weight loss, specialist assessment is likely to be needed. The concerns would need to be discussed as a priority with a child's parent or guardian, if this has not already been done. Initially a child will need to see their GP, and if there are concerns that they are physically unwell they may require assessment by a paediatrician. Alongside this, the child will likely be referred to a CAMHS team or specialist eating disorder service. If concerns remain and the school feels that the child's parent or guardian are not responding appropriately or seeking further support, then this may become a safeguarding matter, which should be handled in accordance with school policy.

What is anorexia nervosa?

Anorexia nervosa is a type of eating disorder in which a person becomes preoccupied with their weight and shape, which in turn affects their relationship with food. Losing weight can become a priority and can dictate all actions and behaviours. The more weight a child loses, the less their brain can concentrate on activities.

Anorexia nervosa has the highest mortality rate of any psychiatric condition (Arcelus *et al*, 2011) and can result in serious physical complications affecting all parts of the body. In particular, the effect of sudden weight loss on the heart can result in low blood pressure and heart rate, which can lead to dizziness and collapse. If a girl has already started her periods these will often stop as the body lacks the fat and nutrients needed to produce adequate hormones to prompt ovulation. If periods have not yet started, their onset could be delayed and this could have long-term effects on both fertility and growth.

A child who is getting insufficient calories is likely to become low in energy, with reduced concentration. A change in their mood may be noticed, and they may become withdrawn and socially isolated. Academic work may be impacted but often a child with anorexia nervosa will have perfectionist traits and will work hard to maintain high standards. This may delay detection of difficulties.

Why does anorexia nervosa occur?

The exact reason why eating disorders, including anorexia nervosa, develop may never be known and can vary between individuals, but it often includes genetic, social and biological factors. Examples of these include being overweight as a child, a family history of eating disorders or extreme dieting and personality traits, such as perfectionism.

How common is anorexia nervosa?

Estimates suggest that over 700,000 people in the UK have an eating disorder, 90% of whom are female (NICE, 2019). These figures only include those presenting to services however, so this is likely to be an underestimate. The lifetime prevalence of anorexia nervosa in women is said to be 2-4% (NICE, 2019).

How is anorexia nervosa diagnosed?

The diagnosis of anorexia nervosa is made when the preoccupation with weight and shape is accompanied by a reduction in weight to less than 85% of that expected (with 100% being the average weight for a child of that age and height). Particular behaviours are often associated with this weight loss, such as a restriction in food intake and exclusion of certain food groups considered by the child as unhealthy, induced vomiting, increased exercise and the use of diet pills or laxatives. Some of these behaviours are more likely to be seen in older adolescent age groups than in younger children.

When further help is needed for anorexia nervosa

Restoration of body weight is the primary aim of initial treatment for anorexia nervosa. Although it is regarded as a psychiatric illness, individual talking therapy is unlikely to help someone who is underweight as their brain is unlikely to be able to engage in this process while malnourished. Instead, current evidence tells us that family-based support to empower parents to take control of feeding to restore a child's weight is the best way of recovering from an eating disorder. Later, there may be a role for individual therapy for the child (NICE, 2017).

Bulimia nervosa

Case example: Bulimia nervosa

I've noticed that Kasey doesn't seem to eat much at school, but her Mum has told me she keeps finding empty packets of crisps and chocolate bars hidden under her bed. On a school trip recently she seemed to eat a big meal at lunchtime but disappeared to the toilet shortly afterwards and another girl thought she had heard her being sick.

What is bulimia nervosa?

Bulimia nervosa is a type of eating disorder in which there are episodes of bingeing; eating an amount of food larger than most people would usually eat during a similar period of time and in similar circumstances. During these episodes there is a feeling of a lack of control and an inability to stop. Binges are then 'compensated' for in order to avoid weight gain. This could be through 'purging' by vomiting, or through using laxatives, diuretics or other medications used to purge the body of this excess food. Alternatively, 'non-purging' compensatory behaviours include restriction of food intake or fasting and excessive exercise. There will also be overvalued ideas around weight and shape, and a fear of being overweight.

The effects of bulimia nervosa may be similar to those of anorexia nervosa in terms of the impact on mood and concentration although the person is often of normal weight. Recurrent vomiting can have additional physical effects including dental problems and changes in the body's electrolytes which can be detected by blood tests. Some electrolyte imbalances can affect the heart and cause abnormal heart rhythms.

Why does bulimia nervosa occur?

The exact reason why eating disorders, including bulimia nervosa, develop may never be known and can vary between individuals, but it often includes genetic, social and biological factors. Examples of these include being overweight as a child, a family history of eating disorders or extreme dieting and personality traits, such as perfectionism.

How common is bulimia nervosa?

Bulimia nervosa is uncommon in children and tends to begin in adolescence or early adulthood. As the person is often of normal weight it can be easier to hide, and may go undetected for some time. There can be some overlap between the eating disorders and a person with anorexia nervosa may also have met the criteria for bulimia nervosa at some point in time, and vice versa. The prevalence of bulimia nervosa in Europe has been reported as less than 1–2% (NICE, 2019).

How is bulimia nervosa diagnosed?

Bulimia nervosa may be diagnosed in a person with a preoccupation around weight and shape associated with binges and actions to counteract the effects of these. These behaviours will be happening at least weekly, for a period of at least three months (American Psychiatric Association, 2013).

When further help is needed for bulimia nervosa

CAMHS professionals will work with GPs and, if needed, paediatricians to ensure the physical wellbeing of a child with bulimia nervosa. They will also offer therapeutic support. This may involve family-based therapy or a type of individual CBT specific to bulimia nervosa (CBT-BN).

Other feeding and eating difficulties

Sometimes a child may be experiencing difficulties around eating, but not fit the criteria for conditions such as anorexia or bulimia nervosa. In these cases, the term 'otherwise specified eating disorder' or OSFED may be used by CAMHS or paediatricians. Management usually follows the eating disorder that the symptoms most closely resemble.

As previously mentioned, some children with a very restricted diet may receive a diagnosis of ARFID. The management of ARFID will depend on the underlying causes, which may be sensory or anxiety related. ARFID is not currently included in NICE guidelines, so management can vary between services.

Eating disorders in school: what do they look like and how can we help?

It is important to consider how eating disorders can present with regard to various aspects of school life and how strategies can be used to help children manage their emotional responses and overcome the subsequent barriers to their engagement and learning. The discussion below explores the potential impact of eating disorders in school and how this can be addressed.

Early identification of difficulties with eating and concerns about weight and shape is of vital importance. A child who is developing an eating disorder may exhibit the following types of behaviours:

- Eating in secret or alone.
- Increased exercise, including tapping feet and fidgeting in chair.
- New eating behaviours, such as cutting out 'fatty' food groups or chopping up food into small pieces.
- Denial of clear attempts to lose weight.
- Denial of hunger or cravings.
- Visiting the bathroom straight after meals.
- New food rules, such as sudden vegetarianism or veganism.
- Social isolation and withdrawal from activities.

Without enough calories for their body and brain to function properly, a child with an eating disorder may also appear tired, lacking in concentration and low in mood. They may appear more withdrawn, spending less time with friends and not seeming to enjoy their usual activities and interests.

Teaching staff may also notice children who appear to have low self-esteem, and who could be at risk of placing more value on their external appearance than on their other skills and attributes. They should be alert to the behaviours above and register concerns with the child's parents and the SENCO as soon as possible.

If a child is clearly having difficulties around eating, a conversation with them and their parents to agree how this will be managed practically during school time can be helpful. This may include extra snacks being sent in from home, and agreeing where meals and snacks will be eaten. The child may require a quieter environment in which to eat.

A child who is underweight and receiving support for an eating disorder may be advised to take time off school to conserve energy during their recovery. While schools may be asked to provide some work to be completed at home, the priority must be achieving weight gain and physical stability during this time. When they are in school, it is often advised that they refrain from participating in sports or PE lessons. This can be distressing for a child who feels that this marks them out as different, and who may have previously been an avid or often competitive player of sport. Decisions around a child re-joining such activities should be led by the professionals involved in their treatment, who will have access to their latest weight, blood results and other measures, which will guide such a decision.

There may be occasions when a child's parents disagree with the decision of professionals, particularly if they feel that abstaining from physical activities is adversely affecting their child's mood. For this reason, it is important that there is good communication between all involved. Consent should be sought from families to enable schools to speak freely to health professionals about their child. Keep in mind that eating disorders often require a multi-disciplinary approach to their treatment including support from CAMHS, paediatrics and GPs and following advice given is essential.

There are many opportunities to promote healthy eating and lifestyles within the curriculum and in doing so, we can support those who are struggling with eating difficulties and those who may be vulnerable to these difficulties developing. It is possible to use science, relevant non-fiction texts in literacy, PSHE and PE to provide specific teaching on the need for a balanced diet (including healthy amounts of fat), appropriate amounts of physical activity relative to a child's age and how to strive for a healthy body image. Encouraging conversations about these areas when they arise is important, as is modelling a healthy approach to food and physical activity. Adults eating with children at lunchtime is the ideal. However, it is difficult to achieve this every day with all the other demands on our time. A weekly rota which includes all school staff can support this regular modelling of healthy behaviours around food.

Summary

- There are many reasons why a child may eat a limited diet, including long-standing food dislikes or aversions, reduced appetite in relation to physical activity or mental illness, or the development of an eating disorder.

- Anorexia and bulimia nervosa usually have their onset in adolescence and young adulthood, but the number of cases presenting in younger children appears to be rising.

- Eating disorders often require a combination of physical health monitoring and psychological therapy.

- As well as weight loss, a child with an eating disorder may also experience reduced energy and concentration and low mood. This can impact on all areas of their development – physical, psychological, social and academic.

- Key strategies to support children involve ensuring that a child is comfortable with the arrangements for eating, following the guidance given from CAMHS regarding physical activity and building opportunities into the school day to foster healthy attitudes and behaviours around food.

References

Adult Psychiatric Morbidity Survey, Results of a Household Survey (2007). Available from https://digital.nhs.uk/data-and-information/publications/statistical/adult-psychiatric-morbidity-survey/adult-psychiatric-morbidity-in-england-2007-results-of-a-household-survey

American Psychiatric Association (2013) *Diagnostic and Statistical Manual of Mental Disorders* (5th ed.). Arlington, VA: American Psychiatric Publishing.

Arcelus J, Mitchell AJ, Wales J & Nielsen S (2011) Mortality rates in patients with Anorexia Nervosa and other eating disorders. *Archives of General Psychiatry* **68** (7) 724–731.

NICE (2017) *Eating Disorders: Recognition and Treatment*. London: NICE.

NICE (2019) *Clinical Knowledge Summary: Eating Disorders*. Available from https://cks.nice.org.uk/eating-disorders#!topicSummary. London: NICE.

Nicholls DE, Lynn R & Viner RM (2011) Childhood eating disorders: British national surveillance study. *British Journal of Psychiatry* **198** 295–301.

Smolak L (2011) Body image development in childhood. In T. Cash & L. Smolak (Eds.) *Body Image: A Handbook of science, practice, and prevention* (2nd ed.). New York: Guilford Press.

Section 4: Transitions

Chapter 15: Transition into the Early Years Foundation Stage

A framework for transition

Although many children now attend a nursery or preschool for several hours a day, with the possibility of additional wrap-around care to support working parents, the transition into the formal learning environment of school is still a hugely significant step in the life of a child. Teaching staff should begin with the expectation that all children will find this transition a challenge, at least initially. It is natural that engagement in a new setting, with new adults, and involving a separation from their primary caregivers, will be appropriately met with some caution or trepidation by young children. Some will adapt quickly and thrive on the routine and challenge. Others may take more time to adjust, needing extra support in school and at home. A smaller number of children will find the transition into the EYFS a significant hurdle. If schools can identify who the children in the latter two groups are likely to be, they will be able to provide them with the appropriate support at an early stage, hopefully pre-empting some issues before they even arise. From the outset of the EYFS, teaching staff must ensure that all children understand that school is a safe place for them to be.

The statutory framework for the EYFS states that the four guiding principles of early years settings are:

1. Every child is unique.
2. Children learn through positive relationships.
3. Children learn well in enabling, responsive environments, in which there are strong partnerships between staff and families.
4. Children develop and learn in different ways and at different rates.

(Department for Education, 2017)

Taking these principles into consideration, all EYFS transition activities need to happen with the intentions of:

- Getting to know the unique child and building relationships with them and their family.

- Enabling the child and family to familiarise themselves with the environments around school and the routines of their new class.

- Identifying which children may need extra support and planning for these additional needs.

Transition opportunities

Getting to know each child as well as possible prior to their start date will enable teaching staff to support their wellbeing effectively from the outset. The information gathered about home life, the child's interests and any additional needs will support planning and provides good foundations for the relationship with the child and parents. Each county council will have their own arrangements and expectations for transition into the EYFS. Schools may take their lead from this, but they can also innovate within the county council guidance and provide creative transition opportunities suited to their school and their new intake.

Handover from external EYFS providers

Formal handover from nurseries and preschools may take the form of individual meetings or cluster-style meetings, whereby several schools and feeder nurseries and preschools come together for a handover. In a cluster-style meeting, each setting is able to highlight those children with additional needs, share the support they have already been providing and which approaches they have found to be particularly effective for an individual child. They can also suggest who may benefit from early interventions and different levels of support.

Home visits

Although the statutory framework for the EYFS does not lay out an expectation for home visits, they are considered by some early years practitioners to be a cornerstone of transition arrangements. Conducting home visits in the summer term rather than in September allows adults to get to know children well in advance of them starting. If supply cover can be arranged, it is really beneficial for both the class teacher and TA to attend. Seeing how a child plays and interacts in their home environment can be useful for teaching staff, and the experience is also beneficial for the child as they begin to establish trusting relationships and develop a perception that these adults are safe. It can also be very helpful for parents, who will feel listened to and supported and will benefit from the opportunity to talk to the new teacher about their child's areas of interest, strengths and difficulties.

School visits

If initial school visits take place early on in the summer term, there is then, potentially, time for additional transition visits for particular children, over and above what would normally be offered. This may take the form of a small group of children and their parents being invited to visit the relevant nursery or Reception classroom on several occasions to try out a range of activities at different times of the day. If children are likely to need specialist support, these visits can also be an opportunity to invite external professionals or on-site teams in to the classroom, or facilitate individual meetings. This may involve speech and language support or school nurses, who can begin to discuss concerns such as communication difficulties and toileting in school. Teaching staff can run activities for the children, while parents are able to speak to these professionals and seek appropriate support and advice where necessary.

Many schools invite children entering Reception to attend for a lunchtime session, either by themselves or with parents. This can familiarise them with lunchtime routines and give them an opportunity to eat with other children in the busy dining room environment. Children can also spend time exploring the playground and getting used to extended outdoor playtime.

Observing children during these all transition visits can reveal much valuable information about their needs, how they interact with others, how stressed or dysregulated they appear to be and what activities they self-select. This can all then feed into the planning process for the autumn term.

Transition journals

It is hugely important that we make it easy for parents to find information about the process of starting school and what the EYFS will look like for their child. It is also helpful if appropriate information is accessible for children too. Designing a journal to support the transition process can benefit all parties. The school can provide important information and helpful tips for preparing children for the start of term; the parent and child can provide key information about interests, strengths, dislikes and areas of need; and the child can view visual prompts, such as photos and a visual timetable to increase their understanding of where they will be and what will happen in the autumn. The 'Thinking about...' box below explores this idea further. The journal should give parents the overall message that all children are unique and, as such, will have different starting points and learning journeys in the EYFS. It should be a working document that a child has at home over the holidays. It can then travel to and from school with the child so that teaching staff can note down key information given by the child and parent. Eventually, this should be kept by the child as a record of their transition (and as a source of information for parents).

? Thinking about ... creating an EYFS transition journal

An EYFS transition journal could include:

- School pages:
  - Information on the school community and the overall ethos.
  - Information on the structure of the school day and expectations around punctuality and attendance.
  - Contact details for relevant members of the school community.
  - EYFS curriculum information.
  - Hints and tips for preparing a child for school:
    - helping a child to recognise their name
    - advice regarding sleep and bedtime routines, eating and diet, hand washing, using a tissue and toileting
    - encouraging children to alert adults to their needs
    - encouraging social interactions with other children
    - encouraging a child to try new experiences
    - encouraging mark making
    - encouraging a gradual increase of responsibility at home e.g. with tidying up or helping in the kitchen
    - information on school uniform, with pictures of children dressed correctly and advice on how to dress and undress independently
    - guidance on gradually matching up the child's daily routine to that of school over the holidays e.g. having lunch at the same time and practising the journey to school
    - suggestions of activities for during the holidays e.g. looking at old school photos of family members and discussing happy memories of school
    - suggestions of books to read with the child about starting school.

- Parent pages:
  - Space for parent to provide key information about their child:
    - likes and dislikes
    - strengths and talents
    - interests
    - areas of additional need.
- Child pages:
  - photos of the EYFS teaching team and other significant adults e.g. the SENCO and headteacher
  - photos of the classroom, dining room, hall and the outdoor space
  - space for photos of the child and special family members
  - basic visual timetable showing the structure of the day
  - space for child to share:
    - What am I looking forward to about starting school?
    - What am I worried about?

Beginning with wellbeing in mind

Making wellbeing a priority from a child's early days in school encourages this concept to become embedded for them. If we can normalise the daily wellbeing practices discussed in *Chapter 4: Wellbeing for All* and encourage children to develop their emotional and social intelligence at this stage, we will provide them with a firm foundation for life.

We know that early intervention is desirable for all children with mental health difficulties. At this stage, especially in the early days of transition, it is hard to know if a concern is simply related to temperament, an overall resistance to transition or an actual emerging mental health presentation. Ensuring that concerns are recorded during the EYFS will greatly support planning for Key Stage 1 (KS1). It is also helpful to begin to put some strategies into place at this early stage, when there are more adults in the classroom.

It is important to highlight that a child's difficulties might not be easily identifiable within the environment and expectations of the EYFS. Demands placed on children are typically fairly low, as a child-centred approach with a high degree of free play and choice is utilised. However, a child may subsequently struggle with the transition to Year 1 due to increased academic expectations, a greater level of structure and daily routine and the need to get used to a different classroom environment and new teacher. However, even during the EYFS, neurodevelopmental differences such as ASC and ADHD may be emerging, and attachment difficulties may also be evident. It is therefore important to remain alert to the signs of these presentations from the very beginning of a child's school journey.

With special thanks to St. Richard Reynolds Catholic Primary, Twickenham for sharing their innovative EYFS transition practices with us.

Summary

- No matter what the nature of a child's previous childcare experiences, the transition to full-time school will be a challenge to all.

- Reinforcing the idea that school is a safe place to be for all children will support the transition from the outset.

- Effective handover from external EYFS providers, home visits and a variety of opportunities for children and parents to visit the school underpin a smooth transition.

- Creative transition journals provide a connection between school and home. Input from all parties make these a valuable tool for the school holidays and beyond.

- Embedding wellbeing practices into the school day from the beginning of the EYFS will provide children with a strong foundation for learning.

- Signs of neurodevelopmental conditions and attachment difficulties can begin to emerge in the EYFS, therefore it is important for all teaching staff to be aware of these.

References

Statutory Framework for the Early Years Foundation Stage: Setting the Standards for Learning, Development and Care for Children from Birth to Five. Department for Education (2017). London: DfE.

Chapter 16: Daily Transitions

Multiple daily transitions are part of the fabric of our lives. As adults, we may move through them on auto-pilot if we don't perceive there to be any associations with threat or loss. Children are less likely than adults to feel in control of transitions and this can contribute to stress. This is especially true when transitions are unacknowledged or hasty and for those with pre-existing mental health difficulties. The stress may be unconsciously or consciously masked by a child, or it may be clearly seen in their emotional state and behaviours. However, if daily transitions are managed well, they can allow children to mindfully close the metaphorical door on one place or activity and move forward to the next with intention.

Movement through the school day can sometimes feel smooth and effortless; at other times it can be an uphill struggle. How can daily school transitions be curated to allow them to support wellbeing for all, and in particular for those children who have mental health difficulties? As always, teaching staff need to know the children well and have a good understanding of what they need at particular times of the day. Keep checking in with the children who seem to be struggling with particular transitions. Key considerations for these children might be:

■ Which moments are especially tricky for them?

■ Do they realise that they are finding these transitions difficult?

■ How do they typically respond?

■ How does this affect the next activity?

■ How does it affect their peers?

■ Can they explain why it is hard for them?

Once these conversations have begun, teaching staff need to work in ongoing partnership with the child to create strategies and solutions that will benefit all. This is another approach that may seem like a huge investment of time on the part of teaching staff, but the results can be transformative. Alongside this, mindfully building in predictable daily routines and rituals for all children will lessen the impact of those unpredictable moments that each day inevitably brings.

This chapter will explore some of the major transition points in the school day: moving from home to school, small transitions within the classroom, moving around the school, playtime transitions and from school to home. Finally, it will look at some specific considerations for children with mental health difficulties.

Daily transition routines and rituals

From home to school

Making children feel welcome, valued and wanted as they enter the classroom is so important. Provide consistency in this first transition of the day, by having either the class teacher or TA on the door greeting children. Many schools now encourage all children to shake hands with their teacher as they enter the classroom, fostering mutual respect. Try to make greetings as personal as time allows. This moment of crossing the threshold into school is immensely difficult for some children. ***Chapter 7: Anxiety, Panic and OCD*** explores separation anxiety in detail and gives strategies for managing the most challenging of situations. Encourage parents to leave the immediate area of the classroom once children are in the building. Though many will enjoy one last wave, for some this only prolongs the transition.

Once children are settled into the classroom, they need a predictable, calm and gentle morning routine: hanging up their bag and coat, placing reading books or homework in the designated boxes and completing self-registration, if necessary. Create the high expectation that all of this will be done without fuss or loud chatter. Making morning starter tasks inviting and inspirational can encourage a reluctant child to begin to engage with the school day. Visual prompts and interesting questions that allow free thinking and creativity may work for some, whereas others may prefer a more structured spelling, grammar or handwriting task. If possible, offer a choice. Perhaps play calming music to support this, if appropriate for all. Above all, teaching staff need to make it easy for the children to want to be in the classroom.

In the classroom

All teaching staff will understand the importance of creating safe and predictable routines within the classroom environment. These support learning activities, help everyone to look after the space and encourage positive interactions between children and adults. There are always certain trigger points during the day, however (and these will be different for every class), that may lead some children to lose focus or become distressed or even dysregulated. Consider what these might be for your class. They could include:

- the transition from the carpet to tables in the middle of a lesson
- movement around the classroom to gather resources
- snack time
- tidy up time
- movement breaks (sometimes the very thing that is designed to calm children can have the exact opposite effect!).

Take time to explore these trigger points and try out possible approaches to calming them. Creating quiet games and challenges to support some may work. It may be that high-energy movement breaks are only appropriate at certain times of the day, for example, just before playtime, and a mid-lesson movement break may need to be gentle yoga instead so that children can maintain their focus on learning. Having resources stored in an accessible central area, or ideally on tables, may help to lessen unnecessary wandering in lesson time.

Ultimately, flexibility is needed, and teaching staff must consider what is needed in the moment. Sometimes the answer is rest and a story, sometimes it is a few minutes' meditation and sometimes the children need a chance to chat with one another and an adult. Sometimes they just need to visit the toilet – even older children can forget or put this off as long as possible until it starts to affect their concentration. It helps everyone to pause in the transition time and reflect on what is needed before becoming ready to embark on the next learning activity.

A visual timetable is a cornerstone of routine in all classrooms and for children of all ages. The 'Thinking about…' box below considers how to make the most of this resource.

❓ Thinking about … visual timetables for all

Displaying a visual timetable benefits all children, but especially those with mental health difficulties.

- Display the timetable in a prominent location, where you can easily refer to it and children can reach it to move events around if needed.
- Use colourful pictures and words, but keep the cards simple and uncluttered so they are easy to understand.
- When time allows, explain events on the timetable in a more detailed way, outlining the rhythms of school life that we must all follow: 'This extra assembly is really important for us all because it's about road safety', 'This spelling test is something I need to do with you all each term' or 'This trip to Forest School is a nice treat at the end of the week for you all'. →

- When speaking to individual children about more personalised (and portable) timetables, highlight any differences in their week and show them any slots where they may be able to choose a favourite activity.

- Explain to all that you always try to provide a balance in the week. Not every child will love every lesson in the same way, so there will always be a variety of activities on the timetable and different types of learning going on

- Make it clear to children each morning that 'This is our plan for the day, as far as I know'. Acknowledge that sometimes changes will happen to the timetable that are beyond anyone's control. Explain that you will tell them about changes as soon as possible (and really stick to that). Remind children that they can ask questions about the timetable during the day or week.

- It is really helpful to recap a visual timetable as a closing ritual at the end of the day. Ask a child to use the visual timetable to tell the 'Story of our day' to the rest of the class. This simple method of positive reflection gives a sense of completion to the day and allows a chance for the class to bond over funny moments or situations where something went wrong. Perhaps they solved a problem together, encountered 'marvellous mistakes' or achieved something impressive. Explain that this is not a time to bring up difficult incidents or squabbles. This is so that everyone leaves class feeling good about something in their day, however small. Encourage all the children to share a highlight of their day with the child sitting next to them. This will help children to leave school each day with a sense of achievement and belonging.

- For older children, even if you think no one in the class is using the visual timetable, don't be tempted to remove it. Even if it is not being referred to, it may be providing reassurance and structure for many who simply glance at it during transitions or those who like to keep track of where they are in the day.

Moving around the school

Transitions from one area of the school to another happen multiple times a day. How smoothly these transitions go depends on countless unpredictable factors – though there are some key considerations that ensure things are not left to chance! A high expectation of how to walk respectfully and sensibly between different areas needs to be embedded in whole-school culture. Appropriate role modelling from the older children can really support those younger children who may be struggling.

Setting a class routine for lining up is essential. There are many different ways to do this, but we suggest choosing a fixed order, which changes once or twice in each half of the term. Some children are acutely attuned to the concept of fairness and at times it is best to completely avoid the debate of 'who gets to go at the front of the line'.

For those children who struggle to regulate their behaviour, lining up can also be a time of negative comparison to other children. If they are not conforming, they may be sent to the back of the line or asked to stand with an adult – neither of which will necessarily help the situation. Remembering to playfully engage children and provide enjoyable distraction at these times can be beneficial. Make lining up a time that children can look forward to – a chance for class bonding, singing a song or reciting a funny poem. However successful this may be, there is no doubt that maintaining this constant engagement throughout the entire day is hard work. Sharing the load between different members of teaching staff can help.

For some children who find these transitions particularly hard, consider if it is possible to decrease the number of transitions in a day. A change of location can be beneficial to learning and can be helpful in diffusing various escalating situations, but equally, many transitions in a short space of time will simply be too much for some children with mental health difficulties.

To and from the playground

The transitions to and from the playground can be some of the most difficult of the day. For children who find this more challenging, consider the following:

- At the start of playtime:
  - Has there been an opportunity to properly 'close' the last lesson? Leaving learning unfinished or unconcluded can be unsettling for some and make the day feel hurried and disjointed.
  - How are children getting out of the classroom? Is it a calm transition or do they rush out all at once? Are there 'bottle-necks' where everyone is pushing and shoving?
  - Do some children delay leaving the classroom as long as possible, or return after they have left? Be alert for these signs that they may be finding the playground environment a challenge.
  - Are children reminded to eat, drink and use the toilet at playtimes? Many children will not think of these important self-care activities when they are desperate to get out of the building and play or run.
- At the end of playtime:
  - How do children come back into the classroom? Do you collect them from a line outside? Is there an opportunity for them to spend a few moments getting ready for learning outside, before they come back in?
  - Are there systems in place for dealing with playtime incidents? Even managing minor squabbles can slow the start of the next lesson. For more significant incidents that involve behaviours that challenge, there may

need to be an agreed procedure to follow, especially if there is a pattern for a particular child. The same applies for any children who do not return independently after playtime. An identified adult (perhaps a TA or member of the pastoral support team) can support these individual children back into class once any concerns have been dealt with.

- Do children know what to do when they return to class? Is there a note on the board telling them where to go and what they need? Perhaps this message has already been given before they went outside? Be as organised as possible so that there is little room for hesitation or wandering around the classroom.

- Once the class are settled, it might be appropriate to take a few quiet moments for reflection, deep breathing, mindfulness practice or a short mediation. This allows all to return to a calmer state, in which they are more likely to be able to listen and focus on the next learning activity. See *Chapter 5: Building Emotional Intelligence* for further discussion on this.

When the transition from the playground to the classroom is causing a child significant difficulty e.g. when incidents involving dysregulated behaviour are occurring on most days, a personalised plan needs to be put into place. It may be that the prospect of returning to learning after the freedom of the playground is too much for the child to cope with on their own and the frustrations caused by this then lead to difficult situations with peers. One option could be a phased transition back into the classroom, where the child spends the last ten minutes of playtime in alternative provision, such a nurture or sensory room. Here they can still play, but activities are calmer and the child can slowly re-regulate to a state in which they are ready to learn. After an agreed amount of time, they can then re-join their class within the classroom once everyone is seated and settled.

From school to home

Closing routines and rituals at the end of each school day and week are incredibly important for all children (and adults!). In the 'Thinking about...' on p.241, we discussed how the visual timetable can be used as a tool for reflection at home time – recapping events, acknowledging tricky moments (but not dwelling on them) and being grateful for the positive moments and successes of the day (see also *Chapter 5*). There are many ways to develop this into a closing ritual that suits each child, depending on their age and preferences. They could use a reflection journal that they have made to draw or write the moments of their day, or they may prefer to share these verbally with an adult or a friend. Crucially, this shouldn't take a long time – keeping it short and sweet is often key to children wanting to take part. It is very important for the adults in the room to take part too and model the process. Teaching staff can share their own highlights and an area to improve on the next day. For example, 'I got quite grumpy when lots of you came running into class after break. Tomorrow, I will work hard to stay calm when I remind you of our class rules.' Some of the following reflection questions could be used at the end of a day or week:

- What have I enjoyed?
- What have I learnt about myself?
- What were my big achievements?
- When was I disappointed? Why?
- What did I find hard?
- What surprised me?
- What am I grateful for?

When time is short, as it often is at the end of a school day, a simple gratitude practice will suffice. Asking the children to share (or think of) one thing they are grateful for (or proud of) still provides a sense of closure and peace to the end of the day. Depending on the specific needs of the children in the class, it is probably not wise to say too much (or anything at all) about the following day. Looking too far ahead and thinking about the uncertainties of the next day or week can increase anxiety for some children.

Of course, a very positive way to end a school day is with a story. We advocate this for all children from EYFS through to Year 6 (and beyond). Enabling children to lose themselves in a story for a few minutes can help them forget the cares and troubles of their day. It can inspire them, make them roar with laughter, challenge them or soothe them – assess the general mood of the class and decide what they might need. If you are reading a chapter book with older children, try to ensure you can read a whole chapter at a time, or at least reach an appropriate break in the story. Whatever you choose, make it come alive for them – the more dramatic voices the better! Bringing the story to a calm close, and ending with a whisper can leave children with a feeling of contentment and wonder ... and hopefully a desire to return for another story the following day.

Sending children out to their parents calmly, slowly and with a kind farewell closes the day well. If your need to speak to parents, for positive or negative reasons, consider how best to arrange this for the individual child.

Considerations for children with mental health difficulties

Children with specific mental health difficulties can find a multitude of daily transitions in school especially challenging. The 'Thinking about…' box below explores considerations for children with insecure attachments and children with ASC.

 Thinking about … daily transitions for children with mental health difficulties

Insecure attachments

Transitions are potentially especially hard for pupils with insecure attachments as they struggle to feel safe and secure. Perceptions of change can trigger anxiety responses. They may take longer to feel confident in new areas or with different trusted adults. Consider the following when addressing daily transitions:

■ Make sure they build a relationship with at least one trusted adult within the school (usually the class teacher), and when the child is transitioning to other adults or settings be clear about when they will see their trusted adult again. Let them know when and where this person is available to them.

■ Keep the school day routine as normal and predictable as possible.

■ Provide structured and mechanical work (e.g. word searches, calculations, handwriting practice, jigsaws puzzles and pattern completion) to form an appropriate distraction at a time when intrusive negative thoughts are more likely for specific children.

■ Let the child know that change does not mean loss.

■ Tell them that you will remember them; recall times that you have enjoyed together.

Autism spectrum condition

■ Children with ASC will often benefit from the use of visuals to support transitions. This could be their own individualised, portable timetable which acts as a visual reminder of where they are going to and what activities they will be doing.

■ They are also likely to have imagination differences. This might impact on their ability to visualise the place they are transitioning to, so photos, reminders or checking with them that they know where they are going can be effective in reducing anxiety.

- Social Stories give an opportunity to validate their feelings about change and might be helpful if certain daily triggers cause distress and a new coping strategy is being tried (see **Further Reading and Guidance**) Social Stories enable a child to be told explicitly what to expect and what they can do to cope with the transition. They aid consistency between adults and build links between home and school – ideally, different people will be reading the story with the child to aid learning and generalisability.

- A transitional object (perhaps in line with their special interest) may provide added security during daily transitions.

Summary

- Take time to identify the children who are finding transitions difficult and explore the reasons behind this. Work in partnership with them to find creative solutions.

- Create a predictable and calm start to the day for the children in your class. Consider which activities will inspire them as they begin their learning for the day.

- Identify the transition trigger points within the classroom. Make classroom routines predictable and smooth for all, but tailor strategies to suit specific children wherever possible.

- Set high expectations for behaviour when lining up and moving around the school, but make this easy for children. Engage them in the moment and use opportunities to facilitate class bonding.

- Pay close attention to how children transition to and from the playground. Consider whole-school procedures for dealing with playtime incidents.

- Create closing rituals for the end of the school day. These may include reflections, a gratitude practice, a story and a kind farewell.

- Be alert for signs that children with ASC and attachment difficulties are struggling with particular transitions. Think about how you can make reasonable adjustments to the school day to support them.

Chapter 17: Yearly Transitions

The end of each school year can be a time of great excitement as children look forward to moving up to the next year group, but it can also be a time of trepidation and worry for many. These commonplace worries may be verbalised by some, demonstrated in behaviours by others and kept hidden completely in some cases. We can safely assume that the majority of children, even the ones who are most excited, will have some reservations about leaving the security of their current classroom and the safety of their known teacher. They will also have plenty of questions about what lies ahead.

It is helpful to identify the children who will find the transition particularly difficult as early as possible and provide specific support for them as the end of the summer term approaches. Schools can then design the annual transition programmes to meet the specific needs of each year group. Some classes will inevitably need more support than others. Transition meetings for parents may take place in the summer or autumn, or both. They are a vital opportunity for the school to share important information about the new year group and for parents to ask questions. Individual transition meetings may be required for children with mental health difficulties or neurodevelopmental conditions.

This chapter will explore the significant events during the yearly transition process and consider how we can use them to support all children, especially those who are struggling. We will consider end of year transition opportunities, the importance of the class handover, start of year rituals that help complete the transition cycle and other significant transitions that children will encounter during primary school, including the transitions in and out of holidays.

End of year transition opportunities

As the end of the summer term approaches, teaching staff should be alert for changes in the children in their class. Listen out for the conversations that will inevitably begin about moving up to the next year group. Note how children are responding to this, particularly those with known mental health difficulties. The PSHE curriculum will naturally move to considerations of change and transition. Building in extra sessions for discussing worries and answering questions about the move is useful. It can also be helpful to ask parents to feed back any worries that are brought up at home.

Teaching staff should try to always frame the transition in a positive light, perhaps highlighting new things that the children will get to do, exciting learning opportunities to come or extra privileges they might be afforded. However, even with these things to look forward to, some children will find discussions about transition difficult. They may need more bespoke transition programmes, which allow them to gradually adjust to their new teacher and environment. This is discussed in more detail below when we consider the class handover.

Encouraging a process of reflection over the last few weeks of term can be beneficial to all. Before the whole-class transition day, it is important to support children to look back on their year, as a class and as individuals, and consider the following questions:

- What have I enjoyed?
- What have I learnt about myself?
- What were my big achievements?
- When was I disappointed? Why?
- What did I find hard?
- What surprised me?
- What am I grateful for?

This process should be modelled fully – for the benefit of children and adults alike. Take time to discuss responses and produce a class reflection that can be displayed. This could include positive thoughts and memories of whole class events, assemblies, visits, residentials and theme days; reflections on how the class has changed over the year; and perhaps consideration of times when things didn't go so well – though it is better to focus on funny mishaps (or 'marvellous mistakes') rather than actual negative events. This encourages a sense of belonging and bonds the class together as a unit before they move on.

After the transition day, support the children to look forward, considering the following questions:

- How do I feel about moving to…?
- How do I think it will be different?

■ What am I most looking forward to?

■ What have I learnt this year that will help me?

■ What am I worried about?

■ What do I want to work on?

■ What do I want my new teacher to know about me?

The frame 'Looking back to look forward' in **Chapter 19: Resources and Lesson Plans** gives a framework for supporting children through this process.

The transition day (or half-day) itself can also be a cause of worry for many. If a particular child is finding the idea of the day difficult, arrange a quiet time for them to meet the new teacher and visit the classroom prior to the actual day. Enabling a fully supported positive interaction like this will go some way to easing their worries – about the transition day, at least. During the day itself, when teaching staff receive their visiting class, it is best to keep activities fun and light-hearted. Commonly, this opportunity is taken to ask children to share information about themselves that may support planning for the autumn. However, arranging an art or craft session or a relaxed PE lesson, with plenty of opportunities for conversation, will do far more to support bonding with the new teacher. Artworks created can then be displayed in time for the arrival of the new class in September. Teaching staff should ensure, though, that they share plenty of information about themselves. Tell funny stories and invite the children to get to know you.

Hopefully, an engaging transition day will help most children to feel more comfortable about the move. For the children with mental health difficulties who are likely to continue to struggle, however, consider other ways in which you can support the transition as the end of term approaches and over the long summer holidays. Make a transition journal following the transition day – a little like the journal discussed in **Chapter 15,** but designed more with the child in mind than the parents. It could contain photos of the new classroom, perhaps a sample timetable, topics that will be covered in the first term and pages for the child to record their thoughts and feelings about the transition. Parents can facilitate this recording over the holiday and then children can share it with their new teacher in the autumn. A page for the child to record 'Things I want you to know about me' is very helpful for new teaching staff and puts the child in charge of imparting this important information.

For children with ASC, Social Stories can be used to support the transition (see **Further Reading and Guidance** for more details). Additional personal information can be included in the pages of the journal to individualise it for the child. Ideas can be given to suggest what the child can do to cope with the difficult feelings they are likely to experience during and after the transition. Some children will benefit from having something that helps them join up their experiences before and after the summer holidays. For example, they could be given a plant to look after for a teacher during the holidays, knowing that it will be returned to the teacher in the autumn. They then have a visual reminder that they will see that teacher again. Other transitional objects, or the idea of 'looking after' a toy, can help bridge the gap between July and September. Some children with ASC, due to differences in their imagination, struggle to visualise their world following the holidays. For this reason, using photos of the new classroom and new teaching staff, and having visual timetables in advance, can be hugely helpful in reducing anxiety. Calendars can also be used so they can mark off the time until term begins.

Class handover

Effective class handover from one teacher to another is essential for maintaining continuity for children and ensuring that significant messages are not forgotten. Having TAs present at a handover meeting will support this process greatly. If this is not possible, we would recommend a TA handover at another time. Schools can support the class handover by providing teachers and TAs with a specific class handover template which covers the following areas for each child, at a minimum:

- interests
- learning preferences
- specific learning needs
- additional physical needs
- SEND and current provision
- mental health difficulties and current provision
- friendships
- ongoing difficulties with peers
- family circumstances.

Any ongoing matters also need to be handed over in full e.g. external assessments and child protection concerns. If any assessments or STAR charts are being completed (see *Chapter 9*), it is helpful to share these so they can be carried on.

Traditionally, at the final pupil progress meeting (PPM) of the academic year, the outgoing class teacher will agree new targets and actions for children. These are then passed on at the handover meeting. However, moving the PPM to the start of the new academic year enables the new class teacher to have input into, and take ownership of, children's targets and implement changes themselves.

When thinking about those with additional needs during the class handover, both related to physical and mental health difficulties, discussing the implications for the learning environment is helpful before you plan your new classroom layout. It may be appropriate to ask where the best place is for a child to sit, how the furniture can be arranged to support them, which type of chair they find most comfortable or if they find any particular sensory stimuli challenging or soothing. Taking time to invite the child into the classroom and come up with a plan for the environment together is ideal. They may wish to sit in a similar place to this year (if the classroom layout is similar), or perhaps they like having their back to a wall. If a child is receiving 1:1 support, ask their TA for their input. Where is best for them to sit with the child during time on the carpet? Do they need their own desk? Ensure that their positioning will not obstruct the view of other children and that conversation between the adult and child can take place without disturbing the rest of the class.

Starting the new year slowly

As the new academic year begins, teaching staff should focus their attention on getting to know children, facilitating class bonding and creating daily wellbeing practices that are suitable for all. Some children will arrive raring to go, but some will find the transition out of the holidays immensely difficult. Make appropriate provision for these children. If they have been identified at the class handover, transition activities can be provided for over the holidays. This is explored further in the 'Thinking about...' box overleaf on school and family holidays.

It is important that teachers do not put pressure on themselves or the children to launch straight into a full, structured curriculum in the first week or so. Having a whole-school expectation that all classes will spend time ensuring children are ready to learn straight after the long holidays is helpful. Ensure the children have plenty of opportunity to share information about themselves. The frame 'This is me...' in *Chapter 19: Resources and Lesson Plans* supports this process, but this can also be done in more informal ways using sharing games and conversation. Build in lots of time for low-key creative activities and games, especially in the afternoons, as children adjust to being back in the school environment. Once the class have settled in a little, begin to co-create a set of class rules or a class code with them. It is vital that they have input into the development of these expectations so that they can engage with them properly and feel a sense of responsibility. As with all transitions, try not to introduce too much, too soon. Bring in new approaches slowly as the weeks go by, so that by half-term the routines and rhythms of the classroom feel more established.

Specific transitions

Early Years Foundation Stage to Key Stage 1

The transition from EYFS to KS1 is a significant one. It is helpful for children if several visits to the new class can be arranged, rather than just one transition day. Creating a 'buddy system' for Reception and Year 1 children in the summer term can be a support for those who are worried about the change. As we discussed in **Chapter 15** opportunities for child-led learning are fewer in Year 1 and it can be hard for children to adjust to the more structured curriculum. The transition should be gradual over the first few weeks of the autumn term, with plenty of free-choice and play-based learning initially. Thorough handover is especially important at this stage as various concerns or emerging behaviours may have been noted, but not yet fully assessed. Continuity in the APDR cycle is essential. The completed EYFS profiles will provide direction for planning a curriculum that meets the needs of individual children in Year 1.

Key Stage 1 to Key Stage 2

The transition from KS1 to Key Stage 2 (KS2) also needs to be considered carefully. Again, more than one visit to the new classroom can be beneficial, especially if KS2 is in a different building. A 'buddy system' for Year 2 and Year 3 children in the summer term can also be a great support, especially to help children slowly adjust to any changes in playground arrangements. Learning expectations will naturally increase and this may be a concern for many children. Designing a specific resilience programme for Year 2 can help them cope with the change, as will frequent communications with parents. Depending on the situation of the school, one significant change in Year 3 may be that class TAs will not be present for the whole school day. Some children will find it a great challenge to only have one adult in the classroom. Identify these children at the end of Year 2 and find ways to build their independence in relevant areas.

School and family holidays

Some children find the school holidays, and the transitions in and out of them, a huge struggle. The 'Thinking about…' box opposite discusses the extra provision that could be considered for these children.

❓ Thinking about ... school holidays and family holidays

Keep in mind that not all children look forward to the holidays in the way we might expect. For some with difficult home circumstances or mental health difficulties, the prospect of a break from school may cause worries – which can present in various ways. Here are some points and ideas to consider:

- Observe children in the week leading up to a break from school. Has their behaviour changed? Is there a pattern?

- A short, whole-class PSHE input on preparing for the upcoming holiday can help to address worries in a low-key way, without singling out any particular child. This may prompt a child to speak to an adult about their worries.

- Losing the routine and predictability of school is a problem for many children. They may dread the start of the holidays and these children are the ones to look out for prior to the start of a break.

- For those children you are concerned about, ensure you or another adult checks in with them briefly before and after the holiday. Offer them a chance to talk if they need it, though of course don't force the issue if they don't seem keen.

- Transitioning back into school routines can be difficult for some. Make allowances for this whenever you can and provide extra support for these children in the first few days after a break.

  - Prepare for the holiday by giving children transitional objects that they can care for while they are away from school, such as a plant or a toy.

  - Encourage children to make (or provide) holiday journals and scrapbooks. These can be shared on their return to school. It is important that this is not seen as homework, but a fun activity that will benefit the child.

  - Children could make an 'All About Me' box over the long summer holiday containing items that tell the story of their life, or simply their holiday. They can then bring this in to share in September. Make one of your own to help children get to know you.

  - Encourage children to send postcards to school from a holiday or day trip. These can then be read to the class and displayed on their return. Send your own postcards to the class too.

- Having to write about what they have done in the holidays can be very difficult for some children. Perhaps they are embarrassed that they haven't done anything as exciting as the child sitting next to them. Perhaps they have had a challenging week at home. Perhaps they had a lovely week, but the prospect of reliving it when they are already worried about returning to school can be very daunting. If possible, leave this sort of activity as a free choice, rather than it being compulsory.

Summary

- When considering how to plan for the end of year transition, it is sensible to anticipate that *all* children will be feeling at least some reservations about leaving their current class and moving on to the next year group.

- End of year transition opportunities include: reflections on the past year, consideration of the year to come, transition day, extra opportunities to meet the new teacher, developing a transition journal and using transitional objects over the Summer holidays.

- The class handover is essential in helping the new teacher form a sufficient overview of the children in the new class. A standard template for the handover will ensure that all matters are covered. Following the handover, consider inviting particular children into the classroom to help design the learning environment to suit their specific needs.

- Begin the year with a focus on class bonding and wellbeing. Spend time ensuring children are ready to learn before beginning structured curriculum learning. Give children the opportunity to share information about themselves with you.

- The transitions from EYFS to KS1 and from KS1 to KS2 can be particularly difficult for children with mental health difficulties.

- Make extra provision for children who find the transitions in and out of school holidays a challenge.

Chapter 18: Transition to Secondary School

A framework for transition

Transition from primary school, to the very different world of secondary school, is a milestone for any child. All need to adapt to new routines and relationships, the complex environment and the increased learning expectations. But for children with mental health difficulties, this transition can be particularly difficult and managing it well is essential. Strong links and liaison between secondary schools and their feeder primary schools are crucial to effective handover and they are valuable not just for transition, but overall, to develop a cohesive local education system. A personal approach to communication, wherein there is a willingness by teaching staff from both schools to share ideas and discuss concerns really makes a difference. Together, schools can support children to develop and internalise strategies that will support them through the change.

It is worth looking for ways in which these relationships can be built in the long term. Potential opportunities include:

- secondary specialist teachers visiting primary schools throughout the year to deliver English, maths or science lessons

- regular sports days at secondary schools for all children of primary age

- identifying secondary sports leaders who can help to facilitate these sports days and build relationships with the younger children

- or running themed-events, for example science days, that are open to the whole community.

When children from primary schools are given the chance to become gradually familiar with the secondary school site, staff and children, the prospect of transition becomes less daunting. Regular discussions at local headteacher and SENCO forums about transition and concerns regarding particular children also underpins the process.

A 2008 report for the Department for Children, Schools and Families identified several aspects of a successful transition to secondary school (Evangelou *et al*, 2008). Three of these are particularly noteworthy: the development of friendships, self-esteem and confidence; becoming familiar with new routines and school organisation; and experiencing continuity of the curriculum. Keeping these in mind when planning transition arrangements will support all children, but especially those with mental health difficulties. In 2019, a systematic literature review of primary to secondary school transitions found evidence from the UK and other countries that the transition is associated with lowered educational and wellbeing outcomes (Scottish Government, 2019). The review gave a number of recommendations for successful transition, many of which are explored in this chapter. These included: helping children to build a 'sense of school belonging', encouraging positive relationships between teaching staff and children, supporting peer networks, improving communication between primary schools and secondary schools, encouraging a problem-based approach to learning, learning of social and emotional skills, having parents as equal partners in the transition process and tailoring transition arrangements to support the needs of individual children.

In this chapter, we suggest a framework for transition procedures which considers: how to form a long-term plan for Year 6 that will support all children; how the primary school and secondary school can embed personalised transition opportunities throughout the year; how secondary schools may continue transition programmes into Year 7; and finally, how to end primary school with wellbeing in mind for all.

Planning ahead for Year 6

Year 6 is a busy year full of significant events: SATs, school productions, residential trips and the culmination of seven years at primary school – exciting for many, but potentially overwhelming for some. When it comes to moving on to secondary school, it is important to strike a healthy balance between facilitating and encouraging the necessary transition opportunities and not overloading children with too much, too soon. As always, the right balance will be different for each child, depending on their specific needs. This is why the conversations between primary schools, secondary schools and parents need to begin early.

The children who are likely to find the transition difficult can be highlighted as early as the class handover from Year 5 to Year 6 (and potentially within EHCP plan reviews). This allows detailed planning for provision in Year 6 and regular liaison with parents from the outset. For the children with mental health difficulties who have been identified as needing extra support, a specific transition programme, perhaps focusing on resilience, can be designed to run throughout the year. This can be run in school by TAs, nurture practitioners or therapists and it can be tailored to the specific needs and concerns that arise. When it is felt that a child may need more than this, external referrals can be made to local behaviour support programmes. The exact provision available will vary between areas: some offer bespoke, transition programmes beginning in the spring term of Year 6, with follow up in the autumn term of Year 7; some may visit a child from the autumn term of Year 6 to address specific behavioural concerns or diagnoses; and some may simply provide the listening ear that a school needs when supporting a particular child. Investigate the options available in your local area and see how they can fit in with the needs of your school.

There are various milestones in the secondary school application process in Year 6 that could potentially cause concerns for children, especially those already struggling with regular or high levels of anxiety. In the early autumn of Year 6, children and parents are invited to attend secondary school open evenings. This invitation could take the form of an individual visit to each primary feeder school by the head of Year 7, which can excite and inspire children about the options available to them. This personal approach can avoid triggering anxiety for some children at this stage. Application forms then need to be submitted around autumn half-term and children receive their school allocation in the spring term. The response at this time will depend on how involved children are in the process and whether or not parents have alerted them to the announcement. Some children may worry beforehand, or if a child isn't allocated one of their top choices, more specific concerns may then emerge. For all children, this can be an overwhelming time, as the idea of transition becomes more real and they consider what is to come.

Throughout Year 6, children are gradually encouraged to build independence in their learning and take on extra responsibilities within the school community. This prepares them for the culture shift that awaits at secondary school. This is valuable for all, but children with mental health difficulties may need graduated support to benefit fully from this; for example, they may need to be partnered with another child who is more confident to take on a regular support role with younger children. The other child can then model the expected behaviours and attitudes. School productions and residential trips also offer a wealth of opportunities for all children to develop their independence and resilience as they approach transition. Again, a graduated approach is likely to be necessary to support children with mental health difficulties – we discuss this in detail in **Chapter 4: Wellbeing for All**.

Transition opportunities

Transition opportunities facilitated by the primary school

In addition to the natural preparation and follow up for visits to secondary schools (see below), and any specific transition programmes that run for children with additional needs, whole-class input on transition is immensely valuable. Using PSHE lessons in Year 6 for this purpose is ideal. A pupil voice survey in the autumn term can highlight particular worries and input can then be targeted accordingly. Concerns and potential dilemmas relating to the transition, or life after the transition, can be discussed and explored. Throughout all conversations, remember to reinforce the message that having these worries about big changes in life is completely normal. All children will be feeling this to some degree, even if they don't verbalise it. Keep demonstrating to children that they are not alone and direct them and their parents to the excellent avenues of extra support available online (see **Further Reading and Guidance**).

Once the transition programme with the secondary school has begun (see below), allow children to make a transition journal to record important information and their ongoing reflections – this is preferably an activity for all, but it is especially helpful for those with mental health difficulties. A template can be provided and opportunities built in to each week for completion of different sections, sometimes in partnership with parents if appropriate. The following ideas could be included:

- Details of how they will get to and from school each day.

- Photographs of the new school environment.

- Names of key adults that will be working with them.

- Example timetables so children can anticipate what their week may look like.

- Lunchtime arrangements – will they be having packed lunches or dinners? Will they be helping their parents to prepare packed lunches?

- Playground arrangements – what are the timings and restrictions for year 7 children? Is there any alternative lunchtime provision for those children who find the playground difficult?

- Reflection spaces for each planned visit to the school – how did they feel before they went? How did they feel afterwards? What was the most helpful or interesting part of the visit?

- Space to record ongoing worries and a reflection area for solutions found.

- Space to record things they are looking forward to.
- Helpful tips for coping with the practicalities of the school day.

This transition journal, along with the information given by the secondary school, can be a useful toolkit and reference over the long summer holiday, as children prepare to begin the new academic year. Teaching staff and parents could also work together with the child to produce a 'What do I need?' template, or weekly plan, to display on the fridge or in their bedroom at home. This is an evolution of the visual timetable, which can help them keep track of all the things that need to be remembered each week, including the timetable, books and resources required, homework deadlines and PE days. It can be completed in full once children have received their timetables in September. Subsequently, colour-coding the timetable and corresponding books with stickers can be an aid to organisation and memory for many children.

It is helpful if children in Year 6 can have the experience of being taught by a range of different teachers as they approach the end of the summer term. They will also benefit from getting used to having lessons in different classrooms at times. Both of these strategies could be built into the transition programme. It is perhaps easier in a two- or three-form entry school, as Year 6 classes and teachers can easily swap around. But in a one-form entry school, Year 6 could exchange classrooms and teachers with Year 5 a few times a week, building in a good transition opportunity for both classes.

As previously mentioned, research has indicated that continuity of the curriculum from Year 6 to Year 7 is linked to a successful transition (Evangelou *et al*, 2008). This is a crucial element of the transition process for primary schools – to ensure that the level and style of learning children will encounter in Year 7 will not be completely unexpected. Good relationships between primary and secondary schools can facilitate communication about curriculum expectations. Moving towards a problem-based learning approach towards the end of Year 6 can be good preparation for what is to come (Scottish Government, 2019). Continuing to help children develop a secure growth mindset and improve their resilience will also give them a firm foundation for the challenges ahead.

Transition opportunities facilitated by the secondary school

Early in the autumn, each secondary school will receive notification from their county council about which children with SEND have selected them as their first choice school. The SENCO from the secondary school will then be able to visit the child in their primary setting, observe them in the classroom and begin to consider what the child needs in place for transition, and beyond, to support them with their learning. They can also use this opportunity to observe all the children in the class, some of whom will also end up attending their school.

For these children with SEND and mental health difficulties, the process of familiarisation with the secondary school and adults needs to begin early. A personalised programme can be planned whereby the child (and parents) can visit multiple times. This could begin with visits in the quiet moments of the day, perhaps after school has finished, and gradually build up to visiting during the busier times of lessons or breaks. It is helpful if different adults can welcome them each time, but a known adult should always be there in the background as a consistent cornerstone of the programme. It is also helpful if the child's 1:1 or class TA can also attend at least one of these visits with them. They can then follow up with discussions and activities regarding areas of concern after the visit.

When secondary schools receive the final list of children accepted in the spring term, the SENCO can identify the vulnerable children with specific needs and organise a separate transition day for them. This would need to take place after SATs, but prior to the standard transition day for every child in July. The 'Thinking about…' box below explores what this day might look like. If the SENCO is able to visit the primary school and deliver a personal invitation for this day to each child, they can also spend a little time getting to know them and asking questions about concerns they may have. Common concerns at this stage might be worries about the older children, getting lost and using the toilets.

 Thinking about … a transition day for children with additional needs

A specific transition day for children with SEND and mental health difficulties can be designed by the secondary school. If this doesn't already take place in your area, use the following ideas to support the conversations you have with secondary schools in the lead up to transition. Ask what might be possible – particularly if you think a specific activity would support a child who is likely to struggle.

Key features of a day like this might be:

■ All food and drink provided.

■ All TAs move away from their usual timetables to support individual children.

■ Time spent walking around the school to get used to the environment.

■ Children could complete a quiz or scavenger hunt with their adult as they move around the school. This encourages them to look all around and take note of significant people and places.   →

- Visiting various toilets is also important, as is general discussion about the movement around the school at different times during the day.
- Following a real timetable with an adult:
  - The prospect of moving from lesson to lesson throughout the school day is daunting for most children.
  - The child can lead the adult from lesson to lesson according to the timetable. This is especially helpful if schools have a two-weekly timetable as it allows discussion about the practicalities of this.
- A computing lesson:
  - Children can create a booklet about themselves to share with staff. This can include a photo taken on the day.
  - A copy can then be printed, laminated and given to the child to take home that day.
- Circle time to discuss worries.
- Opportunity to meet the head of Year 7 and other senior leadership.
- An opportunity for parents to join their children at the end of the day for social time and an introduction from the headteacher.

After the event, surveys can be offered to children, parents and primary staff to assess if the day is a valuable addition to the transition programme. The SENCO, and potentially TAs that have already been allocated to particular children, can then make a further visit to each child. This allows a chance to discuss the information the child gave in their booklet about themselves and another opportunity for them to ask questions and raise concerns.

It is also worth highlighting through the transition process (and EHCP reviews) those children whose levels of TA support may change following the transition from primary to secondary school. This can lead to additional challenges for children whose independence skills are not in line with their chronological age.

During the various visits, considerations for children with specific neurodevelopmental and/or mental health conditions can also be addressed. These may include the following:

- Getting used to the sound of the bell can be a difficult adjustment for children with ASC and anxiety. Therefore, children could record the bell on a phone during one of their visits and then listen to it at home to increase familiarity. Children with known noise sensitivities could be given the opportunity to put on ear defenders to help them manage these trigger times.

- Outline procedures for use of a safe or calm room and the use of a 'self-direct' card to allow a child to move to another space at times of high distress, dysregulation or anxiety.

- For those that struggle in social situations, there can be discussions about peer relationships and friendships in the new environment and plans put in place highlighting the adult that they can go to if they experience social difficulties at different times in the day.

- Finding a way for children with attachment difficulties to connect with the school over the long summer holiday can be beneficial. Perhaps they could keep a holiday scrapbook that can then be shared with their new TA or send a postcard to the new school, which can be displayed and acknowledged when the term begins.

All children will then take part in at least one standard transition day. Further opportunities can be taken here to ensure that every child feels a sense of connection and belonging to their new school before the autumn term begins. This could look like each child being given a school-branded PE bag with corresponding stationery and digital files containing video communications – perhaps including a welcome video from the head of Year 7 or current Year 7 children talking about the school and their experiences in a positive light.

Additional transition arrangements could include:

- a meeting between the head of Year 7 and Year 6 teachers from feeder schools to discuss transition opportunities

- a visit from the primary school SENCO or TA to the secondary school to review the environment and make suggestions around reasonable adjustments for a particular child

- a buddy or mentoring system pairing Year 7 children with Year 6 children to provide a point of contact during visits and then further support in the autumn term

- making plans for some children from the same primary school to be in the same form groups in Year 7.

Throughout all of these visits and meetings, it is crucial to involve the parents as much as possible and keep them informed of transition arrangements. As we have mentioned, we need to encourage an increasing sense of independence for children towards the end of primary school and facilitate connections with secondary school staff, but parents are instrumental in this process too. They know their children best and will be supporting them throughout the holidays. Follow-up phone calls or emails to parents following transition days are helpful, especially if a child was distressed during the visit. Meetings between a child, their parents and their new TAs may be appropriate prior to the end of Year 6.

Planning ahead for Year 7

For children with additional needs that may have attended extra transition days, the transition programme should continue into the autumn. A programme of meetings with the child and their TA can ensure that they have settled in well. A specific transition team can support this process. In the early days, these adults can pop in and out of classes, checking in with particular children. Having these familiar adult faces looking out for them can be a great support and reassurance for some children. Repeat surveys of the transition process can provide opportunities for trouble-shooting and evidence that the process is adding value for children.

Following a settling in period and assessments such as Boxall profiling, more specific provision arrangements for individual children can be made if appropriate. This may involve ELSA sessions, nurture interventions, various therapies or other specific clubs and programmes for social and emotional needs or mental health conditions (see *Chapter 5: Building Emotional Intelligence*). It is important that the child is given the choice about taking part in these sessions. They may feel worried about missing lessons, or perhaps they simply don't want to be singled out as different in this new environment. They must make the final decision – however, there is much the adults can do to encourage them to take part, and the option to return at a later time if they feel they need to can be given.

Transition to secondary school can result in an exacerbation of any mental health difficulties and all staff should remain alert for signs of this. For example, an escalation in anxiety levels in a child with a known anxiety disorder such as OCD may contribute to an increase in obsessions or compulsive behaviours; these may previously have gone unnoticed, or they may emerge for the first time at this point. We need to anticipate that this may happen and liaise with parents appropriately.

Ending with wellbeing in mind

There is sometimes the unfounded belief that once children move to secondary school, all the hard work of inclusion and support that has happened in primary school is undone. This attitude is unhelpful and does a disservice to the really inspirational programmes of support that exist. Throughout all transition arrangements, support from the senior leadership team in both the primary and secondary school is essential. A process of shared responsibility and decision making regarding transition and provision for Year 7 should be encouraged and focus placed on building relationships between secondary schools and their feeder primary schools.

By maintaining a focus on wellbeing right up to the end of Year 6, primary schools can prepare children in good time for what is to come. The transition need not be a horrible shock that unsettles and confuses. We need to allow children to close their primary school chapter with peace and gratitude – encouraging the 'leavers' traditions that the children value so much and seizing chances for reflection before they move on. Addressing concerns as and when they arise (even if they don't fit in with the planned transition arrangements) is essential. All children need to feel heard at this time of change. It is the duty of primary schools to give children the tools and strategies they need to navigate the new world that awaits them. If close connections with secondary schools are fostered, it is possible to ensure that the transition is tailored to the individual child. Primary school staff and parents can then confidently trust that the new school will continue to foster wellbeing for all.

With special thanks to St. Thomas More Catholic Primary School and Knutsford Academy, Watford for sharing their inclusive secondary transition practices with us; and also to Chiltern Hills Academy, Chesham (secondary school) for sharing their innovative primary to secondary transition programme with us.

Summary

- Strong relationships between secondary schools and their feeder primary schools are essential to developing successful transition programmes.

- Identifying children who may struggle with the move to secondary school at the beginning of Year 6 allows bespoke transition programmes to be designed.

- Secondary schools and primary schools can work together to support children and parents through the application process.

- Primary schools can facilitate transition through targeted PSHE teaching, transition journals and adapting the curriculum and teaching arrangements toward the end of Year 6 to more closely match secondary expectations.

- Secondary schools can facilitate transition by visiting primary schools to foster early connection with children, providing specific transition arrangements for children with SEND and mental health difficulties and involving parents in the process as much as possible.

- Secondary schools can continue transition arrangements throughout Year 7 to ensure that all children settle in well.

■ It is the duty of primary schools to provide individual children with the tools they need to make a successful transition to secondary school. Keeping wellbeing in mind throughout Year 6 will support this process.

References

Evangelou M, Taggart B, Sylva K *et al* for DCSF (2008) Research Report: Effective Pre-school, Primary and Secondary Education 3–14 Project (EPPSE 3–14) *What Makes a Successful Transition from Primary to Secondary School?* Available from https://dera.ioe.ac.uk/14069/1/DFE-RR202.pdf

Scottish Government (2019) *Primary to Secondary School Transitions: Systematic Literature Review.* Directorate: Learning Directorate Part of: Children and Families, Education. Available from www.gov. scot/publications/primary-secondary-transitions-systematic-literature-review/

Section 5: Resources and Lesson Plans

Chapter 19: Resources and Lesson Plans

This chapter provides a range of photocopiable resources and lesson plans linking to key areas throughout the book. The resources and lesson plans are also available to download from: https://www.pavpub.com/mental-health-and-well-being-in-primary-education-resources. With each resource and plan, there is a short explanation about the intended use. However, the ideas here can be easily adapted and tailored to suit different ages and needs. The lesson plans can be completed over several sequential sessions if this is more appropriate for your group or class. They are intended for use by all children – those with identified mental health difficulties and those without. All will benefit from exploring the ideas covered here. We hope that the resources and plans will encourage and inspire you to continue the conversation about mental health and wellbeing with the children you teach. If the ideas lead in an unexpected direction, do follow the spark if you are able. Sometimes, that unplanned tangent is really worth it.

Chapter 2: Ready to Learn

Lesson Plan: We are growing hopeful minds

Why use it?

This lesson introduces the concept of growth mindset and helps children to understand the concept of hope. It can be used at any time, but is ideal at the start of a term to help children refocus on the idea that we are all capable of learning and growing. It can be used in full, or the activities can be used on their own in small chunks of time. Some children may find the concept of growth mindset very difficult to grasp. If a child is completely disengaged from their learning, trying to get them to consider what they want to achieve in maths this term is probably not going to be very successful. For that reason, the ideas here are broad and relate to everyday life.

What next?

The intended outcome for this lesson is that children will end up identifying one or two areas in their life that they currently feel hopeful about. These may or may not be related to school. Whatever they are, it is really important to maintain momentum with them. Display the 'seeds of hope' made in the lesson somewhere visible in the classroom and refer to them often. This display can grow as the children do. Encourage them to keep adding shoots and leaves as they take further steps with their hopes. Keep your own record of their hopes so that you can check in with about how things are going. This could look like a simple 'How did your football training go this week?' or a more in-depth chat about how their reading is going. Be their cheerleader as they build on the hopes they have identified. What about those children who didn't feel hopeful about anything or have forgotten their hopes? Keep supporting them to identify areas of hope that can be added later and keep checking in and celebrating the tiniest steps of progress. Have prepared green shoots and leaves always available by the seed display for them to add. Prompt them to do this if they have shown growth in class. Ask their parents to let you know about growth at home. Make it easy for them to watch their seeds grow and see their own progress.

Lesson Plan: We are growing hopeful minds

KS1/KS2 Whole class or small group

Time: 45 minutes (or longer if children make individual seeds). Follow up over several weeks.

Curriculum links:
PSHE, art, design technology

Learning Outcomes:

- To understand that our abilities are not fixed – we can change and develop them over time.
- To understand the idea of having hope for the future.
- To apply this understanding to an area of their own lives.

Key vocabulary: Fixed mindset, growth mindset, hope, future, goals, dreams, seeds, shoots, leaves.

Resources:

- Slides for whiteboard (see plan below)
- Whiteboards and pens
- Paper strips
- Class 'Seed of Hope' - this could be any hollow spherical or cylindrical container (or even a papier-mache sphere) that can be decorated
- Or 2 egg box cups joined by a split pin to make a seed for each child
- Craft materials for decoration (pens, pva glue, tissue paper, glitter, paint, sticky gems)
- Small display board/area
- Pre-cut green shoots and leaves (card or paper)

Introduction: Show a picture of a newborn baby. *When a baby is born, what can they do? What can't they do?* We all begin our lives like this. Day by day we grow and learn new things. *What might this baby be able to do in the future?*

Main teaching:

- Show pictures of 'No Entry' and 'Dead End' road signs. *What do these signs mean?* Explain that sometimes we can feel like this about our lives and our learning. This is called a fixed mindset. If we have a fixed mindset we don't believe that we can learn new things or get better at something. We don't have hope for the future.
- Show picture of a country cross roads in springtime. Paired discussion: *If the road signs show us a fixed mindset, what does this picture show us?* Explain that each of these roads is a hopeful path to the future. The exact path will be different for all us. Paired discussion: *What is hope?* Explain that when we hope for something in the future, we want it to happen and we believe that it can happen. Give an example of something you feel hopeful about e.g. *I feel hopeful that I will improve at running. I am practicing each week and able to run further each time.* When we feel hopeful about something and believe we can get better at it, we have a growth mindset.
- *What do you feel hopeful about for the future? What do you believe you can get better at?* Explain that sometimes we call these hopes our goals or dreams. They are like little seeds that we can help to grow. Children to note down ideas on whiteboard in words or pictures. If they are finding it hard to think of things, encourage them to close their eyes use their imaginations to picture the things they would like to be able to do. It could be related to home, school, sport or other hobby.

Activity: Children to choose one or two hopes to write on strips of paper. Note down hopes for all children on separate sheet for tracking and encouragement. Paper strips to be rolled up and placed into a class 'Seed of Hope'. As they place their hopes inside, children may decorate it with gems or glitter.

Wrapping up: *How will we help our hopes grow?* Reminding ourselves often of what our hopes are, practise, help from others, perseverance.

Extension: If there is time, each child could make their own 'Seed of Hope'.
Follow up: Ideally, place seeds on a surface at the bottom of a display board. As children make progress with their hope/goal they can add green shoots and leaves. Check in with them regularly.

Frame: How I like to learn…

Why use it?

This frame helps to begin the conversation around learning preferences. Some children will instinctively know what works best for them. For others, more support will be needed to help them consider when learning has felt good and when it has felt like a struggle. Some may find it very difficult to discuss this concept at all. In this case, begin slowly. There is no need to complete the whole frame in one go – there is a lot to think about here. Keep it accessible and keep circling back to it when opportunities arise – perhaps when you have tried a completely new learning style in a particular lesson. Also, remember to allow children to change their minds. Be open to them reconsidering learning preferences and as always, avoid putting them in that metaphorical box!

What next?

The information given in response to 'How I feel about learning right now…' and 'How I would like to feel about learning…' can be really illuminating. If children are feeling low, worried or angry about learning, this needs to be addressed as a priority. Helping them to untangle the reasons for this emotion is essential if they are to move forward.

If you are working with an individual child, you should be able to see where you can alter and improve planning to allow for these preferences, at least a few times a week. Of course, all children still need to talk, read and write, but look for opportunities to include more moving, doing or drawing if that is what they need. If you are asking a whole class or group to complete this, look for patterns. Are there ways in which you could incorporate a particular preferred style for the whole class or group? Also, remember to always remain open to children reconsidering their learning preferences and showing a fresh perspective on what currently works for them. Above all, let the children know you that you are listening. They need to understand that you probably can't make everything exactly as they would wish, but that you want to work with them to match learning opportunities with their preferences whenever you can.

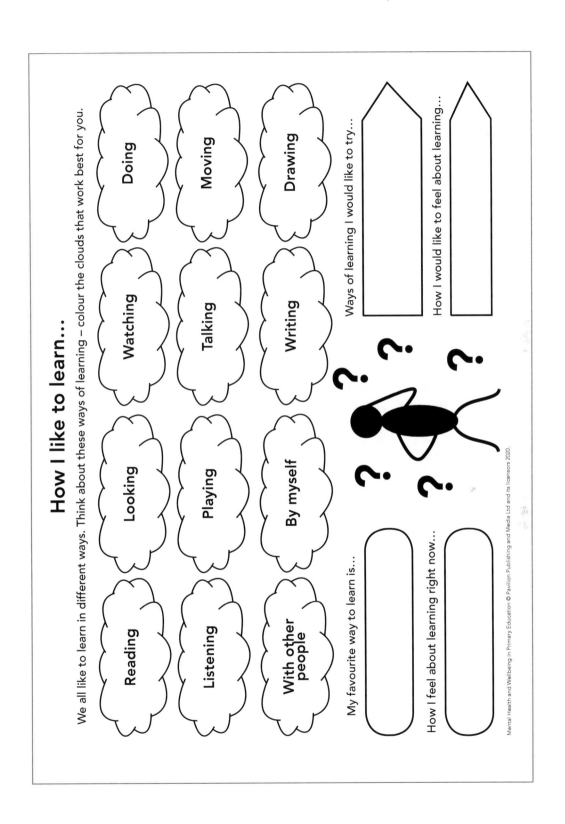

How I like to learn...

We all like to learn in different ways. Think about these ways of learning – colour the clouds that work best for you.

Reading

Listening

With other people

Looking

Playing

By myself

Watching

Talking

Writing

Doing

Moving

Drawing

Ways of learning I would like to try...

How I would like to feel about learning...

My favourite way to learn is...

How I feel about learning right now...

Chapter 3: A Whole-School Approach to Mental Health and Wellbeing

Template: Learning steps

Why use it?

This template gives a suggested format for a personalised proforma for children with mental health difficulties to help track the steps they are taking on their learning journey. Ideally, the child, their parents and relevant school staff will input into a document such as this. It is designed to be child-friendly, but also to include enough useful information about the child and their plan that it is helpful to all adults working with them. We recommend that no diagnosis be written on this document. This allows the child to simply express their needs without a label being placed on them. Some children will find it difficult to contribute to 'Good things people say about me…' – this can be modelled and practised with time. The 'Hopes and dreams' section is really important and should be referred to often with the child. 'My next learning steps…' can be used for specific learning or social and emotional targets e.g. 'I will ask for help when I am feeling angry'. Notes about extra provision and interventions could also be included here e.g. '… will attend afternoon nurture intervention twice a week'.

Learning steps

My name is

I am in class

Photo here

Things I like...

Good things people say about me...

Things I'm not keen on...

How I feel about learning...

My hopes and dreams...

Other things you need to know about me so you can help me with my learning...

My next learning steps...

We agree to use this information to help _____ to make steps in their learning.

Signed _____ (child)   Date _____

_____ (parent)

_____ (teacher and/or TA)   Review _____

What next?

This is a working document that should be used to support all activities that the child is involved in within school. It is easy to spend time creating these, only for them to end up carefully filed away and forgotten. Make them accessible to all – a copy for the child's drawer, one for the parents, a folder in a known place in the classroom (ensuring that any teaching staff covering the class are made aware of this), as well as a copy held centrally with the SENCO.

Frame: I need you to know... card

Why use it?

This card is a useful tool for communicating key messages about a child to cover teachers, supply teachers, different TAs or parent helpers that might be working in the classroom. Once created, it could be laminated to prolong its use! The child can keep it in their drawer or on their table – it will allow the child to let adults know the things that matter to them, without them having to worry about verbally communicating the messages. The responsibility for passing on these messages can be given to the child if appropriate, giving them a sense of control and purpose over their learning experience. Equally, if this is not appropriate for a particular child, a central copy of all the cards for a class can be kept near the teacher's chair or desk, perhaps in a folder of information for new adults.

The card should be written in partnership with the child, TA and parents. Help them to identify things that support them in class ('These things help me to learn') e.g. having instructions repeated, movement breaks or wearing ear defenders to block out classroom noise; and also to identify the reasonable adjustments that may need to be made for this child to allow learning to happen ('Sometimes I need to...') e.g. taking a self-directed break to calm down, moving to a position where they can concentrate better or having a particular toy or resource available to them. These reasonable adjustments are often the more unusual or uncommon strategies that can get missed when a new adult is teaching a class – not through intention, but simply because they are so specific to the child.

What next?

Be prepared to adapt or develop the cards on a regular basis as things evolve for a child. Remember to ask for parental input and updates from home. Alert the child to times when you may be absent from the class and remind them to show their card to the new adult.

🕴 I need you to know...

These things help me to learn: _____

_____

_____

_____

Sometimes I need to: _____

_____

_____

_____

Chapter 4: Wellbeing for All

Frame: My wellbeing wings

Why use it?

This frame is designed to help children consider and track the things that help boost their wellbeing and also identify some of the things that decrease it. It can be used as a standalone activity or as a follow up activity after teaching the lessons relating to specific emotions (see below). Some children may find difficult to work out which things boost their wellbeing and which things drain it. For example, they may say that playing a video game makes them feel good, whereas actually doing this for too long at a time may be harming their overall wellbeing. Helping them to place boundaries around an activity like this is important, but will take time and the support of parents. A step in a positive direction would be to help them recognise that 30 minutes playing a video game, for example, might make them feel good, but a longer time than this might have the opposite effect.

What next?

Ideally, children should keep their 'wellbeing wings' accessible and be able to add things to them as they learn more about what makes them feel good. Look for patterns in the wellbeing boosters that children identify across the class. Try and make time for any recurring ideas e.g. singing, painting or time in nature. If there are patterns in the things that decrease wellbeing, for example, not sleeping well, you could then provide targeted PSHE input on this area over the following weeks.

My wellbeing wings

Which things make you feel good? Maybe playing sport, singing, reading or drawing? These are the things that can raise your wellbeing. Add them to the feathers so your wellbeing wings can fly.

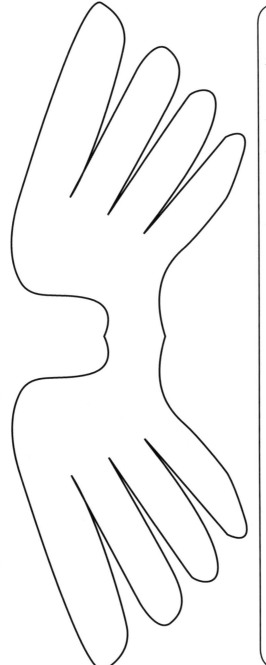

What makes it hard for your wellbeing wings to fly? Maybe staying up late, too much screen time, being hungry or thirsty or not spending enough time with friends and family? These are the things that lower your wellbeing. Write them here and ask an adult to help you find ways to solve these problems.

Lesson Plan and Frame: My school village

Why use them?

All children need support with their friendships at times. For those with mental health difficulties, the social landscape of school can be extremely challenging. This lesson introduces the concept of a 'school village' – a community of children and adults around a child that are there to provide friendship and support. It allows children to identify the friendships that are important to them and the adults that they trust and feel able to talk to. Children are encouraged to think about the peers that they get along with, in learning and in play. However, the lesson also ensures that children can acknowledge that there will always be people around us that we don't get along with so well. They need to know that this is ok. But they also need to know how to manage it well, not upsetting others and not taking things too personally. The more modelling adults can do around these areas, the better. Teachers role-playing with TAs (as described in the lesson plan) is so beneficial in illustrating important ideas around social communication and interaction, especially for those children who are finding this hard. Positive male–female relationship role-modelling is also very helpful to children, some of whom may not see this at home.

What next?

The intended outcome for this lesson is that children will end up with a picture of their key relationships in school, with adults and peers (Frame: My school village) and be able to identify the things that strengthen these relationships and things that undermine them. The frame can be kept in children's drawers where they can access it and also a copy can be kept centrally by the teacher. As always, checking in regularly is a good idea, particularly where there may be difficulties between certain children. Keep reminding children of the chosen adults in their village that they can speak to. And of course, make sure the adults know they have been chosen. Finally, give specific praise when you notice children acting in a way that strengthens relationships (prosocial behaviours) and gently guide them to realise when their behaviour or words are undermining relationships.

Lesson Plan: My school village

KS1/KS2 Whole class or small group

Time: 45 minutes. Follow up over several weeks.

Curriculum links:
PSHE, citizenship, religious education

Learning Outcomes:
- To understand that they have a 'village' or community of people around them in school that care about them.
- To identify times when they have felt part of the school community.
- To identify their special friends and adults that they like to speak to.
- To identify things that can make their relationships stronger.
- To identify things that can harm their relationships.

Key vocabulary: Village, community, friend, friendship, relationships, care, kindness, manners, gratitude, empathy, respect.

Resources:
- Slides for whiteboard - pictures of villages around the world; pictures of school events involving the children
- My School Village frame

Introduction: Show pictures of villages around the world, with people of all ages together. *What do you see?* These are villages. In the past, before we could travel far, most people lived in small communities or villages. *What do you think were the good things about living in small villages? What would have been difficult?* The people in the village looked after each other. Often, it was like a big family. In many countries around the world it is still like that today.

Main teaching:
- Our school can be like a village. It is a community of people that can learn together, have fun together and can look after each other. Explain that we each have lots of people in our school community that care about us – adults and children. *When do you feel happy to be part of the school community?* Think about fun times in class, assemblies, productions and sports days. Show pictures of these events, ideally with the children themselves in. *Why are these times so special to us?* Explain that at these times we are all working together as a team. We feel part of something important, that is bigger than ourselves. Take time to ensure children understand this concept. Ask children to give it a name e.g. 'the village buzz' or 'magic village moments', so that you can refer back to this feeling and help children identify it in the future.
- Paired discussion: *How can we make our school village stronger?* Discuss ideas and record for later reference. Ensure ideas of care, kindness, good manners, helping, gratitude and empathy are covered.
- Paired discussion: *What things can harm our relationships with the special people in our village?* Discuss ideas and record for later reference. Ensure ideas of disrespect, rudeness, unkindness in our words and actions, poor manners and only thinking about ourselves are covered.
- *What happens when we don't get on well with everyone in our village?* Acknowledge that we won't always get on well with everyone. We can find it hard to learn or play with some people. It is normal to feel like this sometimes, but we still need to treat these people with kindness and respect.

Activity: Children to complete 'My school village' frame with support. Some children may need help to identify friends and adults that they can speak to when they need help. Children can use class ideas for things that can make relationships stronger and things that can harm relationships; and add to them if they are able.

Wrapping up: *How will we know if our school village is strong?* Discuss signs that relationships are being looked after and signs that they need our attention.

Extension: Children to identify one relationship in school that needs looking after. Help them to plan one or two actions they can take that week to make the relationship stronger.

Follow up: Check in with them regularly about their school village. Encourage them to discuss problems.

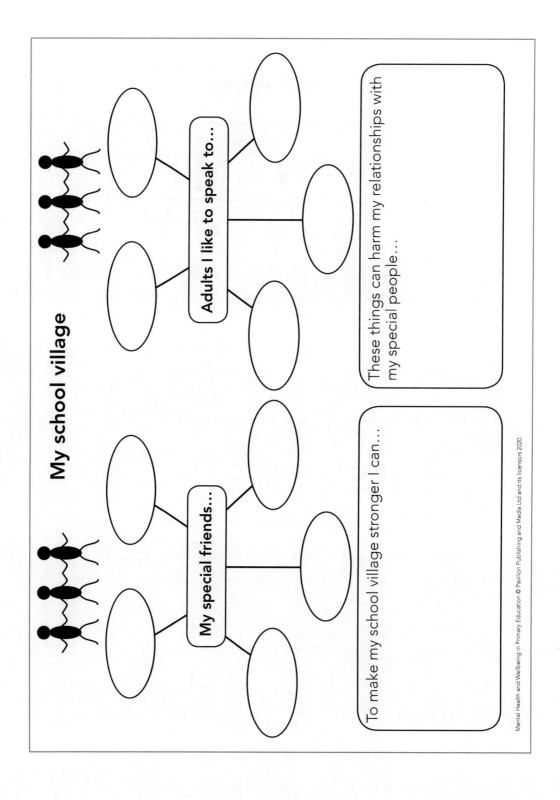

My school village

Adults I like to speak to…

My special friends…

These things can harm my relationships with my special people….

To make my school village stronger I can….

Mental Health and Wellbeing in Primary Education © Pavilion Publishing and Media Ltd and its licensors 2020.

Chapter 5: Building Emotional Intelligence
Frame: Things that make me feel...

Why use it?
This frame helps to continue the conversation around various emotions, and the triggers individual children may have. Ideally, they will need to have had input on naming and understanding emotions before completing this. The frame is not school-specific and can be used for triggers in any area of life. Other feelings to consider could be: jumpy, lonely, excited, embarrassed, bored or confused. This could be adapted into a practical activity using hoops and emotion labels. Younger children could jump into a hoop, name the emotion and share their trigger with a partner or the class. Alternatively, children could write triggers on cards and place them within each hoop.

What next?
Lots of helpful information can be gained from this frame, but children may need support and time to think about the emotions in detail before completing it. For children with mental health difficulties, exploring their specific triggers with them, if they are aware of them, can allow you to make appropriate changes to the environment or routines. Some of the information discovered here may simply be useful for ongoing conversations with children or planning for personalised interventions.

Things that make me feel...

Wriggly or restless

Excited

Comfortable or OK

Scared

Calm

Worried

Happy

Sad

Cross or angry

Frame: All about school

Why use it?

This frame facilitates detailed exploration of various parts of the school day and encourages children to think about the areas they find difficult. A range of activities and lessons are suggested, but don't be limited by these. Adapt as necessary for your class. When you are just beginning to work with a child, focus on the basic building blocks of the day, such as starting the day, sitting at their table, being in the playground and levels of noise. As with some of the other frames, there is no need to rush to complete this all in one session. Keep returning to it each week, or when concerns arise.

What next?

Once children have identified an area that causes them problems, explore this further by encouraging them to identify how they feel before, during and after the event. This may allow a particular trigger to be found e.g. working in a group situation in maths, rather than the actual maths; or it may provide evidence for a child that after a PE lesson they feel good, even though they find the process of getting changed and leaving the classroom a challenge. Try repeating the frame at the end of a term, following the use of specific interventions or strategies, to see how things have improved.

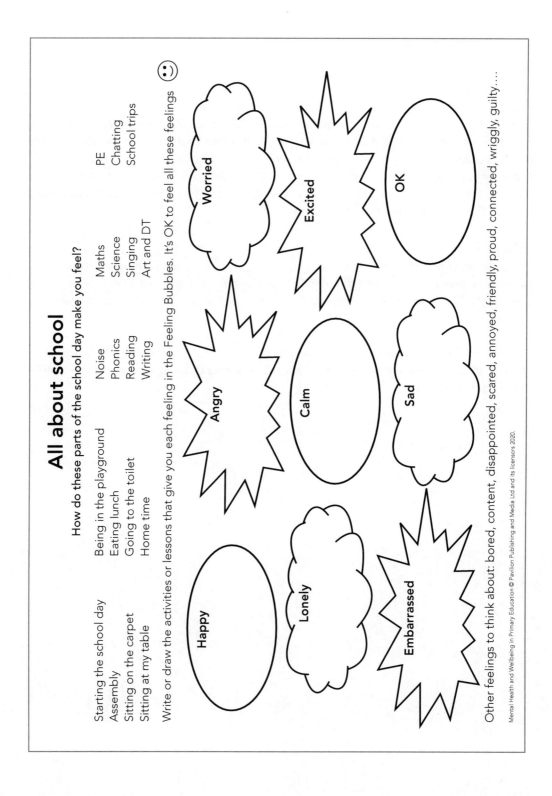

All about school

How do these parts of the school day make you feel?

Starting the school day	Being in the playground	Noise	Maths	PE
Assembly	Eating lunch	Phonics	Science	Chatting
Sitting on the carpet	Going to the toilet	Reading	Singing	School trips
Sitting at my table	Home time	Writing	Art and DT	

Write or draw the activities or lessons that give you each feeling in the Feeling Bubbles. It's OK to feel all these feelings :)

Worried

Excited

OK

Angry

Calm

Sad

Happy

Lonely

Embarrassed

Other feelings to think about: bored, content, disappointed, scared, annoyed, friendly, proud, connected, wriggly, guilty.....

Mental Health and Wellbeing in Primary Education © Pavilion Publishing and Media Ltd and its licensors 2020.

Frame: How it feels for me...

Why use it?

This frame is designed to deepen a child's emotional intelligence and self-awareness. Before children can use this, they ideally need to have had some input on the language of emotions and the importance of naming them as they feel them. The purpose of the activity is to help a child spot an emotion in their body as it arises. An adult needs to support them to consider the physical warning signs that an emotion is present and how these develop if the emotion grows. We can't assume that all children will have the same patterns of physical sensations for a particular emotion – the important thing is that they can say what is true for them.

What next?

If a child is struggling with anger, for example, they may feel a heat rising, or a tight stomach or chest. They might feel themselves clench their fists or jaw. If we can help a child to spot these signs in the moment, we can then support them to step away from the trigger and to feel and let the anger out in a safe and healthy way (see also Frame: The bottle that wants to go pop!). These are two significant steps on the journey to emotional intelligence: regulating the input that causes an emotion, and feeling and expressing an emotion that has already arisen.

How it feels for me...

We feel emotions in our bodies, as well as our minds and hearts.

- Name an emotion that you are finding difficult:

_____

- Mark the places where you feel this emotion in your body.
- If you can, write a few words to explain what you feel.

When you feel the emotion starting in your body, you can ask an adult for help before it grows.

Emotions lesson plans

Why use them?

The following four lesson plans focus on key emotions. They are intended to support other work on emotional literacy that may be going on in class or in interventions. They are suitable for whole-class or small-group use, but if there are particular concerns relating to worry, sadness or anger in your class we recommend that they be used for a small-group session, where discussion can go at a slower pace and be more personalised. For some groups, the learning suggested in each lesson could actually last for several sessions, depending on the depth and diversions required. As we described in ***Chapter 5: Building Emotional Intelligence***, we need to give children the words to support their emotional expression. We can't assume they already have this. Equally, some may have internalised messages they have heard from adults around them. They may report that they have 'problems with anger' without really understanding what this means or knowing what causes the anger. As always, tread slowly and carefully. These conversations can bring up unexpected concerns – always have a second adult (or more!) on hand when teaching these lessons to support those children that need it. Never force an issue if children are reluctant to discuss it, especially in a whole-class situation. A key part of the lessons is the role-play between two adults, firstly modelling appropriate and helpful

responses to emotions, and secondly modelling more negative responses that children may have witnessed or experienced themselves. These can be expanded as necessary to suit the needs of the class. Involving the children in the role-plays or adding this as an extra activity is ideal, but only if you know that the children are likely to be able to cope with this. The discussions following the role-play are essential in order for children to understand why certain responses to emotions are not helpful for the individual concerned.

What next?

Make observations during the lessons and record so you can follow things up later. Ensure that crafts that are made are displayed or kept handy in drawers, or they can be taken home. The outcomes of the lessons on worry, sadness and anger relate to the children being able to identify the emotion in themselves and giving them strategies to help them in the moment and on an ongoing basis. Their 'toolkits' are working documents that they need to be able to refer to often. Keep checking in regularly with how they are getting on and if they need help using them. For those children with mental health difficulties, ensure all adults working with them have copies of their toolkits. Regarding the happiness lesson, another key element that could be explored later is that when we share our happy feelings in an appropriate way we can increase the happiness of others, which further increases our own happiness too. Regarding sadness, it is important for children to understand that the feeling must be acknowledged and felt, to allow ourselves to process it properly. This is obviously a hard concept for children to grasp. For small 'everyday' sad events (i.e. not bereavement or parental separation, for which you need to seek specialist support), we can encourage them to sit with the feeling alongside a chosen adult who helps them to share it, talk about it and move through it. Other considerations here are the issues of disappointment and loneliness, which are linked to sadness, but separate issues that will each deserve their own attention as they arise.

Lesson Plan: Happiness

Lesson Plan: Happiness

KS1/KS2 Whole class or small group

Time: 1 hour or in shorter slots over several sessions. Follow up over several weeks.

Curriculum links:
PSHE

Learning Outcomes:
- To understand what happiness is and that it feels different for everyone.
- To identify how they feel happiness in their body.
- To identify some of the things that make them feel happy.

Key vocabulary:
happiness, happy, wellbeing, joy, contentment, light-hearted, cheerful, pleased, glad, delighted, overjoyed, annoyed, jealous, body language.

Resources:
- Slides for whiteboard (see plan below)
- Whiteboards and pens
- 'Suns of Happiness' - two circles of orange and yellow card (25cm diameter), with cut from edge to centre on each, slotted together to make a 'sphere' with 8 surfaces to write on
- Gold glitter
- Yellow and orange wool or ribbon
- Scissors and hole punch
- Pencils/pens
- Glue and spatulas

Introduction: If appropriate for the class, begin with a teacher and TA role-play. One adult arrives in the classroom, very cheerful and bouncy. They chat away to the other adult about how wonderful the day is. The other adult receives this well and is pleased for them. *What is the adult feeling? How do we know? How do they show this in their body? How does the other adult react to them?* Guide discussion around the feeling of happiness and the body language and facial expressions that communicate this. Explain that the other adult is pleased about their happiness.

Main teaching:
- Show pictures of a variety of smiling faces (from babies to older people). These people are all feeling happiness – they feel good about something. The happiness might be linked to something in the past, the present or the future. Paired discussion: *What other words mean the same as happy?* Discuss ideas and introduce key vocabulary (see box).
- Show basic outline of a person with no features. *Where do we feel happiness in our bodies?* Children to mark ideas on the person e.g. smile, eyes lit up, relaxed body, arms in the air, wanting to jump, warm feeling tummy or chest. Explain that the way we feel happiness will be different for all of us. There is no right or wrong, just patterns that are common for most people. Paired discussion: *Where do you feel happiness in your body? How do we show it with our behaviour?*
- Show pictures of the things that make you and the other adult in the room feel happy. *Can you guess which things belong to which adult?* Short discussion about why some of these things make you happy. Paired discussion: *What things make you feel happy?* Children to write these down on whiteboards for later reference. Explain that the things that make us happy are different for us all – again, there is no right or wrong.

Activity: Explain that the sun is a symbol we often associate with happiness. Children to make 'Suns of Happiness' and write things that make them happy near the centre of each of the semi-circles (put the sun flat for writing). Then cut the rays around each circle and make hole at the top and attach wool or thread to allow it to be hung. To decorate further, children can put glue on rays and cover with gold glitter.

Wrapping up: *How can your 'Sun of Happiness' help you?* Encourage children to hang the sunshine somewhere visible and return to it when they are feeling low or sad.

Extension: Repeat role play, but other adult becomes annoyed by the happiness of the other. *How does this response affect the first adult?* Guide discussion around how sometimes the happiness of other can make us feel jealous or annoyed because we don't feel that way too. *How can we manage this feeling?*

Follow up: Ask children where they hung their 'Suns of Happiness'. Hang your own in the classroom.

Lesson Plan: Worry

Frame: Worry clouds and raindrops

Lesson Plan: Worry
KS1/KS2 Whole class or small group

Time: 1 hour or in shorter slots over several sessions. Follow up over several weeks.

Curriculum links:
PSHE

Learning Outcomes:
- To understand what worry is and that it feels different for everyone.
- To identify how they feel worry in their body.
- To identify things that make them feel worried.
- To identify things that help them feel better when they are worried.

Key vocabulary: worry, anxiety, concerns, uneasy, on edge, fretting, nervous, fear, body language.

Resources:
- Slides for whiteboard (see plan below)
- Whiteboards and pens
- Frame: 'Worry clouds and raindrops'
- Pencils/Pens

Introduction: If appropriate for the class, begin with teacher and TA role-play. One adult starts pacing and talking quickly about something that is worrying them e.g. pet being ill or a test. The second adult notices they are worried and gets them to sit down and take some breaths. *What is the adult feeling? How do we know? How do they show this in their body? How does the other adult react to them?* Guide discussion around the feeling of worry and the body language and facial expressions that communicate this. Explain that the other adult gently helps them to take a breather from the worry and calm down.

Main teaching:
- Explain that worry might be linked to something in the past, present or future. Paired discussion: *What other words mean the same as worry?* Discuss ideas and introduce key vocabulary (see box). *Is it ok to feel worried? Is it ok or normal to feel worried all the time?* Explain that it is normal and ok to feel worried sometimes, but that if we feel worried all the time we need to ask for help.
- Show a picture of a tiger in the zoo. *How do you feel when you see this tiger?* Show a fierce tiger in the wild. *How would you feel if this tiger was chasing you?* Explain that worry and fear have a very important purpose. They tell us when something might hurt us. Millions of years ago, this fear would help us to find the energy to run away from a tiger that wanted to eat us. Today, our bodies can get confused and they can think that normal everyday events are like the tiger that wants to eat us. This can make us very worried about lots of things e.g. tests, conversations, school productions.
- Show basic outline of a person with no features. *Where do we feel worry in our bodies?* Children to mark ideas on the person e.g. wide eyes, pacing or fidgety body, restless arms and legs, bitten lips or nails, 'butterflies' in tummy or chest. Explain that the way we feel worry will be different for all of us. Paired discussion: *Where do you feel worry in your body? How do we show it in our behaviour?*
- Paired discussion: *What things make you feel worried?* Children to write these down on whiteboards for later reference. Explain that the things that make us worried are different for us all. They can be big things or little things. Sometimes we might not know what is making us feel worried. If appropriate, explore some of the themes that arise. Explain that its not fun to feel worried, but we do need to pause and tune into the feeling because it is giving us a message that something is bothering us. Sharing the worry with someone who cares about us is helpful.

Activity: *What can help us feel better when we are worried?* Explore ideas such as: sharing the worry and talking it through, having a 'worry time' each day when you let yourself worry for a short amount of time (to prevent the worry being always present), writing or drawing worries, asking yourself how true a worry is (with support from adult), watching worries float past like clouds (meditating) or doing breathing exercises. Children to complete 'Worry clouds and raindrops' frame to identify things that could help with a worry.

Wrapping up: *How can 'Worry clouds and raindrops' help you?* Remind children to keep it handy and look at it when they feel worried. Encourage them to ask for a further frame if they have a new worry, as they may need different 'raindrops'.

Extension: Repeat role play, but other adult also becomes worried, reinforcing and encouraging the worry. *How does this response affect the first adult?* Guide discussion around how sometimes we can get drawn into the worries of others and end up making ourselves worried and making things worse for them. *What is a more helpful way to respond?*

Follow up: Ask children which 'Raindrop' has been most helpful in easing their worry?

Worry clouds and raindrops

- Think about the things that worry you. Write some of these things in the Worry clouds.
- What can help us feel better when we are worried? Write some of your ideas in the raindrops. These are the things that can make our worries lighter and help the Worry clouds to float away.

Lesson Plan: Sadness

Lesson Plan: Sadness
KS1/KS2 Whole class or small group

Time: 1 hour or in shorter slots over several sessions. Follow up over several weeks.

Curriculum links:
PSHE

Learning Outcomes:
- To understand what sadness is and that it feels different for everyone.
- To identify how they feel sadness in their body.
- To identify things that make them feel sad.
- To identify things that help them feel better when they are sad.

Key vocabulary: sadness, sad, unhappy, upset, miserable, depressed, gloomy, low, down, heartbroken, disappointed, lonely, body language.

Resources:
- Slides for whiteboard (see plan below)
- Whiteboards and pens
- 'Balloons for Sad Times' – coloured card hot air balloon shapes (15cm wide x 20cm high), coloured wool or ribbon, egg box cartons cut into cups.
- Pencils/Pens
- Hole punch
- Scissors

Introduction: If appropriate for the class, begin with a teacher and TA role-play. One adult sits alone, looking down. The second adult arrives and tries to engage them in cheerful conversation. They realise that something is wrong and ask if they can help. *What is the adult feeling? How do we know? How do they show this in their body? How does the other adult react to them?* Guide discussion around the feeling of sadness and the body language and facial expressions that communicate this. Explain that the other adult is concerned for them and wants to help.

Main teaching:
- Show pictures of a variety of sad people (from babies to older people). These people are all feeling sad about something. The sadness might be linked to something in the past, present or future. Paired discussion: *What other words mean the same as sad?* Discuss ideas and introduce key vocabulary (see box). *Is it ok to feel sad? Is it ok or normal to feel sad all the time?* Explain that it is normal and ok to feel sad sometimes, but that if we feel sad all the time we need to ask for help.

- Show basic outline of a person with no features. *Where do we feel sadness in our bodies?* Children to mark ideas on the person e.g. downturned lips and eyes, floppy or hunched body, hands in pockets, wanting to sit still or curl up, heavy feeling tummy or chest. Explain that the way we feel sadness will be different for us all. Paired discussion: *Where do you feel sadness in your body? How do we show it with our behaviour?*

- Paired discussion: *What things make you feel sad?* Children to write these down on whiteboards for later reference. Explain that the things that make us sad are different for us all. They can be big things or little things. Sometimes we might not know what is making us feel sad. Explore some of the themes that arise e.g. friendship problems, when pets die, when someone special is ill or goes away for a while. Only explore if it is appropriate to do so. Explain that its not fun to feel sad, but we do need to pause and tune into the feeling before we can make it better. Sharing the sadness with someone who cares about us is helpful.

Activity: *What can helps us feel better when we are sad?* The thing making us sad can feel very heavy. There are things we can do to make us feel lighter and more cheerful e.g. speaking to one of our special people, having a cry, reading a favourite book, listening to music, spending time in nature, playing a game etc. Children to make a 'Balloon for Sad Times'. Help children attach ribbons to the egg cup basket and onto the balloon. Explain that we can write the sad thing down and put the paper into the basket (this is the heavy thing that keeps the balloon on the ground). Children to then draw 5-6 vertical stripes on the balloon and write things that help them feel better when they are sad in each stripe. These are the things that make us feel lighter (or help the heavy balloon to float). Attach ribbon to the top of the balloon so it can be hung.

Wrapping up: *How can your 'Balloon for Sad Times' help you?* Encourage children to hang the balloon somewhere visible and return to it when they are feeling low or sad. Remind them to tune into the sad thing, write it down and put it in the basket if this helps them.

Extension: Repeat role play, but other adult dismisses their sadness and tells them to cheer up. *How does this response affect the first adult?* Guide discussion around how sometimes we find it hard to hear the sadness of others - we may tell them they are fine and they should cheer up because we don't want to feel this way too. *What is a more helpful and kind way to respond?*

Follow up: Ask children where they hung their 'Balloons for Sad Times'. Hang your own in the classroom.

Lesson Plan: Anger

Lesson Plan: Anger
KS1/KS2 Whole class or small group

Time: 1 hour or in shorter slots over several sessions. Follow up over several weeks.

Curriculum links:
PSHE

Learning Outcomes:
- To understand what anger is and that it feels different for everyone.
- To identify how they feel anger in their body.
- To identify things that make them feel anger.
- To identify things that help them to process their anger in a healthy way.

Key vocabulary: anger, angry, cross, annoyed, irritated, rage, outrage, furious, livid, frustrated, body language.

Resources:
- Slides for whiteboard (see plan below)
- Whiteboards and pens
- Bottle of fizzy water to demonstrate the popping/overflowing bottle (optional!)
- Frame: 'The bottle that wants to go pop!'
- Pencils/Pens

Introduction: If appropriate for the class, begin with teacher and TA role-play. One adult storms in and starts talking/ shouting angrily to the other about something they have done. The second adult notices they are angry, sits down calmly and waits for them to finish. *What is the adult feeling? How do we know? How do they show this in their body? How does the other adult react to them?* Guide discussion around the feeling of anger and the body language and facial expressions that communicate this. Explain that the other adult allows the them to show their anger without becoming cross or shouting back.

Main teaching:
- Explain that anger might be linked to something in the past, present or future. Paired discussion: *What other words mean the same as anger?* Discuss ideas and introduce key vocabulary (see box). *Is it ok to feel angry? Is it ok or normal to feel angry all the time?* Explain that it is normal and ok to feel angry sometimes, but that if we feel angry all the time we need to ask for help. *Is it ok to hurt other people when we feel angry?* Explain when we are angry we can hurt others with our words and actions. It is ok to feel angry but it is not ok to hurt other people.
- Show basic outline of a person with no features. *Where do we feel anger in our bodies?* Children to mark ideas on the person e.g. narrow, stern eyes, tense body, hot and red face, fists clenched, tight tummy or chest. Explain that the way we feel anger will be different for all of us. Paired discussion: *Where do you feel anger in your body? How do we show it in our behaviour?*
- Show a picture of a bottle of fizzy drink with the lid on and bubbles visible (or demonstrate with a real bottle of fizzy drink). Imagine this bottle contains your anger. When we start to feel the signs of anger rising in our body, like the the bubbles rise in the bottle as we shake it, we need to find healthy ways of letting the anger out before the bottle goes 'pop'. If we let the bottle go pop and our anger explodes out of us, we can hurt others with our words or actions.
- Paired discussion: *What things make you feel angry?* Children to write these down on whiteboards for later reference. Explain that the things that make us angry are different for us all. They can be big things or little things. Sometimes we might not know what is making us feel angry. If appropriate to do so, explore some of the themes that arise. Explain that its not fun to feel angry, but we do need to pause and tune into the feeling because it is giving us a message that something is bothering us. Sharing the anger in a healthy with someone who cares about us is helpful.

Activity: *How can we let our anger out before we go 'pop' like the bottle of fizzy drink?* Explore ideas such as: talking about the anger and trying to work out what is causing it, moving to a calm, quiet space, listening to music, squeezing a toy or cushion, writing or drawing the anger, throwing or kicking a ball, eating crunchy foods, going for a safe run, climb or jump, meditating or doing breathing exercises. Children to complete *'The bottle that wants to go pop!'* to identify healthy ways of letting anger out through the holes in the bottle.

Wrapping up: *How can 'The bottle that wants to go pop!' help you?* Remind children to keep it handy and look at it when they start feeling angry. Remind them that adults are always here to help.

Extension: Repeat role play, but other second adult also becomes angry and defensive, worsening the anger of the first. *How does this response affect the first adult?* Guide discussion around how sometimes when people are angry at us or angry near us, we can get angry at them in return and make things worse for them. *What is a more helpful way to respond?* Recap the response in the Introduction of responding with calm and patience.

Follow up: Ask children which of the holes in their bottle has been most helpful in letting their anger out?

Frame: The bottle that wants to go pop!

The bottle that wants to go pop!

When we feel angry, our anger can be like the bubbles in a bottle of fizzy drink. These bubbles of anger try to rise to the surface – they want to get out! If we let our bubbles of anger escape with a 'pop', we might harm ourselves or other people with our words or actions. Instead, we can find healthy and safe ways to feel our anger and let it out – this is like putting little holes in the side of our bottle of anger to release the pressure before it goes pop!

■ Write some things that make you angry inside the bottle.

■ Beside the holes in the bottle, write or draw some healthy and safe ways to feel and let out your anger e.g. kicking a ball, moving to a calm space, squeezing a cushion, listening to music or meditating.

■ When you next start to feel angry, ask to try out one of these ideas.

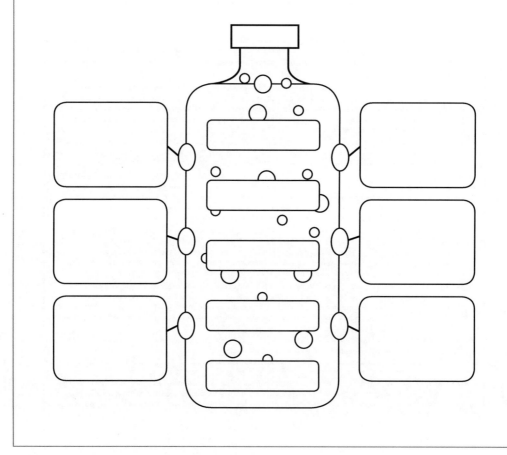

Chapter 6: Managing and Mastering Screens

Lesson Plan: Safe with my screens

Frame: Safe with my screens

Why use it?

There is no getting away from the fact that screens are a big part of everyday life for most children. As adults, we find it very hard to place boundaries around our screen use – for children this is so much harder and they will absolutely need support with it. As we discussed in ***Chapter 6***, we first need to educate them about the risks and dangers of screens and the online world, then help them tune in to how screen use feels for them, and eventually guide them to place appropriate boundaries around their screens, in terms of the time they spend and also the activities they choose. This lesson focuses on the two latter parts of this process. It can be adapted for use with any age group – it is relevant for all.

What next?

This lesson is intended to be a beginning step on the journey to helping children master their screen use. The conversations that arise during this lesson need to be continued and teaching about healthy and responsible interaction with screens will need to be embedded across the curriculum. Use the key issues that come up to plan further lessons and activities tailored to your class. Make a point of having screen-free days or times in school to demonstrate that we can learn and have fun without them. Some children will need specific support around their screen use at home – be mindful of the impact this may be having on them in terms of tiredness, ability to learn and exposure to things that might not be appropriate for their age. Having conversations about this with parents will never be easy, but preparing for them and having an agreed plan in school for these circumstances will help.

Lesson Plan: Safe with my screens

KS1/KS2 Whole class or small group

Time: 1 hour or in shorter slots over several sessions. Follow up over several weeks.

Curriculum links:
PSHE

Learning Outcomes:
- To identify the key screens that they use and how they can be useful.
- To identify how they feel after screen use.
- To understand that there are benefits and drawbacks to using screens.
- To identify some healthy boundaries for their screen use.

Key vocabulary:
screens, digital, internet, online, addiction, boundary, limit

Resources:
- Slides for whiteboard (see plan below)
- Whiteboards and pens
- Frame: 'Safe with my screens'
- Pencils/Pens

Introduction: Show a picture of an old computer from the 1980s. *What do you think this is?* Show a picture of a tablet on the other side of the screen. *Which would you rather have?* Tell funny stories of your own computer use in childhood or adulthood and demonstrate how lucky we are today that screens and the internet can make our lives easier and provide us with entertainment.

Main teaching:
- *What screens do we have?* Show pictures of a variety of screens (TV, laptop, tablet, phone, watch, games console). *What do we use them for?* Discuss the different uses and explore what they can help us with (work, learning, food shopping, connecting with friends, music, films, playing fun games). Paired discussion: *What is your favourite screen?* Share your own and a reason and allow children to share.

- Paired discussion: *Are we always safe when we use our screens? When might things not be safe?* Briefly explore ideas including: sharing personal information and photos, meeting people online who may not be who they say they are and seeing things that aren't appropriate for our age. (This section can be expanded to fill several more lessons, depending on the age of the children and the needs of the class).

- *Can you imagine a life without screens?* We all agree that screens and the internet are fun and helpful, but sometimes we can have too much of a good thing. *What does this mean?* Explain that the more we use screens, the more we want to use them. Our brains love the feeling they get from watching funny things, receiving messages and playing games. But our brains aren't designed to cope with this all the time. Sometimes we find it really hard to put our screens down and we don't feel good when we do – in our minds and our bodies. We sometimes use the word 'addiction' to describe the situation when we can't put things down and keep coming back for more, even when it is not good for us.

Activity: To protect ourselves from the things that are unsafe online and to keep our minds and bodies healthy, we need to put boundaries or limits around our screen use. This is important for adults and children. Model your own 'Safe with my screens' frame, before supporting children to complete their own. Explain that adults in school will help with boundaries in the classroom and at home, they can ask their parents to help. The boundaries might be different in each place. Focus on discussing: *When do I want to use screens and what could I do instead? How do I know when I have had long enough using a screen? What can I do when I see something I don't like on a screen?* This activity may take several sessions, especially if the idea of boundaries is new to children.

Wrapping up: Paired discussion: *What will your target be to make your screen use healthier?* Model your own example e.g. I use my phone late in the evening and it stops me from sleeping. My target is to always put my phone on silent and on charge downstairs by 8pm every evening. Children to share their ideas and write on their frame. Explain everyone can check in with targets over the coming days and weeks and encourage each other. Display yours in the classroom and ask children to prompt you about it.

Extension: Paired discussion: *What helpful ideas can you give to younger children to help them to become masters of their screens too?* Explore further ideas that have arisen during activity. Produce a set of rules in age-appropriate language that the class can share in an assembly with younger children (assuming that consistent messages about screens are being given across the school).

Follow up: Ask how children have been getting on with their targets. Give an update on your progress too.

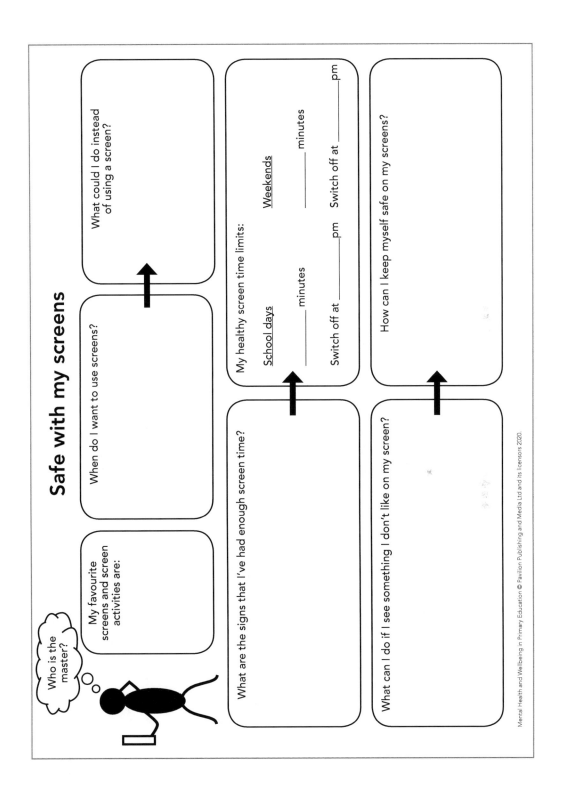

Safe with my screens

Who is the master?

My favourite screens and screen activities are:

When do I want to use screens?

What could I do instead of using a screen?

What are the signs that I've had enough screen time?

My healthy screen time limits:

School days _____ minutes

Switch off at _____ pm

Weekends _____ minutes

Switch off at _____ pm

What can I do if I see something I don't like on my screen?

How can I keep myself safe on my screens?

Chapter 17 Yearly Transitions

Frame: Looking back to look forward

Why use it?

There are many different methods of reflection that can be used at the end of a school year. This frame first takes children through the steps of looking back at the year that is ending – appreciating the good elements and acknowledging the difficult or challenging parts. Second, it encourages them to use these insights to help them look forward to the new year with confidence and hope. Adult modelling of any frame is helpful of course, but with this one in particular, guiding children through elements of your own review of the year, especially how you will look forward to the next year, can show them the long-term benefits of engaging with this process. The frame may need to be simplified for use with younger children or adapted into a more practical activity. However, don't be dissuaded from using it with younger groups – it is never too early to begin learning how to reflect positively on experiences. The frame could also be adapted to include whole-class observations on the year, looking back on their highlights and how they feel they have developed as a team.

What next?

Obviously, the outcomes of this activity will be interesting to the outgoing class teacher and TA, but ultimately, the completed frames need to be passed to the new teaching team to inform their planning for the next year. Children also need to be given the opportunity to review their 'Looking forward...' section, in particular, in the autumn term.

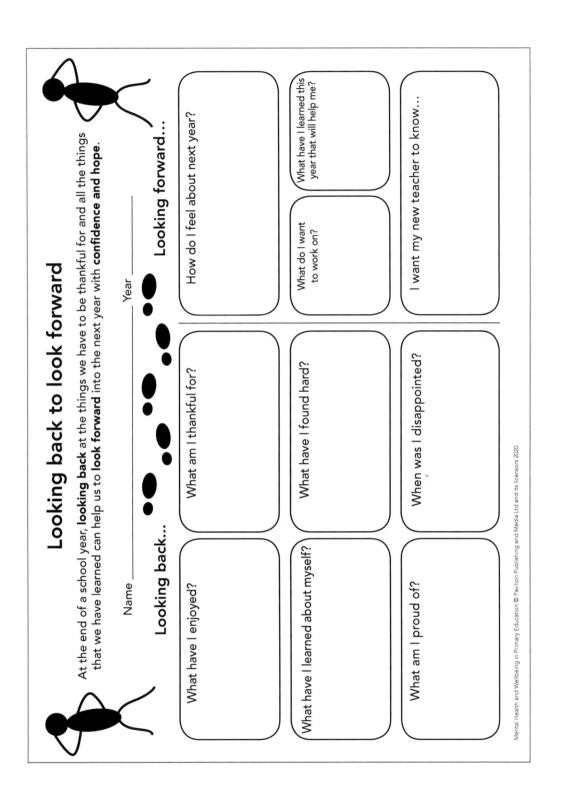

Looking back to look forward

At the end of a school year, **looking back** at the things we have to be thankful for and all the things that we have learned can help us to **look forward** into the next year with **confidence and hope.**

Name _____

Year _____

Looking back...

What have I enjoyed?

What have I learned about myself?

What am I proud of?

What am I thankful for?

What have I found hard?

When was I disappointed?

Looking forward...

How do I feel about next year?

What do I want to work on?

What have I learned this year that will help me?

I want my new teacher to know...

Mental Health and Wellbeing in Primary Education © Pavilion Publishing and Media Ltd and its licensors 2020.

Frame: This is me...

Why use it?

This frame can be used as a transition day activity, at the start of a new year or when a TA begins working with children who are new to them during the year. It will help build an initial picture of the child, their circumstances and any additional needs, which can then be explored further as opportunities arise. 'How I feel about learning right now' is the most important area to explore here. Knowing how a child feels about their learning is critical to being able to target support and make appropriate language choices. If they are feeling positive, they will hopefully be receptive to praise and encouragement. However, if they are ambivalent, despondent or disconnected from their learning, they may find praise and encouragement hard to receive. A gentle approach will be needed to address this over time.

What next?

Keep the completed frame to hand and refer to it often, in order to guide planning and support. Ask children to review the information they gave at intervals and as mentioned previously, allow them to make changes as they wish. Use the information given in 'Things I am curious about...' as much as you can – perhaps for early morning work or homework topics. Valuing and encouraging curiosity is key to helping children develop the love for learning that we wish them all to have.

This is me...

My name is _____. I am _____ years old.

Things I want to practise...

Things I might need help with...

Things I am curious about...

My picture

How I feel about learning right now...

Other important things I want you to know about me...

Things I am proud of...

Things I love...

Things I'm not keen on...

Further Reading and Guidance

Autism spectrum condition

National Autistic Society – www.autism.org.uk

Social Stories – www.carolgraysocialstories.com/social-stories/

ADHD

ADHD Foundation – www.adhdfoundation.org.uk

Anxiety

Anxiety UK – www.anxietyuk.org.uk

Meek L (2019) *Be Your Own Superhero*. London: Penguin.

Attachment and trauma

Beacon House, Therapeutic Services and Trauma Team –
https://beaconhouse.org.uk

Behaviour in schools

UNICEF Rights Respecting Schools – www.unicef.org.uk/rights-respecting-schools/

Restorative Justice for Schools – www.restorativejustice4schools.co.uk

The Incredible Years (The Webster–Stratton Approach) – www.incredibleyears.com

Eating disorders

Beat Eating Disorders – www.beateatingdisorders.org.uk

Emotional intelligence and regulation

Zones of Regulation – www.zonesofregulation.com/index.html

The Incredible 5 Point Scale – www.5pointscale.com

Decider Skills – www.thedecider.org.uk

Emotional and social interventions

Nurtureuk – www.nurtureuk.org

ELSA Network – www.elsanetwork.org

Thrive – www.thriveapproach.com

Gender identity

The Gender Identity Research and Education Society (GIRES) – www.gires.org.uk

Mermaids UK – https://mermaidsuk.org.uk

Growth mindset

Growth Mindset Culture – www.mindsetworks.com/schools/culture

Low mood and depression

Depression UK – http://depressionuk.org

Mental health

Royal College of Psychiatrists –www.rcpsych.ac.uk/mental-health

Mental Health Foundation – www.mentalhealth.org.uk

Mind – www.mind.org.uk/information-support/for-young-people/

Young Minds – www.youngminds.org.uk

Youth in Mind – www.youthinmind.com

Child Mind Institute – www.childmind.org

Kooth – www.kooth.com

Mental health in schools

Mentally Healthy Schools – www.mentallyhealthyschools.org.uk

The National Nurturing Schools Programme – www.nurtureuk.org/news/national-nurturing-schools-programme

Anna Freud – Schools in Mind Programme – www.annafreud.org/what-we-do/schools-in-mind/

Mental health policy

Department for Health and Department for Education (2017) *Transforming Children and Young People's Mental Health Provision: A Green Paper.* Available at: https://assets.publishing.service.gov.uk/government/uploads/system/uploads/attachment_data/file/664855/Transforming_children_and_young_people_s_mental_health_provision.pdf

Department for Health and NHS England (2015) *Future in Mind: Promoting, Protecting and Improving Our Children and Young People's Mental Health and Wellbeing.* Available at: https://assets.publishing.service.gov.uk/government/uploads/system/uploads/attachment_data/file/414024/Childrens_Mental_Health.pdf

Department for Education (2018) *Mental Health and Behaviour in Schools.* Available at: https://assets.publishing.service.gov.uk/government/uploads/system/uploads/attachment_data/file/755135/Mental_health_and_behaviour_in_schools__.pdf

Mindfulness and meditation

Mindfulness in Schools Project – www.mindfulnessinschools.org

Relax Kids – www.relaxkids.com

Online safety

Child Exploitation and Online Protection command – www.ceop.police.uk/safety-centre/

Childnet International – www.childnet.com

UK Safer Internet Centre – www.saferinternet.org.uk/advice-centre/teachers-and-school-staff

PSHE

Department for Education (2019) *Relationships Education, Relationships and Sex Education (RSE) and Health Education Statutory Guidance* [online]. Available at: https://assets.publishing.service.gov.uk/government/uploads/system/uploads/attachment_data/file/805781/Relationships_Education__Relationships_and_Sex_Education__RSE__and_Health_Education.pdf

PSHE Association – www.pshe-association.org.uk

Safeguarding

HM Government (2018): *Working Together to Safeguard Children* [online]. Available at: https://assets.publishing.service.gov.uk/government/uploads/system/uploads/attachment_data/file/779401/Working_Together_to_Safeguard-Children.pdf

Child Protection Online Monitoring System – www.cpoms.co.uk

My Concern Safeguarding Software – www.myconcern.co.uk

Tics and Tourette's

Tourettes Action UK – www.tourettes-action.org.uk/

Wellbeing

Bethune A (2018) *Wellbeing in the Primary Classroom*. London: Bloomsbury Education.

New Economics Foundation (2011) *5 Ways to Wellbeing* [online]. Available at: https://neweconomics.org/uploads/files/d80eba95560c09605d_uzm6b1n6a.pdf

Action for Happiness – www.actionforhappiness.org

The Schools Advisory Service: Pupil and Staff Wellbeing Programmes – www.schooladvice.co.uk/whole-school-wellbeing-services/

The Daily Mile – www.thedailymile.co.uk

Skip2bFit – www.skip2bfit.com

Glossary of Terms

Abuse – A behaviour which causes deliberate or intentional harm to another. Abuse can take many forms, including verbal, psychological, physical, sexual and discrimination. (See also neglect.)

Adverse childhood experiences (ACEs) – Potentially traumatic events that may have negative and long-lasting negative effects on a person's development and wellbeing. Encompasses a wide range of events such as parental separation, abuse and parental mental illness.

Affect – This refers to a person's 'in the moment' emotional state which can change rapidly. Sometimes affect is compared to 'the weather', whereas mood is the 'climate' which has a longer term, more pervasive pattern.

Anorexia nervosa – A type of eating disorder in which a person has a preoccupation with their weight and shape, alongside a reduction in weight to less than 85% of that expected.

Anxiety – A normal human emotion and is most often transient. Whilst 'worry' tends to refer to the repetitive negative thoughts in our heads, anxiety can affect our entire body in a physical way too.

Attachment difficulties – These are emotional and behavioural patterns in children that are largely determined by their relationships with their primary caregivers and the nature of the caregiving they receive. These include insecure attachment and disorganised attachments patterns.

Attention deficit hyperactivity disorder (ADHD) – A neurodevelopmental condition, affecting the frontal cortex, in which an individual has difficulties with concentration, hyperactivity and impulsivity.

Autism spectrum condition (ASC) – A neurodevelopmental condition in which an individual has difficulties with social communication and interaction, restricted or stereotyped behaviours, interests, and activities and also sensory challenges.

Avoidant and restrictive food intake disorder (ARFID) – A term sometimes used for individuals who eat a very restricted diet and experience restriction in growth and/or impaired functioning because of this. Although the person is often underweight, weight loss is not intentional as in eating disorders such as anorexia nervosa.

Behavioural activation – This refers to strategies designed to increase positive activity level, with the aim of increasing access to positive reinforcement and experiences that support positive mental health.

Behaviours that challenge – Behaviours which are considered to be socially unacceptable and which are of sufficient frequency and/or intensity that they impact on the quality of life of the child and those around them.

Biomedical model – A model of health which looks primarily at the physical causes of illness, and may not fully consider the role of psychological and social factors.

Boxall profile – An online tool for the assessment of children's emotional, behavioural and social development and levels of need.

Bulimia nervosa – A type of eating disorder in which there are episodes of uncontrolled bingeing on food, followed by compensatory 'purging' or 'non-purging' behaviours.

Child and Adolescent Mental Health Service (CAMHS) – A service for children and young people experiencing mental health difficulties and/or neurodevelopmental difficulties. They are commissioned to support children and families from 0 to 18 years of age.

Clinical psychologists – Psychologists specifically trained in the assessment and treatment of mental, emotional and behavioural conditions.

Cognitive behavioural therapy (CBT) – An evidence-based therapeutic intervention designed to highlight the relationship between our thoughts, feelings and behaviours.

Comorbidity – The presence of one or more co-occurring conditions which may be overlapping and have similar aetiology.

Conduct disorder – A condition closely linked to ODD, which occurs in adolescents. The defiant behaviours are also associated with persistent aggression or other antisocial acts such as vandalism, fire setting or harm to animals.

De-escalation – This refers to a process designed to reduce escalations of conflict and distress behaviours and the risks associated with this.

Depression – A mental health condition characterised by low mood, reduced energy and a loss of interest and pleasure. In children, it may also lead to irritability.

Depression may be classified as mild, moderate or severe, depending on the number of symptoms and the impact on a person's functioning.

Designated Senior Lead (DSL) for Mental Health – All schools need to appoint a DSL for Mental Health by 2025. They will be appropriately trained to enable them to be responsible for leading a whole-school approach to mental health and wellbeing.

Diagnosis – Primarily a system of classification that uses a biomedical model to understand a child's difficulties.

DSM-5 – The Diagnostic and Statistical Manual of Mental Disorders, 5th edition, published by the American Psychiatric Association, offers a common language and standard criteria for the classification of mental health conditions.

Early help assessment (EHA) – This school-led assessment is designed to identify what help a child and their family needs in order to prevent a situation escalating to a level where a statutory assessment under the Children Act 1989 would be necessary.

Eating disorder – A mental health condition in which an unhealthy relationship with food affects functioning. It is associated with behaviours centred around weight and shape, such as fasting, bingeing or excessive exercise. Examples include anorexia nervosa and bulimia nervosa.

Education and Health Care Plan – If, following an education, health and care (EHC) needs assessment, it is deemed that a child needs more support than can be provided through standard school SEND support, then an EHCP will be drawn up to provide detailed guidance on how to meet their needs.

Educational consequences – These demonstrate the connection between a child's action and the outcome. They need to be logical, meaningful and appropriate for the individual and the incident.

Educational psychologist – Psychologists work within local authorities, in partnership with families and other professionals, to help children and young people who are having difficulties with their learning.

Emotional dysregulation – The inability to manage the intensity and duration of negative emotions such as fear, sadness or anger.

Emotional intelligence – This encompasses the capacity of an individual to be aware of, control and express their emotions, and to handle interpersonal relationships judiciously and empathetically.

Emotional literacy – The ability to express one's emotional state and communicate one's feelings using language.

Emotional literacy support assistant (ELSA) – An ELSA provides targeted emotional support for children during focused, short-term interventions, in order that they can learn more effectively and develop social and emotional skills and coping strategies.

Exposure and response prevention (ERP) – This involves exposure to a feared situation with a focus on reduction of 'safety behaviours', such as using hand gel or checking dates in germ-related OCD. It is recommended as part of CBT.

Fight or flight response – The fight or flight response is a physiological reaction that occurs in response to an actual or perceived threat or danger.

Formulation – Psychological formulation refers to an understanding of a child's current presentation using a psychosocial model.

Functional analysis of behaviour – This refers to the examination of why a specific behaviour occurs. It looks at the antecedents and consequences of the behaviour to highlight its function and maintaining factors.

Gender dysphoria – A descriptive term for an individual who is not content with their assigned gender. Also used as a diagnostic term.

Gender identity – An individual's identification as male, female or another category such as gender neutral. It does not always correspond to one's biological sex.

Generalised anxiety disorder (GAD) – An anxiety condition in which a person feels persistently anxious. The anxiety is not restricted to, or dominated by, any particular circumstances. Symptoms may include persistent nervousness, trembling, sweating and dizziness.

Graduated approach – The graduated approach of Assess Plan Do Review (APDR), as described in the Special Educational Needs and Disability (SEND) Code of Practice (SEN Code of Practice, 2015), can provide a template for the initial response to mental health concerns. It involves teaching staff noticing, talking, providing initial support and monitoring the impact.

Growth mindset – This mindset asserts that one's innate intelligence, talents and temperament are the foundations from which you can grow – through effort, experience and drawing on the support of others.

Hyperarousal – This refers to difficulties with relaxing which can lead to irritability, anger outbursts and impaired concentration.

Hyperkinetic disorder – A term used in ICD-10 to describe a condition in which there are difficulties with inattention, impulsivity and hyperactivity. In the UK it is often used interchangeably with ADHD, which is the term used in DSM-5.

Hypervigilance – This is a state of increased alertness where a person demonstrates a high level of sensitivity to their environment.

International Statistical Classification of Diseases and Related Health Problems (ICD), versions 10 and 11 – A medical classification list by the World Health Organisation used to aid diagnosis. ICD-11 was published in 2018 and is due to come into clinical use in 2022.

Learning disability – An umbrella term used to describe a range of conditions defined by three core criteria: an IQ of below 70, functional impairment and onset in childhood.

Learning environment – The physical areas in school in which learning takes place, including the classroom, the hall, corridors, the library and the outside space.

Learning preferences – The notable preferences for learning activities and styles that an individual has.

Limbic system – This refers to structures in the brain which work together to regulate some of the brain's most important processes, including those relating to motivation, emotion, learning and memory. It is made up of the amygdala, hippocampus, thalamus, hypothalamus, basal ganglia and cingulate gyrus. It operates by influencing the endocrine system and the autonomic nervous system.

Looked after children (LAC) – Children under the care of the local authority, such as in foster placements or children's homes.

Meditation – A more formal extension of mindfulness, in which an individual concentrates on fostering a peaceful mind and a relaxed body. It emphasises the importance of the breath in creating calm and developing an awareness and acceptance of thoughts.

Mental health – A person's psychological and emotional wellbeing.

Mental health difficulties – Problems with a person's psychological and emotional wellbeing which may or may not meet the threshold for the diagnosis of a particular condition.

Mental health condition – Mental health problems which meet the diagnostic threshold for a particular disorder.

Mental health support team – This team will work with clusters of schools to support early intervention for mental health difficulties. They will be jointly managed by health and education sectors.

Meta-analysis – Statistical analysis that combines the results of multiple scientific studies on the same subject.

Mindfulness – A practice concerned with being in the present moment, developing one's awareness of what is happening right now and remaining with that. Developing the ability to be mindful is a vital component of building emotional intelligence.

Mood-enhancing thinking – Thinking patterns which encourage feelings of wellbeing and happiness. These can be encouraged using gratitude and positivity practices.

Motivation – The internal drive for our actions and behaviours. This can be intrinsic, related to personal values, morals and interests; or extrinsic, related to external factors, such as the desire for positive outcomes or the avoidance of negative outcomes.

Neglect – This refers to the failure of adequate provision of care.

Neurodevelopmental differences – Differences in the brain which may affect emotion, learning ability, self-control and memory.

Nurture – Nurturing provision and interactions focus on the importance of the social environment around a child – specifically, giving targeted opportunities to children who may have missed out on early nurturing experiences, to enable them to thrive emotionally and socially in school and later in life.

Obsessive compulsive disorder (OCD) – A mental health condition is characterised by recurrent obsessional thoughts or compulsions. Obsessional thoughts are intrusive and unwanted – they may take the form of ideas, images or impulses. Compulsions are acts or rituals which are repeated again and again – they are performed in order to prevent an unlikely harmful event occurring.

Occupational therapist – A healthcare professional who provides support to enable people to do the things that matter to them. They focus on developing, recovering or maintaining the skills needed to perform daily living and working activities.

Oppositional defiant disorder (ODD) – A mental health condition occurring in younger children which is characterised by persistently defiant, disobedient and disruptive behaviour.

Paediatrician – A medical doctor specialising in the treatment and management of physical health problems in children. They may be hospital- or community-based.

Panic disorder – An anxiety disorder characterised by recurrent attacks of severe anxiety or panic which are not restricted to a particular situation and often 'come out of the blue'.

Pastoral support team – A team of staff in school responsible for the pastoral care and wellbeing of children. This may include therapists, learning mentors and Designated Safeguarding Persons for Child Protection, among others.

Pervasive developmental disorder – A diagnostic term encompassing a range of conditions in which there is a delay in the development of social and communication skills. ASC is an example of a pervasive developmental disorder.

Post-traumatic stress disorder (PTSD) – A mental health condition defined by clusters of symptoms including re-experiencing, avoidance or numbing and anxiety following a traumatic event.

Prosocial behaviours – These behaviours help children to foster positive relationships with others, view mistakes as opportunities for growth and consider the impact of their actions on those around them. They can relate to tone of voice, body language and positive language choices.

Protective consequences – These consequences look forward to provide future protection for the child or others in the event that difficult behaviours continue. They should be viewed as measures to keep everyone safe, rather than as a punishment.

Psychiatrist – A medical doctor specialising in the diagnosis and treatment of mental health conditions.

Psychoeducation – The process of providing information about the reasons for, symptoms of and treatment for psychological disorders. It is an important intervention in its own right, which can empower people to feel more in control of their experiences.

Resilience – This refers to the ability of an individual to cope with setbacks, respond flexibly and adapt to change.

Ritual – A repeating, predictable and comforting action or activity.

Safety behaviours – In this book this term refers to reassuring, anxiety-reducing behaviours, such as the use of antiseptic hand gel in a person with germ-related OCD. Although the behaviour may reduce anxiety temporarily it ultimately perpetuates a condition by creating false reassurance and reliance.

Selective mutism – This is a childhood anxiety disorder characterised by a child's inability to speak and communicate effectively within a specific social setting, such as at school.

Self-awareness – This encompasses the knowledge we have about our own fundamental nature and also the knowledge we have about ourselves in the moment.

Self-efficacy – This is the belief an individual has in their ability to perform. It will fluctuate and develop over time and affects emotions, thoughts and actions.

Self-esteem – This involves an individual's overall subjective emotional evaluation of personal worth. It is related to the messages conveyed to them through their attachment relationships and experiences.

Self-harm (or self-injury) – These terms refer to behaviour which is an expression of distress, and which results in harm to an individual. The reasons for this will vary from child to child, but may include anger and frustration, a desire to feel something when feeling numb, a desire to let others know of their distress and unhappiness or a desire to punish oneself if feeling worthless.

Self-referral – The ability for a family or a young person over the age of 16 to refer themselves to a service such as CAMHS, rather than being referred by a professional such as a teacher or GP.

Separation anxiety – Refers to an emotional response triggered when an individual is being separated from another person. Separation anxiety is typical for all children at different stages within their development.

Social modelling – Refers to the process of learning through observation of others and imitation.

Special educational needs and disability (SEND) – The umbrella term for the learning difficulties and disabilities that require extra educational provision to be made for a child. The needs may relate to communication and language; cognition and learning; social, emotional and mental health; and sensory and/or physical needs.

Special educational needs co-ordinator (SENCO) – The individual responsible for SEND assessment, provision and liaison in a school. The terms SENDCO or Inclusion Lead may be preferred in some schools.

Speech and language therapist – Therapists trained to assess, diagnose and treat speech, language and communication impairments in children of all ages and in adults. They also assess difficulties with eating and drinking.

Social Stories – These story-based interventions were created by Carol Gray in 1991 to support children with ASC. They are short descriptions of a particular situation, event or activity, which include specific information about what to expect in that situation and why. The terms 'Social Story' and 'Social Stories' are trademarks originated and owned by Carol Gray.

Strengths and difficulties questionnaire (SDQ) – This is a brief behavioural screening questionnaire for use with children aged 3–16 years, the outcomes of which can give an overall picture of a child's social and emotional presentation. It can be completed by children (aged 11 or above), parents or teaching staff.

Temperament – This the evolving nature of an individual and the tendencies that determine the differences in their emotions, thoughts and behaviours as compared to others.

Theory of mind – The ability to attribute mental states (beliefs, perspectives, intents, desires, emotions, knowledge) to oneself and to others, and to understand that others have mental states that are different from one's own.

THRIVE model – A model of mental health care provision in which needs are agreed collaboratively between all involved, and not based purely on severity, diagnosis or health care pathways. It is replacing the traditional tier model in some areas of the UK.

Tics – These can be classified as motor, involving an involuntary, fast, repeated twitching movement, or vocal, involving a noise which is made involuntarily and repetitively. They are more likely to occur at times of stress, tiredness or worry. Some medications may also worsen tics.

Tier system – The traditional model for mental health services for children in the UK, based on graded levels of support ranging from universal (available to all) at Tier 1, to specialised in-patient care at Tier 4.

Tourette's syndrome – A hereditary mental health condition which may be diagnosed when both vocal and motor tics are seen over period of greater than a year, and they cause distress and/or functional impairment for a child.

Transgender – An individual who identifies with a gender different from their gender assigned at birth.

Transition – The change between one place, activity or situation and another.

Transitional object – An object which supports an individual through a transition, providing familiarity, consistency and comfort.

Trauma – In this book this term is used to describe psychological trauma, which is the damage to the mind sustained following a traumatic event.

Trigger – An object, event or experience that leads to a particular response in an individual.

Wellbeing – A desirable state of welfare and contentment, which is a precursor to good mental health and also provides essential support for mental health.

Index

A

abuse 18, 19, 34, 90, 111, 137, 176, 179, 311

adrenaline 92, 152, 161

adult emotional regulation 84, 91, 161

aggression 74, 111, 116, 117, 126, 151, 152, 153, 172, 178, 312

anger 17, 37, 39, 76, 90, 91, 92, 98, 126, 140, 148, 151, 152, 153, 156, 157, 160, 171, 178, 207, 289, 291, 298, 313, 315, 318

anorexia nervosa 29, 221, 222, 223, 224, 225, 226, 311, 312, 313

antisocial behaviour 5

anxiety
  separation anxiety 123, 128, 129, 130, 139, 140, 240, 318

anxiety see also obsessive compulsive disorder panic worries vii, 4, 13, 21, 29, 62, 64, 75, 76, 94, 98, 106, 121–147, 153, 154, 156, 160, 162, 169, 171, 172, 177, 179, 180, 181, 187, 188, 189, 193, 194, 195, 198, 210, 211, 214, 216, 219, 221, 226, 240, 245, 246, 252, 259, 263, 264, 265, 307, 311, 314, 317, 318

assemblies 41, 47, 52, 57, 65, 83, 84, 102, 124, 134, 163, 190, 199, 241, 250

assessment iv, 7, 11, 20, 22, 23, 28, 29, 32, 51, 62, 63, 64, 84, 85, 100, 140, 151, 156, 165, 183, 190, 195, 196, 200, 201, 206, 210, 222, 223, 252, 265, 312, 313, 319
  external assessment 22, 252
  specialist assessment 11, 165, 210, 223

atomoxetine 207

attachment 2, 11, 36, 39, 43, 44, 55, 89, 92, 94, 128, 129, 146, 155, 156, 160, 166, 167, 168, 169, 170, 171, 172, 173, 174, 175, 179, 180, 181, 221, 238, 247, 264, 307, 311, 318
  ambivalent attachment 169, 171, 172, 180
  attachment difficulties 11, 39, 43, 55, 146, 160, 167, 168, 169, 174, 175, 180, 221, 238, 247, 264, 311
  attachment disorder 167, 168
  attachment styles 92, 169, 170
  disorganised attachment 167, 168, 169, 172, 173, 180
  insecure-avoidant attachment 169, 170
  primary attachment figure 172
  reactive attachment disorder 167, 168
  secure attachment 36, 167, 169, 170, 180

attention deficit disorder 201

attunement 169, 176

auditory stimuli 79

autonomic arousal 36, 121, 160

B

behavioural activation 145, 149, 312

behaviour policy 51, 55, 56, 58, 60, 62, 69, 95, 161, 204

behaviours that challenge 20, 62, 96, 126, 151, 152, 154, 156, 162, 163, 243, 312

belonging vii, viii, 36, 82, 83, 84, 85, 86, 101, 197, 242, 250, 258, 264

bereavement 42, 137, 144, 153, 292

bingeing 225, 312, 313
biomedical model 23, 312, 313
body language 54, 56, 160, 317
bonding 82, 243, 247, 251, 253, 256
Boxall Profile see also nurture 20, 34, 99
brain development 89, 112, 116, 167, 184
buddy system 139, 254
budgets 8, 27, 64, 81
bulimia nervosa 221, 225, 226, 228, 312

C
class handover see also transition 21, 249, 250, 252, 253, 256, 258
Clinical Commissioning Group 19, 27
Common Assessment Framework 22
community engagement 84
competition 57, 96, 193, 194
concentration 74, 75, 76, 79, 103, 127, 144, 171, 172, 180, 189, 193, 199, 200, 201, 205, 206, 210, 223, 225, 227, 229, 241, 311, 315
confidentiality 31, 65, 97, 100
connection 35, 40, 42, 43, 44, 49, 55, 58, 60, 67, 77, 82, 95, 115, 125, 156, 170, 238, 264, 266, 313
coprolalia 208
counselling 30, 85
creative activities 100, 101, 104, 253
curriculum interventions 66

D
de-escalation 60, 61, 125, 157, 160, 165, 174, 312
defiance 43, 151, 152, 153, 154, 164
depression 81, 143, 144, 145, 147, 148, 149, 187, 216, 219, 308, 312, 313
Designated Safeguarding Persons for Child Protection see also safeguarding 19, 317
diagnostic model see also DSM-5 ICD-10

ICD-11 24
diet 74, 86, 222, 224, 225, 226, 228, 236, 311
digital technologies see also internet screen use 109, 110, 111, 112, 116
disappointment 36, 54, 95, 292
dissociation 178
domestic violence 18, 92, 172, 176, 177, 180
dopamine 111, 200, 206
dyslexia 23
dyspraxia 23
dysregulation 53, 60, 92, 98, 103, 143, 146, 148, 190, 264, 313

E
ear defenders 75, 79, 124, 190, 263, 278
early intervention vii, 6, 17, 26, 234, 237, 316
eating disorders see also: anorexia nervosa bulimia nervosa 29, 221, 222, 224, 225, 226, 227, 228, 229, 307, 311
educational consequences 58, 60, 61, 204, 313
emotional development 25, 43, 173, 197
emotional intelligence see also interventions for building emotional intelligence 9, 69, 89, 90, 92, 93, 96, 99, 100, 103, 104, 105, 106, 107, 126, 160, 161, 289, 308, 313, 316
emotional literacy 89, 90, 98, 99, 103, 160, 172, 174, 291, 314
emotional literacy framework 98
emotional skills 44, 258, 314
empathy 24, 55, 57, 91, 99, 116, 160, 173, 178
Equality Act 189, 202
external agencies 7, 9, 10, 20, 63
eye contact 54, 160, 183, 185, 191, 203, 205

F

fasting 17, 53, 143, 144, 148, 225, 311, 313

fiddle toys 77, 146, 203

fight or flight see also stress response 92, 133, 140, 160, 161, 314

flashbacks 177, 179, 180

fluoxetine 147

food culture 74

formulation 23, 24, 28, 33, 34, 147, 314

friendships 115, 132, 145, 147, 167, 170, 183, 185, 192, 204, 252, 258, 264, 282

frontal lobe 199, 200, 207

functional analysis see also STAR chart 62, 155, 165, 314

G

GDPR 32

gender dysphoria 216, 217, 218, 219, 220, 314

gender identity 216, 217, 218, 219, 308, 314

graduated approach 21, 22, 23, 33, 55, 58, 62, 63, 259, 314

gratitude v, 102, 245, 247, 266, 316

greetings 240

growth mindset 2, 37, 39, 261, 272, 308, 314

guanfacine 207

H

happiness 52, 73, 90, 106, 291, 294, 310, 316

Health Education 6, 7, 12, 96, 116, 219, 310

healthy eating 74, 82, 86, 228

holidays 40, 100, 207, 236, 238, 249, 251, 252, 253, 254, 255, 256, 261, 264
    family holidays 40, 253, 254, 255
    school holidays 207, 238, 254, 255, 256

home visits 234, 238

homework 47, 138, 147, 207, 210, 240, 255, 261, 304

hope v, 2, 7, 8, 9, 11, 24, 37, 53, 60, 63, 91, 92, 95, 163, 174, 175, 190, 194, 244, 247, 251, 254, 271, 272, 291, 302, 318

hyperactivity 20, 24, 126, 199, 200, 201, 202, 203, 211, 311, 315

hyperarousal 176, 178, 180, 315

hyperkinetic disorder 201, 315

hypervigilance 132, 167, 171, 178, 179, 180, 315

I

impulsivity 194, 199, 200, 201, 202, 203, 204, 205, 211, 311, 315

inattention 20, 200, 203, 205, 211, 315

independence 41, 70, 89, 90, 96, 147, 170, 189, 196, 236, 244, 254, 259, 263, 264

internet 109, 110, 111, 112, 309
    online activities 111, 113
    online safety 48, 69, 113, 114, 309

interventions for building emotional intelligence 100

irritability 144, 145, 148, 168, 178, 312, 313, 315

K

kindness 52, 57, 67

KS1 237, 254, 256

KS2 48, 254, 256

L

language choices 51, 53, 54, 56, 62, 304, 317

leadership skills 48, 82, 83

learning disability 27, 90, 93, 148, 152, 187, 200, 315

learning environment 77, 81, 86, 124,

134, 137, 145, 156, 170, 171, 173, 179, 189, 202, 203, 209, 210, 214, 233, 253, 256, 315

calm area 58, 59, 100, 124, 146, 156, 204

classroom layout 78, 253

class rules 113, 192, 205, 245, 253

displays 52, 59, 74, 79, 80, 92, 189

seating 52, 78, 203, 211

learning preferences 42, 252, 274, 315

learning styles 40, 42, 49

limbic system 89, 315

listening skills 83, 94

local authority 19, 22, 27, 30, 32, 34, 184, 313, 315

low mood 29, 143, 144, 145, 146, 147, 148, 169, 229, 308, 312

lunchtime 61, 74, 80, 82, 83, 125, 127, 183, 192, 193, 204, 223, 225, 228, 235, 260

lunchtime staff 80, 125

quiet lunch club 82

M

mania 143

Maslow's Hierarchy of Needs 35

mastery 37, 42, 96, 103

meditation 85, 104, 105, 174, 179, 241, 309, 315

melatonin 75, 112

memory 89, 103, 128, 140, 183, 196, 201, 205, 261, 315, 316

menopause 85

mental health

incidence of mental health difficulties 3

mental health policy 6, 8, 10, 309

mental wellbeing ix, 1, 5, 6, 18, 26, 27, 89

mentoring 30, 163, 264

methylphenidate 206, 207

mindful activities 103, 104, 125

mindfulness 85, 102, 103, 104, 105, 106, 146, 179, 244, 309, 315, 316

mistakes 36, 37, 46, 54, 56, 96, 201, 202, 242, 250, 317

mood disorder 143, 148, 164

mood-enhancing thinking 102, 105, 316

motivation 13, 35, 36, 38, 39, 45, 49, 55, 56, 57, 89, 93, 94, 96, 148, 172, 187, 189, 315, 316

extrinsic motivators 38

intrinsic motivators 38

movement 44, 64, 76, 78, 79, 86, 101, 190, 203, 208, 239, 241, 263, 278, 320

breaks 64, 76, 101, 190, 203, 241, 262, 278

daily movement 76

music 30, 47, 79, 80, 81, 104, 174, 240

N

negative thoughts 122, 144, 178, 246, 311

neglect 18, 19, 90, 167, 168, 176, 311, 316

neurodevelopmental conditions 29, 95, 152, 207, 238, 249

neurodevelopmental differences 75, 90, 197, 238, 316

neuroplasticity 36

nightmares 177, 180

noise see also auditory stimuli sensory sensitivities 64, 75, 79, 124, 186, 190, 208, 263, 278, 287, 320

noticing 4, 17, 21, 66, 102, 133, 147, 161, 314

nurseries 234

nurture iv, vi, 20, 34, 43, 44, 49, 67, 99, 127, 147, 156, 162, 174, 244, 259, 265, 276, 316

nurture groups 99, 174

nurturing practices 44, 49, 59, 69

O

occupational therapist 28, 29, 317
Ofsted Education Inspection Framework
7, 68
outdoor learning 81, 86, 87

P

paediatrician 209, 223, 317
panic 121, 123, 133, 134, 135, 139, 140,
143, 160, 162, 177, 240, 317
   panic attack 133, 134, 135, 140
   panic disorder 123, 133, 134, 135,
140, 317
parents
   parental engagement 45, 46
   parental separation 18, 144, 292,
311
   parenting support 165
pastoral care 29, 68, 317
pastoral support team 9, 63, 244, 317
peer relationships 20, 110, 136, 173,
185, 192, 264
periods 65, 76, 145, 202, 203, 213, 214,
215, 223
personal development 7
personalised learning 63, 69
personalised planning 63, 98
personality 40, 41, 49, 53, 106, 153, 176,
224, 225
   extroversion 41
   introversion 41
pervasive developmental disorder 317
pets 42, 83, 84
phobias 123
photos ii, 9, 42, 74, 82, 101, 111, 113,
146, 235, 236, 237, 246, 251, 252,
260, 263, 271
physical contact 59, 124
physical education (PE)
   sports days 257
physical needs 23, 252, 319
playground 17, 21, 46, 48, 61, 80, 86,
125, 151, 152, 158, 163, 171, 199,
223, 235, 243, 244, 247, 254, 260,
287
   alternative provision 80, 125, 244
   arrangements 32, 64, 78, 82, 85, 169,
211, 218, 229, 234, 254, 258, 260,
264, 265, 266
   play leaders 83, 193
   playtime 151, 176, 192, 235, 240,
241, 243, 244, 247
policies 1, 6, 7, 8, 10, 19, 33, 46, 51, 52,
53, 55, 56, 58, 59, 60, 62, 67, 69,
85, 95, 106, 112, 113, 114, 161,
204, 210, 215, 217, 218, 219, 223,
309
positivity 39, 56, 60, 316
poverty 3, 4, 8, 13, 14, 172
PPA 33, 85
praise see also recognition 39, 45, 46,
48, 52, 56, 57, 81, 91, 101, 127,
147, 148, 157, 164, 165, 174, 204,
282, 304
preoccupation see also special interest
111, 186, 192, 221, 224, 226, 311
problem-based learning 261
prosocial behaviours 20, 39, 55, 56, 57,
60, 61, 62, 69, 86, 111, 282, 317
protective consequences 58, 60, 61, 69,
317
psychiatrist iv, 1, 147, 209, 317
psychoeducation 135, 206, 318
psychologist iv, 1, 11, 43, 44, 49, 91, 93,
313
   clinical iv, 1, 11, 19, 23, 24, 26, 27,
28, 29, 32, 33, 34, 43, 91, 149, 165,
166, 169, 173, 181, 185, 198, 211,
219, 229, 312, 315
   educational viii, 5, 8, 17, 19, 21, 23,
26, 44, 49, 58, 60, 61, 69, 73, 93,
99, 106, 107, 152, 171, 181, 194,
204, 258, 313, 314, 319
puberty 213, 214, 215, 218, 219, 222

pupil voice 83, 260
purging 225, 312

R

reasonable adjustments 64, 81, 83, 189, 190, 202, 247, 264, 278
recognition see also praise vii, 13, 30, 36, 39, 52, 56, 57, 60, 62, 69, 90, 93, 98, 157, 166, 198, 200, 211, 229
reconciliation 55, 58, 61, 62, 69, 161
referral 13, 19, 22, 25, 28, 32, 99, 139, 148, 169, 175, 180, 195, 196, 198, 206, 259, 318
reflection 49, 52, 55, 58, 60, 61, 62, 69, 102, 161, 165, 242, 244, 245, 250, 260, 266, 302
relationships vii, 2, 6, 12, 20, 23, 32, 43, 45, 48, 56, 61, 62, 73, 74, 82, 83, 84, 86, 89, 91, 94, 95, 96, 110, 111, 116, 128, 136, 167, 168, 169, 173, 174, 180, 185, 188, 192, 205, 215, 219, 233, 234, 235, 257, 258, 261, 264, 266, 282, 285, 310, 311, 313, 317, 318
relaxation 174, 179
repetitive behaviours 138, 189, 191
reporting 3, 18, 19, 33, 97, 112, 190
residential trips 83, 258, 259
resilience vii, viii, 1, 2, 12, 18, 52, 57, 64, 81, 84, 91, 93, 95, 96, 99, 105, 107, 122, 126, 156, 170, 254, 259, 261, 318
respect 31, 52, 80, 83, 91, 215, 240
responsibility 12, 40, 66, 83, 84, 91, 163, 236, 253, 265, 278
restoration 55, 58, 60, 61, 62, 69, 161, 224
rewards 38, 49, 56, 57, 156
rituals 35, 100, 136, 137, 186, 239, 240, 242, 244, 247, 249, 316, 318
role-modelling 62, 282

role-play 162, 291
routines 35, 66, 76, 86, 173, 186, 188, 191, 196, 234, 235, 236, 239, 240, 244, 247, 253, 255, 257, 258, 285

S

sadness 90, 92, 98, 144, 145, 168, 291, 292, 297, 313
safeguarding v, 19, 29, 30, 32, 34, 40, 112, 114, 148, 223, 310, 317
    Designated Safeguarding Persons for Child Protection 19, 317
    safeguarding concerns 29, 30, 148
    safeguarding procedures 112, 114
    safeguarding software 19
safety 5, 6, 11, 31, 35, 36, 48, 52, 55, 59, 68, 69, 100, 112, 113, 114, 138, 140, 170, 171, 174, 195, 241, 249, 309, 314, 318
    safety behaviours 138, 314, 318
SATs 258, 262
school-based support 29, 63
school community vii, 9, 11, 43, 46, 48, 52, 56, 67, 73, 80, 82, 83, 86, 102, 163, 197, 236, 259
school productions 258, 259
school refusal 129, 139
science curriculum 213, 215
screen use see also digital technologies internet social media video games 75, 109, 110, 112, 113, 114, 115, 116, 299
secondary school 9, 147, 257, 258, 259, 260, 261, 262, 263, 264, 265, 266, 267
    secondary school application 259
    transition opportunities 234, 249, 256, 258, 260, 261, 264
selective mutism 139, 318
self-awareness 93, 105, 156, 289, 318
self-efficacy 36, 37, 49, 93, 94, 105, 318
self-esteem vii, 6, 17, 36, 38, 39, 76, 81,

93, 94, 96, 99, 102, 105, 109, 144,
147, 157, 164, 170, 171, 172, 174,
210, 211, 227, 258, 318
self-harm 7, 18, 29, 143, 147, 148, 318
self-injury 143, 147, 148, 151, 318
self-referral 318
self-reporting 97
SEND Code of Practice 21, 22, 23
senior leadership 8, 9, 20, 21, 48, 55, 57,
62, 67, 85, 164, 263, 265
sensory needs 137, 191
sensory processing 23
sensory room 80, 126, 146, 244
sensory sensitivities see also auditory
stimuli noise visual stimulation
146, 155, 190, 197
separation anxiety 123, 128, 129, 130,
139, 140, 240, 318
sex education see also RSE 215
sexualised behaviours 151
sexual orientation 215
shyness 41
sleep 3, 6, 75, 86, 87, 112, 115, 138, 144,
177, 187, 201, 207, 236
social care ii, 5, 10, 25, 29, 30, 152, 164
social interaction 110, 111, 127, 162,
163, 183, 185, 187, 193, 198, 236
social masking 191, 197
social media see also internet 1, 109,
115
social modelling 37, 53, 319
social regulation 124, 125, 127, 145,
147, 156, 162, 165, 170, 171, 172,
173, 189, 190, 192, 202, 203, 204,
209, 210, 214, 215
social skills see also emotional skills 84,
97, 99, 100, 101, 162, 164, 166,
172, 187, 192, 197
Social Stories 193, 198, 247, 251, 307,
319
speaking and listening 83, 127
special interest see also preoccupation

67, 111, 190, 191, 193, 247
staff ratios 61
staff wellbeing 84, 85, 93
STAR chart 155
stories iv, 54, 82, 94, 97, 127, 146, 193,
247, 251, 307, 319
strengths 20, 24, 34, 35, 40, 42, 47, 54,
55, 82, 93, 94, 95, 128, 196, 197,
207, 235, 237, 319
stress response see also fight or flight
59, 161
suicide 7, 144
summative assessment 64

T
television 109, 115, 177
temperament see also personality 37,
41, 49, 109, 237, 314, 319
therapeutic support 30, 147, 226
family therapy 29
in-house therapists 30, 68
music therapy 30
play therapy 30
psychological therapy 29, 229
THRIVE model 25, 27, 28, 319
tics 199, 201, 207, 208, 209, 210, 211,
310, 320
motor tics 208, 209, 210, 320
vocal tics 208, 209
tier system 25, 26, 27, 320
timetables 62, 63, 171, 172, 173, 189,
193, 197, 241, 242, 252, 260, 261,
262
personalised timetables 62, 63
visual timetables 170, 171, 173, 189,
241, 252
toileting 125, 235, 236
Tourette's syndrome 207, 208, 209, 211,
320
transgender 216, 217, 218, 219, 320
transition viii, 44, 78, 100, 101, 125,
129, 130, 131, 139, 214, 219, 233,

234, 235, 236, 237, 238, 240, 241, 243, 244, 247, 249, 250, 251, 252, 253, 254, 256, 257, 258, 259, 260, 261, 262, 263, 264, 265, 266, 267, 304, 320
daily transitions 76, 239, 246, 247
end of year transition 249, 256
EYFS transition 234, 236, 238
transition from KS1 254
transition journal 236, 251, 256, 260, 261
transition meetings 249
transition programmes 249, 250, 258, 259, 260, 266
transitional object 131, 247, 320
trauma see also post-traumatic stress disorder (PTSD) 11, 137, 167, 176, 177, 178, 179, 180, 307, 320
trusted adults viii, 30, 171, 246

U
uniform 218, 223, 236

V
values ii, 38, 51, 52, 56, 57, 60, 69, 80, 83, 98, 316
video games 109, 110, 111, 116
visual prompts 164, 235, 240
visual stimulation see also sensory needs sensory sensitivities 78, 146
visual timetables 170, 171, 173, 189, 241, 252
voluntary organisations 10, 26
vomiting 221, 224, 225

W
weight 79, 128, 184, 203, 221, 222, 223, 224, 225, 226, 227, 228, 229, 311, 313
wellbeing for all 10, 69, 73, 77, 78, 86, 239, 266

wellbeing practices 69, 85, 237, 238, 253
whole-school approach ix, 7, 51, 69, 103, 140, 217, 313
whole-school culture 9, 40, 51, 205, 242
whole-school ethos 56, 68, 69, 74
worry see also anxiety 40, 41, 75, 98, 102, 122, 123, 126, 127, 130, 132, 135, 140, 157, 208, 249, 251, 259, 278, 291, 294, 311, 320

Y
Year 6 9, 143, 245, 258, 259, 260, 261, 264, 265, 266, 267
Year 7 258, 259, 260, 261, 263, 264, 265, 266
Yerkes–Dodson Law 121
youth justice 5, 29